REFLECTIVE PRIMARY
MATHEMATICS

SAGE was founded in 1965 by Sara Miller McCune to support the dissemination of usable knowledge by publishing innovative and high-quality research and teaching content. Today, we publish more than 750 journals, including those of more than 300 learned societies, more than 800 new books per year, and a growing range of library products including archives, data, case studies, reports, conference highlights, and video. SAGE remains majority-owned by our founder, and after Sara's lifetime will become owned by a charitable trust that secures our continued independence.

Los Angeles | London | Washington DC | New Delhi | Singapore

E. JACKSON

REFLECTIVE PRIMARY
MATHEMATICS

A Guide For Student Teachers

Los Angeles | London | New Delhi
Singapore | Washington DC

Los Angeles | London | New Delhi
Singapore | Washington DC

SAGE Publications Ltd
1 Oliver's Yard
55 City Road
London EC1Y 1SP

SAGE Publications Inc.
2455 Teller Road
Thousand Oaks, California 91320

SAGE Publications India Pvt Ltd
B 1/I 1 Mohan Cooperative Industrial Area
Mathura Road
New Delhi 110 044

SAGE Publications Asia-Pacific Pte Ltd
3 Church Street
#10-04 Samsung Hub
Singapore 049483

Editor: James Clark
Assistant editor: Rachael Plant
Production editor: Tom Bedford
Copyeditor: Elaine Leek
Proofreader: Jill Birch
Indexer: Cathy Heath
Marketing manager: Dilhara Attygalle
Cover design: Naomi Robinson
Typeset by: C&M Digitals (P) Ltd, Chennai, India
Printed in India at Replika Press Pvt Ltd

MIX
Paper from
responsible sources
FSC
www.fsc.org   **FSC® C016779**

© Elizabeth Jackson 2015

First published 2015

Library of Congress Control Number: 2014959110

British Library Cataloguing in Publication data

A catalogue record for this book is available from the British Library

ISBN 978-1-4462-9510-6
ISBN 978-1-4462-9511-3 (pbk)

At SAGE we take sustainability seriously. Most of our products are printed in the UK using FSC papers and boards. When we print overseas we ensure sustainable papers are used as measured by the Egmont grading system. We undertake an annual audit to monitor our sustainability.

Table of contents

About the author

Elizabeth taught mathematics for sixteen years across the UK from the Channel Islands to the North West of England in various primary and secondary schools. For fourteen years she was a Senior Lecturer at the University of Cumbria (formerly St Martin's College) teaching mathematics at degree level, mathematics education with secondary and primary student teachers and supervising Masters students' research into primary mathematics. Her Honours degree from Manchester University is in mathematics and education. She explored the use of IT as a tool for learning and teaching mathematics for a Masters from the University of Lancaster, and conducted research into mathematical perceptions for her PhD, also from the University of Lancaster. Liz has always taken a keen interest in how children learn mathematics and how adults, including teachers, perceive mathematics.

Acknowledgements

Profound thanks to the many student teachers whose descriptions of their experiences and perceptions of mathematics informed the research underpinning this book. Sincere appreciation also goes to the University of Cumbria for affording me the opportunity to study, the University of Lancaster for research guidance, and colleagues from both universities and SAGE for their support and advice. Heartfelt gratitude goes to Gary for his unwavering faith and encouragement. Thank you.

SAGE would like to thank the following reviewers whose comments have helped shape the original proposal:

- Janet Baker – Oxford Brookes University
- Nigel Hutchinson – Bishop Grosseteste University
- Sandy Pepperell – University of Roehampton
- Stefanie Sullivan – University of Nottingham

Introduction

As a university lecturer I encounter student teachers on their primary teacher training courses whose confidence in mathematics varies considerably. If you are amongst the many student teachers who feel in any way anxious about teaching mathematics to children or about returning to a classroom yourself to learn mathematics again as part of your initial teacher training, then this book is intended for you.

Do you want to be a primary school teacher but does the thought of entering a mathematics classroom again in order to train and to teach fill you with dread?

Are you already teaching mathematics in primary school but do not like to admit to how lacking in confidence you are, and how you feel as if somebody is going to find out you are not good enough?

Maybe you teach mathematics at a higher level and know that you can do it yourself, but struggle to aid your students to develop their understanding.

Although written with student teachers specifically in mind, this book may also prove useful if you feel reasonably confident about your own mathematical ability but want to find out more about how people learn mathematics and the ways in which it is taught, or how you might develop your understanding of teachers' difficulties with mathematics if you either support teachers in primary school or teach in initial teacher training.

Whatever your purpose, the book will guide you through a reflective process of considering various aspects of mathematics, your own perceptions of mathematics based on your past mathematical experiences and your awareness of the different mathematical perceptions that student teachers may have which can affect the way mathematics is learnt and taught. The aim is for you to think about the kind of mathematics teacher you want to be and to plan what is needed to achieve your aspirations.

If you do have any anxieties about mathematics, you are not alone. Not only is it an all too frequent occurrence for people in everyday life to admit they 'don't like maths' or to say they 'can't do it', there have been many student teachers over the years who have confided to me that they are terrified of having to learn mathematics during their teacher training course and are worried about having to teach mathematics in a primary classroom.

Those who agreed to talk to me explicitly about their perceptions of mathematics have allowed me to gain a better understanding of the many difficulties student teachers can face at the outset of their training course for primary teaching. In so doing, they shared a desire to try to help future students raise their awareness of mathematical perceptions so that they could be in a better position to answer queries they may have. As a result of their accounts of their mathematical experiences, this book is based on a framework for reflection using analysis of student teachers' mathematical experiences so that you can identify your own, compare with others and think about potential changes you would like to make about your relationship with mathematics.

All names have been changed to ensure the anonymity of the participants, whose contributions to the research that led to the writing of this book are much appreciated.

Throughout the chapters, you will be encouraged to think about mathematics and to explore what it means to think mathematically. A range of literature and research carried out with student teachers is drawn upon to exemplify the mathematical experiences of people just like you. This theoretical and practical background is brought together to provide you with reflective tasks so that you can personally examine your own relationship with mathematics. Case studies are also provided in some chapters in order to share individual contexts that may help you think further about your own circumstances and perceptions of mathematics.

Through reflective tasks that get you thinking about mathematics and what it means to think mathematically, you will be encouraged not only to raise your awareness of mathematical perceptions, but to identify your own perceptions of mathematics, analyse them by comparing and contrasting your own perceptions with those of others, consider pedagogy that may be associated with mathematical perceptions, identify potential implications of your own mathematical perceptions on your learning as you study to become a teacher or take part in continuing professional development, create a personal mathematical philosophy on which to base your teaching of mathematics, identify potential need for change and plan to make changes as necessary.

As you work through the book, you will be able to consider the nature of mathematics and pedagogical associations, set goals for your own mathematical learning, make explicit your aspirations for teaching mathematics and develop a personal philosophy for mathematics that will prepare you for doing your best to improve provision for children's mathematical learning.

Your ambition is to become a primary teacher and, since mathematics is a core subject on the primary curriculum, there is no getting away from it; you will learn about teaching mathematics on your training course and you will end up teaching mathematics. You will undoubtedly aspire to be the best teacher you can possibly be and the children you teach in the future deserve the best mathematical learning opportunities you can provide for them. You certainly will not want to pass on to them any anxiety about mathematics or dislike for the subject, and you will want to feel confident in your ability to teach mathematics effectively. By working through this book, you can begin to address the issues that are pertinent to you. You will read about different factors that may have an impact on how you feel about mathematics. You will be guided through a process of reflection so that you can face any fears you may have and plan to overcome them. There will be no magic wand waving, as you will have a lifetime of mathematical experiences that have led to feeling the way you do about mathematics, but by becoming more aware of how you perceive mathematics you can consider what you can do to achieve your goal of being an effective teacher and, if necessary, change your mindset and increase your confidence.

In Chapter 1 you will read about historical difficulties with teaching and learning mathematics and compare your own learning experiences with various approaches taken over the years, to think about what was, or was not, useful to you in your own learning of mathematics. You will begin to think ahead to ways in which you would like to teach primary mathematics that you consider are beneficial to children's learning.

You will be encouraged in Chapter 2 to think about using a process of reflection to consider whether your mathematical perceptions need to change if you are to achieve your goals for teaching primary mathematics. It is argued that the way you perceive mathematics can affect the way you understand mathematics, and as such you will be guided throughout the book in recognising and analysing your perceptions.

Chapter 3 presents a framework for reflection, as based on a group of student teachers' experiences of mathematics. Consideration of this framework will allow you to make conscious your mathematical perceptions, compare them with those of other student teachers and begin to ascertain your goals for your future learning in initial teacher training and your practice as a teacher.

Chapter 4 concentrates on identifying and reflecting upon your attitudes towards mathematics and how these might affect the way you understand mathematics and therefore the potential impact upon your future learning and teaching.

In Chapter 5 you will take your reflections a stage further to consider how your engagement with mathematics is affected by your perceptions. If you have negative associations with mathematics, it is crucial that you examine these and think about how you might change them in order to get the most from your teacher training and to do right by the children you will teach.

Any anxieties about mathematics are usually tied up with subject knowledge, and in Chapter 6 you will reflect upon how you understand mathematics so that you can ascertain any change that you may need to bring about in order to develop your mathematics subject knowledge further.

Chapter 7 brings together some of the aspects of mathematics teaching and learning that you have been analysing to specifically consider your mathematical beliefs and how these may affect your future learning and the kind of primary mathematics teacher you aspire to be.

The relevance of mathematics is explored in Chapter 8 so that you can consider why we learn mathematics and add to your developing philosophy of both why we teach mathematics and how it can be taught.

In Chapter 9 you will consider the notion of being a mathematician and ascertain the extent to which you see yourself as such and why. Alongside these reflections you will be encouraged to think about how these perceptions may affect the way you learn mathematics and the impact it could have upon your teaching.

Throughout the chapters so far, you will have been raising your awareness of your mathematical perceptions and developing your personal philosophy for learning and teaching mathematics. Chapter 10 encourages you to draw together your reflections on contrasting perspectives in order to firm up your aspirations for the kind of teacher of primary mathematics you want to be and how you want to be able to learn mathematics in initial teacher training.

In Chapter 11 you will build on your developing philosophy and your reflections so far to consider your relationship with mathematics so that you are in a better position to achieve the goals you have set yourself for learning and teaching mathematics.

Having raised your awareness of different aspects of mathematics, reflected upon your own mathematical experiences, compared them with those of others, set goals for your mathematics learning and teaching, created your philosophy of mathematics learning and teaching and determined changes you may need to make in order to meet your aspirations, in Chapter 12 you will be guided through a process of beginning to bring about change.

You may not find reading this book an easy process and might even find it unsettling as you make explicit your thoughts about mathematics, but stick with it … you know you want to be the best teacher of mathematics that you can be, so now's the time to confront the dragon!

1
History of difficulties in learning and teaching mathematics

Learning objectives

Having read this chapter you will …

- Raise your awareness of some of the historical difficulties faced in learning and teaching mathematics
- Begin to compare these with your own experiences
- Consider potential factors that may have contributed to your own perceptions of mathematics

---

Introduction

The notion of mathematics being difficult to learn is not new. Approaches to teaching mathematics change from time to time, but despite continued efforts to find the best ways of teaching the subject, mathematics education seems to have proved problematic for many years. This chapter outlines the changing face of mathematics education over time so that you can expand your awareness of the wider picture of learning mathematics and of some of the difficulties faced in mathematics education. There are opportunities for you to reflect upon your own mathematical experience and perceptions, allowing you to consider your own thoughts about mathematics teaching and learning and some of the difficulties that colleagues and children you will work with may have. Perhaps your own mathematical experience may resonate with those of others. This chapter begins with a case study of a student about to begin initial teacher training who is keen to become a primary teacher but who has her own concerns about mathematics and is worried about being back in a mathematics classroom as a learner herself. The case study is followed by discussion of a history of difficulties in teaching and learning mathematics based on theoretical substantiation and student teachers' descriptions of their experiences.

Case study

Judy was a Bachelor of Arts graduate when she enrolled on an initial teacher training course in the North of England. With several years' experience working in the tourist industry, she had decided to retrain and enter primary teaching. The course for which she successfully applied started with a registration day, at the end of which the group were invited to take part voluntarily in a research project looking into student teachers' perceptions of mathematics.

She was confident in her enthusiasm for her new career, her general academic ability for the course, her communication skills for working alongside adults, patience with young children, her organisational skills for coping with largely online study and time management techniques for fitting the course around her job, which she had arranged to reduce to part-time hours. Mathematics was the one area that Judy was really anxious about. The research sounded interesting as she had concerns about the way she thought of mathematics, but those very concerns discouraged her from getting involved.

Sitting there in the lecture theatre with her new peers she felt inadequate. As the various lecturers had talked about their subject areas and given presentations about what students could expect to cover during the course, she had felt a rising anxiety about the mathematics element. It seemed ridiculous to put herself forward to be involved in the research as she felt such a fraud, but the researcher seemed friendly and approachable and had emphasised that anyone who expressed an interest could back out at any time with no obligation. Judy thought it could be a chance to have some of her own questions answered and so at the risk of being exposed as unsuitable for a primary teaching course, she filled in the slip in her information pack and decided she might as well be sure sooner rather than later if she was going to be able to manage the mathematics part of the course.

The researcher subsequently contacted her and arranged to meet in a café close to Judy's home. Despite her reservations, Judy soon felt at ease as the research interview turned out to be quite therapeutic. She had never really given her full attention to how she felt about mathematics before, or really thought about the various incidents of learning mathematics and having to do mathematical stuff in public that had happened over the years. It almost felt like a counselling session, as she did all the talking, and there was a lot of nodding and smiling and agreement as she was gently prompted with various questions.

When the interview concluded and the tape recorder was switched off, the researcher talked more herself and explained the reason for the research, now that it wasn't liable to influence Judy's responses. Judy was relieved to realise how valuable her answers were and that she hadn't just talked rubbish for the last forty-five minutes. As she had presumed, people were involved in the research who really liked mathematics as well as people like herself who were worried about it, but it was a huge relief to find out there were many other students like her who didn't feel confident about learning mathematics again and who were anxious about teaching it to children. She learnt more about the course and how she and other students would be supported in learning mathematics for primary teaching and she was given lots of sources of support to brush up on her own knowledge of mathematics.

The main thing Judy came away with, however, was the realisation that maybe it wasn't her. She'd always assumed she was particularly bad at mathematics but now she was beginning to think that learning and teaching mathematics was a problem for a much wider range of people. Although she knew she was going to have to work at it, she felt much less of a fraud and could stop worrying that she'd be the only one on the course struggling with this part of learning to be a teacher. However, she couldn't help thinking that it was even more worrying that this problem seemed to be widespread and was now thinking of the poor kids out there who had teachers who still felt like her.

Post-Script: Judy went on to enrol and successfully complete the teacher training course, finding that the mathematics element was tailored to her needs and enabled her to learn a lot about how children learn mathematics, how she herself understood mathematics, how ways of teaching mathematics had changed since she herself was at school and what she needed to develop for her own mathematics subject knowledge and her ability to teach the subject well. Upon completion of her training, Judy secured a full-time teaching post in a primary school and kept in touch with the researcher, who was delighted to hear that she was not only confidently teaching mathematics, but was thoroughly enjoying the experience too.

Difficulties with mathematics education

Judy's case study may resonate with you, as she is certainly not the only new teacher to begin a teacher training course with a degree of trepidation about entering a mathematics classroom as a learner again and about having to teach mathematics. As Judy had begun to realise, and would learn more about during her course, mathematics education has been, historically, widely recognised as problematic.

Let's step back in time and think about how mathematics education has developed over the years. During your career as a primary teacher there will no doubt be a time when you organise a school trip or an in-school history day where the children get to experience what life was like for a child in a Victorian classroom, chanting multiplication tables and repetitive practice of arithmetic. Schools in this era operated on an early form of performance pay since, together with attendance, academic results determined the income for schools via government grants. In an effort to ensure successful assessment figures through testing, the content of a Victorian mathematics lesson would be mainly number work with a teaching approach of drilling facts into children who learnt by rote (Sharp et al., 2009).

Reflection points

- Is this approach to teaching mathematics confined to the classroom from over a century ago?
- Do children in twenty-first century classrooms chant number facts or routinely practise arithmetic by rote?
- Are teaching methods in any way similar to the Victorian era?
- In what ways are they different?
- How effective are the different methods you are aware of?
- How do you know they are effective?

It is a natural reaction to say that such an old-fashioned way of teaching no longer exists, yet on reflection such pedagogy is not left so far back in history as we might first surmise. Some student teachers, recounting their own experiences of being taught mathematics far more recently than the nineteenth century, describe a learning environment where they sat separately or in rows and talking was discouraged. They describe mathematics lessons limited mainly to number and remember being required to recite and constantly repeat number facts, such as multiplication tables, in an effort to memorise and be able to recall them. What they describe is a transfer of mathematical knowledge consisting of number from the teacher to the learner using a transmission mode of teaching dependent on memorisation. Alan, for example, found this method of learning useful as he thought the only way to learn multiplication tables was to keep practising and for the repetition to help the facts 'sink in'.

However, what exactly is it that sinks in? Francesca recalled her father bribing her with extra pocket money to learn her multiplication tables when at primary school as he was alarmed that she did not know them, but she struggled to remember the numbers to be able to recite them as expected by her teacher in class and also to instantly recall a particular fact when asked. She described an example of finding the answer to 7 × 5 where in her head she would halve the 7 to get 3.5 then multiply it by 10 to get 35. She had developed her own technique that allowed her to mentally work out the answer as quickly as her teacher expected, but without being entirely reliant on her memory. She would later develop an understanding of why her system worked, although at the time she was not sure why and her teacher never asked her since all that was required was a quick and correct answer. It was not until Francesca became a teacher herself that she realised the worth in having children really understand the meaning of numbers and the calculations they could work out, as opposed to the limitations of trying to recall number facts that held no meaning for them. She was able to look back on the ways she had coped in primary school and to analyse how she had used her understanding of number to work out things she did not instantly know the answer to.

Reflection points

- What of your own memories of learning mathematics and your most recent experience observing and teaching in today's classrooms – does rote learning take place where children are presented with mathematical facts and required to memorise and recall them?
- Is it useful to have a set of mathematical facts that you just know and can instantly recall?
- How beneficial is it to understand the meaning behind those mathematical facts rather than being reliant on having simply memorised them?

In some ways, today's mathematics teaching retains elements of what, on the surface, we would consider outmoded practice. Nineteenth-century mathematics pedagogy must have been sufficient for the needs of the day if the mathematical understanding required for the advance of industry and technology during and after that period is recognised. However, dissatisfaction with teaching methods led to a wider curriculum in British schools in the early twentieth century, with a move in the 1930s to suggest a prescribed curriculum. This did not come into being, interrupted as it was by war, after which it was not considered to be the best way forward (Mathematical Association, 1955). Instead, it was thought that children should learn mathematics at their own rate through play, talk and experimentation in order to explore mathematical relationships and develop their ability to think mathematically. In contrast to the focus on passing tests linked to government funding from the previous century, the Mathematical Association (1955) advocated mathematics being taught as a necessary language, a scientific tool, for pleasure and for its use in everyday life.

Children learning mathematics through play, investigation and talk and for the purpose of enjoyment and not just necessity may resonate with your recent experiences of observing mathematics in primary schools and it may even surprise you that such a philosophy for teaching mathematics is not a relatively new one. Indeed, student teachers have expressed their confusion regarding the purpose of learning mathematics with Julie, for instance, who questioned its relevance and wondered about what relation mathematics has to the world, surmising that there must be value in learning mathematics, but she could not articulate what that value might be.

Reflection points

- From your observations of mathematics teaching and learning in today's classrooms, what seem to be the main drivers and reasons for teaching this subject?
- Will you teach mathematics solely because it is a core subject in the statutory curriculum or what other reasons are there?

Child-centred perceptions of learning mathematics continued into the 1960s and beyond, with the Plowden Report (DES, 1967, para 9) suggesting that 'at the heart of the educational process lies the child'. Depending on the period in which you were at school, you may recall child-centred approaches with individualised learning. However, the advent of published schemes of work tailored to children's individual progress in mathematics perhaps led to an over-reliance on mass-produced resources. Some student teachers recalled working on their own through various series of work-cards, sheets or books and describe teaching approaches that were not proactive, with Lois suggesting that she was not actually taught anything, as she remembers having to get on with it herself, working through a series of worksheets that she found very boring.

Reflection points

- What are your recollections of being taught mathematics?
- What was useful to your learning and what did you not find as useful?

By the 1980s there remained dissatisfaction with the quality of children's learning and the depth of their mathematical understanding. A detailed study into mathematics education reported that it was 'a difficult subject both to teach and learn' (Cockcroft, 1982, p. 67) with advice that mathematics should include 'exposition by the teacher ... discussion between teacher and pupils and between pupils themselves ... appropriate practical work ... consolidation and practice of fundamental skills and routines ... problem solving including the application of mathematics to everyday situations ... investigational work' (Cockcroft, 1982, para 243). Previous pedagogical developments had not led to mathematics being learnt sufficiently well and a range of teaching approaches were advocated.

Lee recounted her experience as a teaching assistant working alongside a teacher evidently keen to embrace the findings of the Cockcroft Report and to implement a structured curriculum that replaced the somewhat haphazard approach to mathematical content she had witnessed at her previous school, yet which had scope to teach in proactive ways as advocated by Cockcroft in order to develop children's mathematical understanding. What Lee observed, however, was adherence to the school's existing scheme of work and a reluctance of colleagues to change the whole-school approach of children working individually through a published scheme of workbooks. Rather than children learning in collaborative groups through discussion, practical experience, investigation and problem-solving, Lee recalled the class teacher being informed by the mathematics curriculum leader that was 'not the way maths was taught in that school'. Instead, they were required to continue the children's individual use of textbooks, with what Lee saw as the unavoidable labelling of children dependent on what level of book they reached, and a steady stream of individual children queuing at their sides needing help to know what was required of them.

Lee's critique of practice resonated with the government's 'Better Schools' paper (DES, 1985) that highlighted a lack of approaches to teaching mathematics through practical contexts to aid children's understanding of its use and application.

Reflection points

- Do you see children in today's mathematics lessons working through a series of books, work-cards or sheets individually without proactive teacher input?
- How much teacher exposition, discussion, practical work, consolidation and practice, problem-solving, everyday application and investigation do you observe in your recent school experience?
- Which of these approaches are more prevalent than others?
- Which approaches are most beneficial for children's learning?
- How do you know they are beneficial?

To address recommendations raised by Cockcroft (1982), the 1988 Education Reform Act (DES, 1988) brought about a statutory National Curriculum in England and Wales in 1989 (DES, 1989) whereby the responsibility for mathematical teaching content was removed from teachers and replaced by a prescribed mathematics curriculum as had been suggested, but rejected, half a century earlier. Although the mathematical content of a school syllabus became statutory, pedagogical approaches were not prescribed and so methods of teaching remained varied, other than a programme of study within the new curriculum devoted to 'using and applying' mathematics which, in response to the Cockroft Report (1982), attempted to promote the learning of mathematics through means such as problem-solving, developing mathematical communication and children's use of logic and reasoning.

Despite the advent of the statutory curriculum, standards in mathematics continued to be criticised a decade on (Askew, 1998). The National Curriculum had been revised to form a more concise version than the original and, in the interest of developing further mathematical understanding, the 1999 version (DfEE, 1999a) incorporated the use and application of mathematics into the other programmes of study, so as to avoid being seen as a separate teaching element and to instead encourage teaching of the use and application of all mathematical content, whether number, shape, space, measures or data handling through problem-solving, communication and the use of logic and reasoning.

Reflection points

- Were you at school when the National Curriculum for England and Wales came into being?
- How aware were you of teachers linking mathematics to everyday contexts and developing your ability to communicate mathematically, building in problem-solving to your mathematics learning and encouraging your use of logic and reasoning?
- Were such approaches helpful to your mathematical learning and why?

The non-statutory National Numeracy Strategy (DfEE, 1999b) was also introduced into primary schools, and extended later into secondary schools. While Ofsted (2005) reported that the National Strategies had a positive impact upon teaching and learning, further change was brought about when the National Numeracy Strategy (DfEE, 1999b) was superseded by the Primary National Strategy (DfES, 2003a), at which point the term 'numeracy' was replaced by 'mathematics' in the strategy's title.

At this time, the Excellence and Enjoyment strategy for primary schools (DfES, 2003b) encouraged creativity and innovation in teaching, advocating that teachers 'take ownership of the curriculum' (2003b, p. 5) to provide a 'rich and exciting curriculum' including 'building and applying mathematical skills' (2003b, p. 6) and suggesting that teachers 'have great freedoms to exercise their professional judgement about how they teach' and that 'teachers have the power to decide how they teach' (2003b, p. 16).

The National Curriculum remained statutory with its focus on content, whereas the Primary National Strategy provided more detailed prescription, including age-related learning objectives, recommended calculation strategies to be taught and suggested blocks of mathematical content to be taught in particular time periods. On the one hand, new teachers described feeling more confident in planning as the wider learning objectives of the National Curriculum were broken down into more manageable learning objectives for their short-term planning, and they indicated that learning various mental and written strategies for number calculations was useful. However, student teachers described feeling overwhelmed by the lists of objectives, personal difficulties in learning mental and written calculation strategies, confusion concerning when they were required to teach particular units of work and worried about meeting children's needs, with May, for example, commenting that she felt sorry for the children she observed in school. She described teachers 'ploughing' through objectives as if they were trying to get to the end of them but May was not convinced that they were necessarily making sure children fully understood before they moved on to the next set of objectives. Her view was that both the children and the teachers seemed to be like 'hamsters running round wheels'.

Experiences such as May's are supported by research into mathematics education at the time. ACME, for example, noted teachers feeling pressured about children reaching certain levels due to a focus on standards, with evidence of teachers focusing on mathematics for a particular year group rather than on overall progression and making connections between different aspects of mathematics, suggesting that 'changes to curriculum guidance and documentation that increase the number of bulleted teaching and learning objectives only serve to decrease the ability of teachers – especially non-specialists – to see this bigger picture' (ACME, 2006, p. 13).

Consideration of such changes to curriculum were under way, with the Education Act of 2002 (DfES, 2002a, p. 53), suggesting a revision to the National Curriculum for England. Mathematics was to continue to be a core subject with a curriculum including attainment targets and assessment arrangements alongside programmes of study (2002a, p. 57) whereby 'matters, skills and processes are required to be taught to pupils of different abilities and maturities by the end of that stage' (2002a, p. 59), although it suggested that particular periods of time may not be allocated for the teaching of the programmes of study.

Such was the continued concern about mathematics education that a government-initiated review was set up in 2007 resulting in the Williams Report's examination of effective pedagogy for primary mathematics (DCSF, 2008). Although considerable progress was noted in mathematics learning, Williams reported that there remained issues in learning and teaching mathematics and that government assessment targets had not been met. Williams (DCSF, 2008, p. 1) recommended that every primary school should have a mathematics specialist 'who will champion this challenging subject and act as the nucleus for achieving best pedagogical practice'.

There was further feedback from the Cambridge Primary Review (Alexander, 2010), which criticised the National Strategies' emphasis on number and computation for being not so far removed from nineteenth century approaches to mathematics pedagogy, particularly assessment-driven transmission modes of memorisation as opposed to the wider mathematics curriculum of the statutory National Curriculum. While Victorian teaching methods may have largely focused on passing tests to make the most of assessment results and therefore funding, the philosophy of resulting committees (Mathematical Association, 1955) seemed to change the focus to child-centred learning wherein children's understanding was fostered through more active approaches to learning. However, as Lee commented during her student teacher experience, there is evidence in today's classrooms of teaching being assessment-focused, perhaps not for funding purposes so much as national and parental interest in league tables and Ofsted performance gradings.

In response to the need to ensure effective educational provision for all primary children, the Rose Review was set up (DCSF, 2009). This noted that 'experience from the National Strategies shows that schools are sometimes unaware of all that numeracy should cover and so limit opportunities for children to apply the full range of numeracy skills across the curriculum' (DCSF, 2009, p. 68). It also suggested that the primary curriculum was too prescriptive, stating that 'the trend, usually motivated by the desire to strengthen particular aspects of learning, has been to add more and more content with too little regard for the practicalities and expertise needed to teach it effectively' (DCSF, 2009, p. 3).

Hence, despite attempts to improve mathematics education via the implementation of the National Strategies, dissatisfaction expressed of over-emphasis on number, memorisation, knowledge transmission, lack of application and over-prescription indicated a need for more concentration on the development of mathematical understanding and more effective teaching approaches. A revised National Curriculum to include exploration of the use and application of mathematics was recommended by Williams (DCSF, 2008), with the Rose Report (DCSF, 2009) advocating cross-curricular work to enrich and enliven children's learning. It also recommended a less prescriptive curriculum with 'greater flexibility to meet pupils' individual needs and build on their prior learning' (DCSF, 2009, p. 10).

Such increased autonomy for teachers was further supported in a subsequent British government White Paper which stated that the National Curriculum was too prescriptive (DfE, 2010) and intimated 'allowing schools to decide how to teach' (2010, p. 10), indicating that 'teachers must be free to use their professionalism and expertise to support all children to progress' (2010, p. 42).

Reflection points

- Government reports and guidance are freely available online – access a selection from the reference list at the back of the book for more details of what has been advised for mathematics teaching in primary schools.
- Reflect upon the curriculum you think is needed for children to develop mathematical understanding.

(Continued)

(Continued)

- What is your understanding of 'the use and application of mathematics'?
- How do you see this being incorporated into the teaching you observe in today's classrooms?
- How do you think it could be further embedded into children's learning opportunities?
- Do you think it is worthwhile to do so and why?

The Primary National Strategy is now decommissioned and a revised statutory National Curriculum (DfE, 2013) was implemented in September 2014. This includes a 'mathematics' as opposed to 'numeracy' section and a breadth of mathematical areas, although there remains an emphasis on number in that 'the principal focus of mathematics teaching in Key Stage 1 is to ensure that pupils develop confidence and mental fluency with whole numbers, counting and place value' (DfE, 2013, p. 101). Despite suggestion of developing understanding of number as opposed to memorisation of fact through, for example, the use of resources, there is indication that practice, as opposed to developing understanding, might be advocated since it is proposed that 'by the end of year 2, pupils should know the number bonds to 20 and be precise in using and understanding place value. An emphasis on practice at this early stage will aid fluency' (2013, p. 101) as well as a requirement to memorise number facts since it states that 'by the end of year 4, pupils should have memorised their multiplication tables up to and including the 12 multiplication table' (2013, p. 113).

While less prescriptive than the National Strategies, it is more prescriptive than the former National Curriculum, in that it sets out programmes of study for year groups as opposed to the previous key stages. Despite this age-related content, however, there is specific information provided regarding the use of these as guidance in terms of schools introducing 'content earlier or later than set out in the Programmes of Study' as well as schools introducing 'key stage content during an earlier key stage if appropriate' (2013, p. 100). It is stated that progression through the age-related content should 'always be based on the security of pupils' understanding and their readiness to progress to the next stage' (2013, p. 99).

Although it is advocated that those children achieving conceptual understanding are 'offered rich and sophisticated problems' (2013, p. 99), there remains an emphasis on practice in that the new National Curriculum states that 'those who are not sufficiently fluent with earlier material should consolidate their understanding, including through additional practice, before moving on' (2013, p. 99). Assuming that a child who is not sufficiently fluent is a child who needs to expand their mathematical understanding of a concept, there is apparent suggestion that additional practice may fulfil this need, iterated in the stated aim 'to ensure that all pupils become fluent in the fundamentals of mathematics, including through varied and frequent practice with increasingly complex problems over time, so that pupils develop conceptual understanding and the ability to recall and apply knowledge rapidly and accurately' (2013, p. 99) suggesting an emphasis on fluency related to practice is the prerequisite for development of problem-solving and conceptual understanding.

The notion of 'using and applying' mathematics previously identified as crucial is included in the new curriculum in that children are to be engaged in problem-solving 'by applying their mathematics to a variety of routine and non-routine problems with increasing sophistication, including breaking down problems into a series of simpler steps and persevering in seeking solutions' and encouraged to 'reason mathematically by following a line of enquiry, conjecturing relationships and generalisations, and developing an argument, justification or proof using mathematical language' (2013, p. 99). Although it states that pupils are to be taught to apply their understanding within number, measurement, geometry, algebra and probability and to apply mathematics to problems (2013, p. 9) with some reference to problem-solving within some of the various programmes of study for different year groups, this is not universally included. For example, there is no indication of specific problem-solving for measurement and geometry in Year 1; for fractions, geometry or statistics in Year 2; for measurement, geometry or statistics in Year 3; for geometry in Years 4 and 5; nor for algebra, geometry and statistics in Year 6, which is unusual given the apparent importance previously stated for applying mathematical understanding.

However, the new National Curriculum does recognise mathematics as 'an interconnected subject in which pupils need to be able to move fluently between representations of mathematical ideas' (2013, p. 99) with the recommendation that mathematical connections are made and that mathematical knowledge be applied to other areas of the curriculum, stating that 'teachers should use every relevant subject to develop pupils' mathematical fluency' and 'develop pupils' numeracy and mathematical reasoning in all subjects', although their rationale for this is for pupils to 'understand and appreciate the importance of mathematics' (2013, p. 9) as opposed to a means to develop mathematical understanding in a wide range of relevant contexts for the learner.

Pedagogy is not prescribed, with an indication for teacher autonomy in how the content can be taught as it provides 'an outline of core knowledge around which teachers can develop exciting and stimulating lessons to promote the development of pupils' knowledge, understanding and skills as part of the wider school curriculum' with schools being 'free to choose how they organise their school day, as long as the content of the national curriculum programmes of study is taught to all pupils' (2013, p. 6).

Reflection points

Access the new National Curriculum –

- What are your initial thoughts regarding its content?
- What do you think you need in order to be able to effectively teach the National Curriculum?

Changes over time show that there have been and still are difficulties in the way mathematics is taught and learnt and mathematics education continues to be subject to review. Both student and qualified teachers continue to work in a difficult sociopolitical climate with regard to quality mathematics provision for children and at a time of frequent policy and curriculum change. The new curriculum appears to address a sense of progression in children's mathematical learning but has a previously criticised focus on age-related objectives, no longer contains the previous Attainment Targets by which children's learning was measured in what was denounced as an assessment-driven curriculum, recognises the need for a range of mathematical connections to be made beyond an emphasis on number, recommends cross-curricular mathematical links and advocates the use and application of mathematics through problem-solving, reasoning and language. In terms of teachers having the expertise to put this into practice in order to develop mathematical understanding, it indicates a degree of autonomy in line with previous recommendations (DCSF, 2009). However, as was recognised by ACME (2006, p. 5), putting curriculum content into practice effectively 'is reliant on teachers' ability and attitude' whereas a lack of confidence has been seen in primary teachers of mathematics (ACME, 2006, p. 23) and mathematics is known to not always be 'embraced with enthusiasm and confidence' (DCSF, 2008, p. 1). So, we have the new curriculum, but are left with the question of how to implement this with confidence and efficacy.

While pedagogy has been identified as an underlying reason for the problem with mathematics education (Ryan and Williams, 2007), addressing this issue is not straightforward, as shown in over a century of changing approaches to teaching mathematics that have not as yet resulted in successful results for learners of mathematics. It is apparent that difficulty in teaching mathematics is international (Goulding et al., 2002), with MacNab and Payne (2003) suggesting that insecurities in teaching mathematics are widespread globally. Elements contributing to teachers' practice are many for, as so aptly described by Desforge and Cockburn (1987, p. 2), 'the problem of mathematics education is a many headed monster'. To attempt to tackle this decades-old problem with its underlying multi-faceted aspects is, therefore, no mean feat, but necessary when one considers the raw deal that children may be facing in some classrooms, since, as Bibby et al. (2007, p. 16) purport, 'something is going wrong for learners in mathematics classes and … this needs remedying'. Mathematics education remains a concern today, a thought that may not be encouraging to you as a new recruit to primary teaching, but which may reassure you in the sense that if you are somewhat apprehensive about teaching primary mathematics effectively, you are not alone.

This may not be a comfort; you may be feeling even more apprehensive, thinking that if the many who have gone before you have apparently not entirely succeeded in providing mathematical education that is up to scratch, then what hope do you have? What you *can* do, like Judy in the case study, is strive to be the best teacher of mathematics that you can be, because the children you will teach deserve it. To do that, you can begin with raising your awareness of the factors that may contribute to what has evidently been an historical problem. You have started with awareness of the ongoing difficulties with mathematics teaching and learning and it is intended that subsequent chapters will help you to develop your thinking further.

Chapter summary

In this chapter, changes in approaches to teaching primary mathematics have been explored alongside reflection on the impact on learners of mathematics, from the perspective of drill and practice a hundred years ago, through movement to encourage mathematical thinking in the early twentieth century, child-centred provision of the 1960s and suggested development in the 1980s for practical application, investigation and problem-solving. Associated changes in curriculum have been outlined to include the National Curriculum, National Numeracy Strategy, Primary National Strategy, government recommendations, independent reviews and the most recent version of the National Curriculum.

Mathematics education has proved difficult for over a century and continues to be a subject for review and development in terms of provision for learners. Considering pedagogy as a reason for these difficulties is not straightforward and, as such, subsequent chapters in this book will seek to encourage you to develop your awareness of learning needs relating to mathematics and ways to work on developing mathematical understanding.

As a student teacher reading this book, however, don't be disheartened. Maybe, like Judy in the case study, you are starting out on teacher training with some apprehension regarding your mathematical ability for the course and teaching children or perhaps you work alongside colleagues who share those anxieties and you are in a position to support them. Anyone experiencing concerns about teaching mathematics in the future and learning mathematics on an initial teacher training course can be reassured that they are not alone. The ensuing chapters in this book will guide you through various aspects of mathematics education to help you form your own philosophy of teaching and learning mathematics and to consider how you can fulfil your aspirations as a teacher of primary mathematics.

2
Considering a need for change

Learning objectives

Having read this chapter you will ...

- Consider your position as a future teacher of primary mathematics
- Begin to take on responsibility for your learning within teacher training
- Gain awareness of your learning needs during teacher training
- Prepare to make conscious your beliefs and assumptions about mathematics

Introduction

Whether you are a teacher who wants to improve your own mathematics teaching, a mathematics specialist teacher who wants to support colleagues in improving teaching or a student teacher wanting to get the most from their teacher education course, this chapter guides you through changes that may need to be considered. Written specifically with student teachers in mind, the content is also useful for practising teachers and anyone in a position to support colleagues who are less than confident in their mathematics teaching.

In order to develop as a teacher you will need to begin with awareness of your starting point and your current situation, as the responsibility and the power for your development and learning about mathematics and mathematics education lies in your hands. In this chapter you will be encouraged to gain an awareness of your own learning needs so that you are more able to identify and prepare for development that may be needed. In so doing, you will consider that any mathematical anxiety that you or your colleagues may have is not irrational, contrary to what some people believe! You will be encouraged to ascertain the roots of such mathematical anxiety and to begin to face any fear there may be. If you are to develop to the best of your ability as a teacher of mathematics, then it is important to consider that negative perceptions can affect your ability to engage in mathematics as a learner during initial teacher training and also your engagement with mathematics as you teach it.

The chapter includes guidance on raising awareness of mathematical perceptions to consider development, if needed, of positive perceptions of mathematics, since these have been shown to have a strong influence on understanding how to teach effectively. Also included is exploration of the possible effects of prior mathematical experience upon learning: the personal, intrinsic nature of mathematical perceptions and the difficulties faced in challenging negative perceptions and making changes, together with examination of long-held beliefs and consideration of their implications upon mathematical learning. There will be guided reflection on your own perceptions of mathematics to consider a personal philosophy for learning and teaching mathematics. The chapter includes a case study of a primary teacher who is in a position to support colleagues identified as needing improvement with regard to mathematics, as well as examples of student teachers' concerns about mathematics.

Case study

James is a primary teacher who has found himself in the position of mathematics curriculum leader through no particular desire but instead due to being the most likely candidate in the school to take on the role. He has made the most of training for mathematics specialists in primary schools, provided as a result of the Williams review (DCSF, 2008). James considers himself to be a competent mathematician and has experienced success in his own classroom, but leading colleagues in the subject is a relatively new venture for him. Although keen to develop mathematics in his school, he feels somewhat daunted by the prospect, especially since recent Ofsted feedback highlighted the need for the school to improve in this area. James has analysed assessment data across the school, finding no specific aspects of mathematics to be more problematic than others. Similarly, he has, with his colleagues' full permission, observed their practice, but no individual teachers in particular were identified as needing more support than others. The school follows a pre-agreed scheme of work, based mainly on the Primary National Strategy, following blocks and units of work in set timeframes in an agreed order. James has worked on various areas in order to make a difference to the school's approach to teaching mathematics, including subject knowledge sessions for colleagues, finding problem-solving resources to use across the school, trialling a new published scheme for mathematics, analysing the new National Curriculum in terms of content to be taught and revising means of assessment and recording if attainment target levelling is not to continue.

At this time, James began studying for a Master's degree in Education and focused on researching approaches to teaching and learning mathematics in order to learn more about how the subject can be taught effectively in the hope it would help him to understand what other support might help his colleagues improve the quality of teaching across the school. Despite the pressures of studying on top of his full-time job and his increasing worries about his responsibility for improving mathematics within the school, James found his research fascinating. Through his MA work he posed the hypothesis that alongside the various ideas he had intended to try out or had tried out within the school, the basis for considering how changes could be made might be to first identify how school staff felt about teaching mathematics, and where their strengths and weaknesses lay. He needed to consider how he might elicit such information since this was bound to be personal and maybe in some cases uncomfortable, as well as exploring the ways in which their thinking about mathematics affected the way they taught.

He began to question the extent to which children were given the opportunity to think mathematically within their learning, as he realised that, although the school as a whole used existing National Strategy guidance for planning their lessons, there was little overt indication of how these were planned over the longer term with regard to children's understanding. He suspected that not enough time was provided within the whole-school planning to really give children the chance to consolidate their mathematical thinking, carry out practical work and get involved in problem-solving. He had, during his observations, gathered evidence of children understanding the tasks provided for them and on the surface having achieved the intended learning objectives, but his questioning of the children in informal settings had intimated that their understanding of the various mathematical concepts underlying the set tasks did not perhaps go deep enough. James was interested in finding out whether his colleagues had also identified this as an area for further development across the school, but to delve deeper into this was difficult if colleagues felt their professional quality was under scrutiny. James felt the need to carry out his research within the school, in the interests of improving the teaching of mathematics, was his remit as curriculum leader, but knew from his MA study that considering and addressing the ethical implications were the crucial next stage for his research.

Post-Script: James' research is ongoing. There has been whole-school agreement, on the basis of the ethical guidelines that James has put in place with regard to staff anonymity, to the research project taking place in the interests of whole-school improvement in the area of mathematics teaching and learning.

Identifying a need for change

As we saw in Chapter 1, it would appear, given the many changes in teaching approaches over the years and the apparent ongoing dissatisfaction with the quality of learning, that mathematics is not a straightforward subject to teach and learn. As a student teacher, this may not fill you with confidence, but if you believe that children deserve better and you are determined to ensure that those in your care have good quality mathematics teaching and learning experiences, then it is important for you to seek a solution to this issue from your own perspective. You are a teacher of the future and part of either the problem, or the solution, depending on your outlook.

It is evident that mathematics education has been subjected to frequent change and this is likely to continue. Such changes are underpinned by apparent difficulties in learning and teaching mathematics. This is unlikely to be resolved easily and, if you are a student teacher setting out into primary mathematics teaching, it is similarly unlikely that this boosts your confidence in your ability to teach the subject well and indeed perhaps your confidence in learning mathematics within your initial teacher training course and beyond as a practising teacher. While this book cannot overcome any difficulties for you, it can give you the means to reflect on the situation and to focus those reflections in a meaningful way for your professional development.

It may be that you feel confident in both your mathematical knowledge and your ability to teach mathematics, or your mathematical knowledge may be good but you are unsure how you will teach the subject. Perhaps your confidence in mathematics is not strong, or you may even feel a degree of anxiety about not only teaching the subject, but having to go back to learning more about mathematics in an educational setting once more if your previous experiences were not positive. You want to be a primary teacher and teaching mathematics is part of the package, whether you like it or not, and this can be quite daunting for many student teachers.

Reflection points

- How confident do you feel about your own mathematical ability?
- How do you feel about learning to teach mathematics?
- Do you have any particular concerns about learning mathematics within initial teacher training and if so, what are those concerns?
- What might help you overcome those concerns?

It is, of course, the responsibility of the initial teacher training provider to ensure that your course meets the needs of a new teacher, including the teaching of primary mathematics. However, there is a wide and diverse range of needs amongst student teachers in terms of subject and pedagogical knowledge, alongside a wide and diverse range of attitudes towards the subject, ranging from the confident to the terrified. It may be surprising to some that an individual who dislikes mathematics would consider becoming a primary teacher, given that mathematics has to be taught in the primary school. An example is Trudi, who explained that she was genuinely frightened of beginning her course and extremely worried that she would be asked mathematical questions that she would not be able to answer. She described her concerns that she would feel that everyone would be looking at her, causing her embarrassment as well as adding to her fear and anxiety. The bravery of such individuals has to be recognised; they are determined to tackle their problems and fears head on in order to be able to achieve their career aspirations.

Meeting diverse needs of student teachers is an important task, but whatever the quality of your teacher education course, the ultimate responsibility lies with you, the student teacher. Only you can truly establish what your needs may be and ensure that these are met, either through your course or self-study. The power for learning lies in the hands of the learner and it is therefore crucial that you are aware of your learning needs and are prepared to identify what is necessary for your development in order to be in the best position possible in terms of your expectations, organisation and aspirations as a future teacher of mathematics.

Student teachers have expressed feelings of fear at the thought of learning mathematics on their initial teacher training course and have described their own previous experiences of learning mathematics as possible reasons for feeling as they do, such as Cheryl, who said she had all the confidence knocked out of her by a teacher who told her she was 'behind' everyone else. This had a strong, long-lasting effect as her mathematical confidence remained very low. Cheryl was able to identify the judgement of a previous teacher as being at the root of how she felt about mathematics as an adult. Research also indicates that negative associations with mathematics are not unfounded. Mathematics has been shown to cause rational anxiety (Hodges, 1983). As well as affecting confidence levels, negative perceptions amongst some learners can affect their ability to engage in mathematics. If you do not feel entirely positive about mathematics and you think this may have a knock-on effect on your ability to cope with teacher training and your future career, then try to avoid feeling despondent as this is not only recognised, it is mendable.

As outlined in Chapter 1, there is 'an urgent need to teach mathematics differently' (Hogden and Askew, 2007, p. 470). Perhaps your own experiences of having been taught mathematics have affected your perceptions of the subject. Daniel, for example, suggests that it is not mathematics itself that causes him problems but the thought of having to engage in mathematics again, stating that he thought it was his pre-conceptions of mathematics that caused him difficulties. You will be encouraged in later chapters to review different approaches to teaching mathematics and experiences of learning mathematics to establish the reasons for how you feel, so that you are in a better position to do something about it.

It has been established that teachers themselves have an enormous influence on what is taught and on learning (Cross, 2009), so not only might your previous mathematical experiences affect how you now perceive the subject, but the way you think about mathematics is also likely to influence your own practice (Nespor, 1987). Reflecting on your past experiences can help you to identify teaching and learning approaches that were not helpful to you as well as considering what approaches may have suited you better. Gina, for instance, remembers her experience as lacking practical opportunities. She identified that the way she was taught by a teacher standing at a board as opposed to her being able to use resources affected the way she learnt, as she remembered not being able to understand what the teacher was talking about. Through the guided reflections in this book, you can raise awareness of the way you think about mathematics, identify potential changes that you may need to work on and consider potential development of positive perceptions (Noddings, 1992) and how these might have an impact upon your teaching; they are crucial if your ultimate goal is to be the best teacher of mathematics you can be.

Reflection points

- What are your general memories of learning mathematics?
- What are the positive aspects of your experiences of learning mathematics?
- How do these positive experiences perhaps affect the way you view mathematics now?
- Do you have any negative memories of learning mathematics?
- How do any negative experiences affect the way you view mathematics now?

It is recognised that learners' 'prior conceptions of the nature of the subject matter they are studying needs to be taken into account in the design and teaching of courses in higher education' (Prosser et al., 1998, p. 94). However, while there is a need for teacher training providers to be aware of these perceptions in order to consider what to include in their courses (Swars et al., 2009), teachers have different experiences, attitudes, knowledge and pedagogical understanding of mathematics and flexible opportunities for development are needed to meet individual needs (Smith, 2004). Since the way in which you perceive mathematics now will have an effect on your learning of mathematics during initial teacher training, which in turn will impact upon the ways in which you teach primary mathematics in the future, it is important for you to be aware of your perceptions so that you can analyse the potential effects they may have on your own learning and future teaching. By doing so you can also identify changes that you may need to make and how they could be brought about, whether these arise from your teacher training or form part of your own plans to develop as a confident mathematician. You may feel like Trudi, who began her teacher training aware that she was not in the position she would like to be, yet was looking forward to being able to address her problems, stating a desire to enjoy mathematics and not be frightened or feel anxious about it.

Being determined to address any worries you have about mathematics is a must, as perceptions are a personal and intrinsic entity and direct involvement on behalf of the learner is needed in terms of taking responsibility for learning (Tolhurst, 2007). As such, it is essential for you to examine your own perceptions of mathematics and to take control of a subject that may have caused you anxiety in the past. Subsequent chapters of this book will provide you with the means to reflect on your own mathematical experience and practise in more depth in order to make the improvements you wish to make (Cooney and Krainer, 1996). Gattegno's (1971) notion that 'only awareness is educable' is valid here, in that addressing and potentially changing perceptions as may be warranted needs to start with you, for perceptions cannot be taught (Ernest, 2000) and as such the starting point lies in your own hands.

This may seem a daunting prospect, especially if you feel anxious about mathematics, but there is a wealth of research to assure you that this can be remedied. With regard to improving mathematics teaching, negative perceptions can be challenged (Uusimaki and Nason, 2004). You are certainly not alone if you do experience mathematics anxiety, which has been recognised amongst adults, and yet it can be overcome, for educationalists have shown that 'adults can get over a negative disposition towards maths' (Pound and Lee, 2011, p. 16). According to some researchers, mathematics anxiety is learnt and as such can be unlearnt (Ashcraft and Kirk, 2001). That is not to say the journey will be easy, but with your goal of wanting to do the best by the children you will teach, you can focus on making the necessary improvements and perhaps surprise yourself along the way as your confidence improves. Daniel is one such example. He began by ascertaining what it was about mathematics that was off-putting and concluded that his difficulties lay in how he thought about the subject. During his course, he worked specifically to address his personal issues as he wanted to change his mindset. By the end of his course, he was sure he had done so, resulting in him feeling much more confident and treating mathematics as 'a friend rather than an enemy'. However, he recognised that the journey had been difficult.

Change is always difficult, not least changing ingrained beliefs. You will have spent a long time in mathematics lessons, coping with mathematics in the everyday world and thinking about your career aspirations of becoming a teacher and what that involves, all of which will have contributed, consciously or not, to the perceptions you now have of mathematics and the associated effect that will have on your ability to learn about primary mathematics education and teach mathematics in the future. However, increasing your awareness of the range of perceptions people have of mathematics is an effective starting point for considering your own, and heightening awareness in such a way is recommended (Houssart, 2009). Mathematical perceptions need to be identified before they can be challenged, which is a process entirely personal and unique to anyone 'with the capability to influence their environment and determine their own actions' (Christou et al., 2001, p. 44). Although your perceptions of mathematics are a result of a lifetime of experience and may be difficult to change (Liljedahl, 2005), it is a worthwhile process to engage in so that you can determine your personal philosophy of mathematics in order to become the best teacher you can be, for as Pound and Lee (2011, p. 16) suggest, 'we owe it to them [children] to do all that we can … to develop our own enthusiasm and, in the process, our expertise'.

Reflection points

- What kind of teacher of mathematics do you aspire to be?
- How do you want children in your class to learn mathematics?
- How does this resonate or differ with your own experiences of mathematics?
- What are your initial thoughts about changes you maybe need to make if you are to fulfil your aspirations of becoming a primary teacher?

To establish your mathematical perceptions and analyse the development you may need is not straightforward. Mathematical perceptions are 'the indirect outcome of a student's experience of learning mathematics over a number of years' (Ernest, 2000, p. 7), developed over considerable time, 'implicitly and unintentionally' (Bishop, 1991, p. 195). Up until now you may never have really been aware of those perceptions or given them any conscious consideration (Ambrose, 2004), but this book will encourage you to 'examine these beliefs and consider their implications' (Schuck, 2002, p. 335). If you are already a confident mathematician, perhaps in a position to support less confident colleagues, such a reflective process may confirm your perceptions of mathematics as being valid and worthwhile, expand your awareness and gain understanding (Valderrama, 2008) as well as provide an opportunity for critical reflection leading to change. If you are not so confident, taking these first steps to confront your anxieties is a brave thing to do, as it is recognised that there can be 'great psychological difficulty for teachers of accommodating [restructuring] their existing and long standing schemas' (Skemp, 1978, p. 13). It will prove worthwhile in the long run if you emerge as a more confident mathematician who is able to provide children with good learning experiences. It is not only worthwhile, but a long-needed general approach to take since, according to Ernest (1989, p. 249), 'teaching reforms cannot take place unless teachers' deeply held beliefs about mathematics and its teaching and learning change.'

By first ascertaining your mathematical perceptions, you can then consider them with regard to whether they match your aspirations for teaching, or whether they need to change and, if so, what those changes may be. So, to begin with you will need to raise your awareness, which, according to Whitmore (2009, p. 34), involves 'gathering and clearly perceiving the relevant facts and information, and the ability to determine what is relevant'. You have a wealth of mathematical experience, much of which may not be part of your conscious thought. You need to access these experiences in order to reflect upon them and decide what is relevant to your current and future relationship with mathematics. Only once you have made conscious such awareness will you be in a position to act upon it, develop your professional knowledge and aptitude for learning and teaching, for as Whitmore (2009, p. 37) suggests, 'when we truly accept, choose, or take responsibility for our thoughts and our actions, our commitment to them rises and so does our performance'. As part of this process, you will be able to establish your own philosophy, the kind of teacher of mathematics that you aspire to be and the kind of opportunities you believe that young children should have to learn mathematics, so that you can then consider how you can achieve your aspirations.

As you embark upon teacher training you bring with you a lifetime's general experience. As Dodd (2008, p. 203) indicates, 'adults returning to learning bring with them a wide range of mathematical experiences. Memories from formal education processes have interacted with experiences from the home and workplace to bring new understandings.' Your current mathematical perceptions, whether you are fully aware of them or not, will be a result of a lifetime of both specific educational activity and also a myriad of mathematical engagement, conscious or otherwise, in everyday life. There will be mathematical situations that you are relatively confident with, others that may be new to you, and some that you may be apprehensive of. You will have skills, strategies, knowledge and understanding that you may be unaware of, aware of yet not perhaps entirely confident with, or which you are competently able to use and apply to different circumstances. You may even find there are elements of mathematics that you thought you understood but come to learn that you actually held misconceptions about. It sounds like a maze to negotiate, but what is certain is that 'an individual's personal experiences shape their values and attitudes which in turn influence how they see themselves as teachers and what kind of teacher they are' (Dunne, 2011, p. 39), and so it is essential that you gain awareness of your experiences and the influence these may have on how you feel about mathematics and your ability to learn and to teach.

Reflection points

- What experience do you have of mathematics in your everyday life?
- How confident are you at coping with the mathematics you need in life?
- Make a wish list of what you would improve if you could.

If at this stage you are increasingly aware of your insecurities about mathematics, then take comfort that this book will help you address various issues and also that you are not the first student teacher with concerns. Barry, for example, reflecting on his past experiences of learning mathematics, had asked himself whether problems had lain with him or with his teachers. He was a student teacher who knew that his mathematical confidence was not where he wanted it to be, yet was initially unsure about the reasons for this, questioning at first whether it was his own mathematical ability that he felt had let him down or whether it was the teaching he had experienced. He had a strong desire to improve his mathematical confidence and ability and began with considering past experiences to consider what had not worked for him as a starting point for ascertaining what he could do to improve. Dunne (2011) suggests that there are various influences that have an impact upon teacher 'identity', including experiences of life that have led to beliefs, values and attitudes; professional development and school experience during teacher training; and reflection on practice.

For educators, time to reflect is a precious commodity (Carson, 1995). It is difficult to find the time to step back from the everyday in order to think critically about past experiences, how these have shaped our perceptions, how we subsequently act and how we think. Reflection gives us the chance to deepen our awareness (Taylor, 2006) as we bring thoughts that were perhaps otherwise unconscious to the fore. Within education the term 'reflection' is associated with various different forms (Harvard and Hodkinson, 1995), with 'reflective practice' having many meanings (Adler, 1991). In general, to reflect means to carefully consider your own experiences and, according to Schön (1996), to apply knowledge to practice. In this case, your mathematical experiences lead to your personal beliefs, assumptions and perceptions of mathematics and to your mathematical knowledge and understanding which you will apply to mathematical practice via everyday life and specific experiences during your teacher training and in the classroom.

Considering the various elements of mathematics that are presented in this book should enable you to engage in a form of reflection that allows you to consider your own beliefs and assumptions. Such reflective practice can help you to form a professional identity (Larrivee, 2000) and in this context can facilitate your formation of a personal philosophy of mathematics education in accordance with your personal beliefs.

According to Ferraro (2000), reflective practice can lead to improved classroom effectiveness, insofar that, by engaging in reflection, you gain a better understanding of your mathematical perceptions and this greater understanding can have an impact upon your own learning and teaching. According to McGregor (2011, p. 2), 'thoughtful reflection can help you to recognise more swiftly what is effective practice and what are the key characteristics of a successful teacher'. Reflecting upon your mathematical experience, establishing your mathematical perceptions and relating what you read here to these considerations, can facilitate your recognition of what effective mathematics education might be and your contribution to this. As McGregor (2011, p. 4) suggests, 'being reflective requires active considerations about actions and their consequences' and she emphasises the importance of understanding that 'how you view yourself as a teacher (and a person) will have a bearing on the way you perform in the classroom' (2011, p. 11). Addressing your perceptions of mathematics in order to reflect upon the kind of teacher you want to be and what you might need to do to bring that about is a good start since 'reflection can inform the development of practice' (2011, p. 18).

Reflection points

- Do you have any particular concerns about teaching mathematics?
- What might help you overcome those concerns?
- Look ahead to the chapter titles in this book and identify which areas reso-
  nate with any of the concerns you have listed.

While reflection can help you to establish awareness of your mathematical perceptions, there is a need to establish how your perceptions were formed and how this influences the way you teach and learn mathematics. During initial teacher training you will develop your own professional learning as you take on the role of teacher. Napper and Newton (2000, p. 13) define learning as

> the bringing together of information, abilities and experiences – both internal and external – to create a new insight or competence which becomes freshly integrated into an individual's understanding of the work. Learning thus requires a change in an individual's frame of reference – the unique way each of us sees our world. The change may involve an altered perspective, or may be a reinforcement of previous learning.

They suggest that learning is a process of change as we develop knowledge and understanding, skills and behaviour through changing attitudes and values. This can be intentional, as we plan to learn, or incidental, as we are constantly learning even if at a subconscious level, but either way is developed through all our experiences as we consolidate meaning or construct new meaning and make sense of that which is around us. With regard to mathematics, therefore, the information, ability and experience you have built up over your lifetime, whether overt, conscious learning through your education or more implicit, informal mathematical learning through everyday life has brought you to your current level of confidence, ability and liking for mathematics. Everyone's levels are different and, especially if you are someone who lacks mathematical confidence and perceives a lack of mathematical ability and harbours a dislike for a subject that you know you have to teach if you are to become a primary teacher, it is important to recognise that it is OK. You do not need to judge or indeed be harsh on yourself if, at this time, you feel inadequate with regard to mathematics. By the very fact you have taken the time to read this, you are committed to doing something to rectify your personal situation and to seek to improve as you feel is necessary.

Charlotte was a student teacher who began her teacher training feeling terrible about mathematics. She admitted that she had never been able to do anything involving mathematics that had not resulted in her getting frustrated. A lifetime of struggling with mathematics had left her feeling that she was never going to be able to understand it. Far from anyone being judgemental about Charlotte or anyone feeling similarly negative about mathematics, she is to be admired in her courage in setting out on a course that would include learning more about the subject, engaging in mathematical situations and being responsible for children's learning of the subject. Charlotte was determined to learn, overcome difficulties, change the way she felt about mathematics and to develop the knowledge and understanding required to improve her perceptions of mathematics and be able to teach it effectively. This began with 'confronting the dragon' – being aware of the position she was in and ascertaining what she needed to do to make the necessary improvements. Charlotte knew that this would not be an easy process but it was, and indeed did transpire to be, doable. It was not just a case of learning about mathematics and mathematics education, but a cognitive and behavioural development process by which she came to change the way she perceived mathematics. As Van Nieuwerburgh (2014, p. 86) indicates, 'sometimes people have to change the way they think before they can alter what they do, especially if they are trying to make long-lasting changes'.

Just as James had identified in the case study at the beginning of this chapter, there are many elements of mathematics education provision that can affect the way in which children learn. However, an over-riding aspect of effective teaching concerns the way in which a teacher thinks about mathematics. Even the best planning, curriculum, resources or assessment strategies are dependent on the teacher who implements them and a lifetime of mathematical experience influences the mindset of the teacher and how they teach.

You may find upon reading this book that there are no changes to be made and you can go ahead with your teacher training bolstered by an affirmation that you are fully prepared for the primary mathematics component. It is more likely that you have chosen to read this book because you are either aware of colleagues who need your support, or that you need to develop in this area. If your previous mathematical experiences have led you to have negative mathematical perceptions, it is acknowledged that challenging and potentially changing established perceptions is problematic for 'beliefs tend to be highly resistant to change' (Cross, 2009, p. 327). These beliefs have been considered particularly painful with regard to the teaching of mathematics (Clarke, 1994), because the subject can evoke emotional reactions when learners reflect on past experiences. If this resonates with you, then all the more reason to do what you can to rid yourself of those demons and to ensure that the children you will teach will not have the same difficult experiences in your mathematics classroom as you endured in the past.

Chapter summary

In order to teach primary mathematics effectively, mathematical understanding and pedagogical knowledge is needed. The perceptions we have of mathematics, based on our prior experiences, affect how we understand, learn and teach mathematics. It is important, therefore, for student teachers to reflect on their prior experiences, consider their mathematical perceptions and think about the effect these may have on their future learning in initial teacher training and on their future teaching in schools. In so doing, you may identify a need for change in order for you to develop into the kind of teacher of mathematics you want to be. There is value in considering what your aspirations are for teaching and for clarifying your own philosophy in terms of how you think children should learn mathematics and how you want to be able to teach them.

Subsequent chapters will encourage you to reflect upon your own perceptions of mathematics and to establish a mathematical philosophy whereby you ascertain what mathematics means, determine your understanding of mathematics, acknowledge your attitudes towards it and consider your intentions regarding how it should be taught, so that your perceptions can be acted upon to develop effective practice during initial teacher training and beyond.

3
A framework for reflection

36 Reflective primary mathematics

Learning objectives

Having read this chapter you will ...

- Raise your awareness of a range of mathematical perceptions amongst student teachers at the outset of teacher training
- Reflect upon your own mathematical experiences and compare them with those of others
- Begin to consider how your mathematical perceptions could affect the way you learn and teach mathematics in the future
- Consider the kind of mathematics teacher you aspire to be and what changes might be necessary for you to achieve your goals

---

Introduction

Chapter 2 posited that your mathematical perceptions, based on prior experiences, can influence how you learn and teach mathematics. If you can bring your mathematical perceptions, which may have lain unconscious until now, to the fore you can raise awareness of how you think about mathematics and analyse the ways in which your thoughts may affect your future learning and teaching.

This chapter provides a framework for you to reflect upon and analyse your mathematical perceptions, and identify and plan for any changes that may be needed, if you are to learn and teach mathematics in the way to which you aspire. The reflective framework is followed by a case study of a learner and teacher of mathematics who has used the framework for her own reflection, to give you an example of how it can be used to analyse personal mathematical perceptions.

Framework for reflection

You have so far been encouraged to reflect upon a range of elements pertaining to mathematical development and to consider your own mathematical experience, including how you learnt and were taught mathematics, the way you aspire to teach mathematics, and the way you want to learn mathematics yourself as part of initial teacher training. It is important for teachers to be aware of their understanding of mathematics, what it means to them, how they feel about it, how mathematics can be learnt and how they believe it is best taught. Here follows a framework for reflecting on your past mathematical experience in a structured way.

This framework arose from in-depth interviews with a group of student teachers about to begin their teacher training. They described their past experiences of mathematics and reflected on their aspirations for becoming primary teachers of mathematics, together with their thoughts on the courses they were due to begin. All of the student teachers' responses were pooled anonymously so that no individuals could be identified from the material, but so that all responses could be analysed in order to provide a theoretical and hierarchical framework of mathematical perceptions. Rather than focusing on individual descriptions of experience, the framework provides a basis for reflection by teachers in order to ascertain their own perceptions of mathematics from the perceptions of others grouped hierarchically. As with the individual interviewees, it is likely that your own experiences will resonate with differing elements of the framework, rather than finding yourself 'fitting' in to any one part, just as the individual interviewees did not. Instead, it is intended that you identify with the elements of the framework relevant to your own experience, so that you can reflect upon the potential implications for your own mathematical learning and your aspirations for teaching. The framework provides a range of student teachers' mathematical perceptions at the outset of their initial teacher training so that you can use it to aid your reflection on your own previous mathematical experiences, raise awareness of your own mathematical perceptions and be able to compare these with others.

Based on your previous experiences of mathematics in everyday life, learning mathematics, observing mathematics being taught and your aspirations for teaching, consider which of the following descriptions from student teachers resonate with you (see Figure 3.1). You may find you associate with more than one section.

Tier 1 Mathematics: Knowledge learnt from an external relationship	Tier 2 Mathematics: Knowledge learnt from an internal relationship	Tier 3 Mathematics: Understanding learnt from an internal relationship	Tier 4 Mathematics: A way of thinking
Do you dread doing maths?	Do you wish you could be better at maths?	Do you look forward to learning to teach maths well?	Are you excited about learning and teaching maths?
Does maths bewilder you?	Are you acutely aware of your lack of mathematical understanding?	Have you begun to identify what is effective practice in teaching maths?	Have you a clear notion of what constitutes effective maths teaching?
Does it make you feel afraid, stupid, upset or ashamed?	Do you feel anxious about maths?	Do you enjoy maths?	Do you find maths stimulating?
Do you feel a sense of failure about maths?	Do you think your teachers' approaches let you down?	Do you think it is socially acceptable to not be good at maths?	Do you embrace the challenge of maths with fascination?
Do you avoid maths when possible?	Do you struggle to engage with maths?	Do you find maths interesting?	Do you think we develop mathematical understanding through an active process?
Do you tend to give up when maths is hard?	Does maths frustrate you?	Have you considered how you can improve your relationship with maths?	Do you think maths is an intrinsic part of life and part of our being?
Have bad experiences of maths stayed with you into adulthood?	Do you think your perceptions of maths impede your learning?	Do you think some people are naturally good at maths?	Do you think maths is a way we observe, think, explore and communicate what we make sense of as we interact in the world?
Does maths render you unable to think clearly?	Do you struggle to remember what you learnt because you didn't really understand maths?	Do you think maths is elusive because it is scientific as opposed to creative?	Does maths involve a creative process, based on the relation between phenomena and the experiencer?
Do you find maths pointless and difficult to relate to?	Do you see maths as something to learn to pass exams?	Is maths learnt for its purpose in applying to everyday life?	Do you see maths as an internal experience unique to the individual and a way of thinking?
Is maths mainly about number?	Is maths mainly about the real life application of number?	Does maths extend beyond the use of number?	Is maths a means by which humans seek to make sense of the world?

(Continued)

Figure 3.1   (Continued)

Tier 1 Mathematics: Knowledge learnt from an external relationship	Tier 2 Mathematics: Knowledge learnt from an internal relationship	Tier 3 Mathematics: Understanding learnt from an internal relationship	Tier 4 Mathematics: A way of thinking
Is maths really only understood by clever people?	Is maths better understood by logical people with mathematical brains?	Does maths have a particular logic and structure of its own?	Do you think we are all mathematicians who create our own unique understanding?
Does maths seem like an alien language you don't understand?	Do you find mathematical language difficult?	Have you experience of development of mathematical vocabulary and communication?	Do you aspire to develop children's sense of what is around them using mathematical language to communicate and learn?
Were you ever ridiculed by teachers for not understanding?	Did you find your teachers impatient or unhelpful?	Have you experienced teachers who encourage learners to work at their own level and speed?	Do you aspire to be an approachable, inspirational teacher who promotes interest, enjoyment, fun and excitement in learning mathematics?
Did you feel pressure to not get left behind with maths?	Did you experience competition between classmates?	Do you feel overwhelmed by maths objectives to be taught?	Do you believe children should learn the statutory curriculum at their own pace?
Were you expected to memorise mathematical facts via rote learning?	Were you taught facts, rules and procedures via demonstration and practice?	Is maths about using and applying known scientific facts, rules and procedures?	Has the science of maths been created to pose and answer questions, to develop thinking and understanding?
Was learning maths a passive experience?	Was there an emphasis on mechanically completing tasks as opposed to working with understanding?	Do you have experience of interactive, practical maths with a variety of methods, games, learner autonomy, development of mathematical thinking and children being encouraged to ask questions?	Do you aspire to learn and teach maths through active thinking, collaboration, discussion, pattern seeking, playing, experimenting, noticing, describing, articulating, testing, developing new situations, investigating, problem-solving and questioning?

Figure 3.1   Reflective framework – perceptions of mathematics

Such reflection may be a challenge, but is also an interesting journey to take. There appears to have been little engagement with philosophising about mathematics in terms of teachers questioning what their views are of mathematics and what they are teaching (Bibby, 2002b) and their associated perceptions of mathematics (De Corte et al., 2002). Perceptions are intangible and often unconsciously held, so perhaps the lack of research into eliciting mathematical perceptions is due to the difficulty that lies in capturing something so elusive (Hofer and Pintrich, 2002). The student teachers whose descriptions of mathematical experience formed the reflective framework here were very honest in their reflections, given the anonymous nature of the interviews and analysis and the non-judgemental stance of the resulting framework. It was evident as the interviews progressed that this was the first time that many of them had really thought about how they understood or felt about mathematics, which is not unusual. Existing research suggests that students may be unaware of variations in thinking about the nature of mathematics, learning the subject and using it professionally, and also that they tend 'to assume that their fellow students think in the same way that they do' (Petocz and Reid, 2005, p. 798). This chapter offers a broad view of how people think about mathematics so that you can compare and contrast with your own perceptions and link to your own aspirations for learning and teaching.

Mathematics – Knowledge learnt from an external relationship

At the beginning of the framework is the notion, presented within student teachers' descriptions, that mathematics exists as a body of knowledge that is learnt through external imposition by transference. Recollections were of being taught with little evidence of gaining mathematical knowledge beyond memorised numeric facts as recounted experiences described mathematics constituted of number, with passive learning being teacher-led via rote methods. Mathematics beyond the recall of facts was regarded as 'pointless and difficult', understood only by clever people who were seen as 'weird' and associated mathematical language was described as incomprehensible. Mathematics was regarded as an entity to be feared, a subject that learners were made to do, with fearful associations including learning experiences and expectations of finding the 'right' answer, with pressure being imposed from parents, peers and teachers. A lack of mathematical confidence was described as affecting self-esteem, with physical and mental feelings of tension, bewilderment, confusion and prevention of clear thought leading learners to switch off, get lost and seem unable to engage mathematically. Mathematics was accepted as something that cannot be understood, resulting in a tendency to give up, procrastinate, rely on others, disguise apparent lack of ability and avoid mathematical situations where possible.

Educational experiences transcended into adult life with confidence detrimentally affected and future mathematical involvement met with fear.

Reflection points

- Is there a body of mathematical knowledge 'out there' to be learnt?
- How can mathematics be taught by teachers transferring knowledge to learners?
- Were you expected to take a passive role in learning mathematics?
- Was your mathematical learning mainly concerned with number?
- Do you question the point of learning mathematics?
- Is learning mathematics difficult?
- Is mathematical language very difficult to understand?
- Does the thought of doing mathematics fill you with dread and fear?
- Was mathematics a subject at school that you felt 'made to do'?
- Was learning mathematics at school something to fear?
- Was there an expectation to find the right answer?
- Did you feel pressure from your parents, peers or teachers about learning mathematics?
- Do you lack confidence in mathematics?
- Does this affect your self-esteem?
- When you engage in mathematics, do you feel tense, bewildered or confused?
- Does this affect your ability to think clearly?
- Do you tend to switch off if you are required to engage in mathematics?
- Do you lose track when engaged in mathematical activity?
- Is it something you cannot understand?
- Do you tend to give up, put it off, rely on someone else or hide your apparent inability to do mathematics?
- Has your previous experience of mathematics affected your confidence now as an adult?
- Are you looking ahead to your initial teacher training with a degree of fear with regard to the primary mathematics education content?

If you answered yes to any of the questions above, this could be quite a painful process for you, but keep in mind your goal of overcoming your fears with a view to becoming the primary teacher you aspire to be.

Take some time to think about why you answered the questions the way you did, unpicking what it is about your past experiences that has perhaps led you to feel bad about mathematics. Try not to feel discouraged if this process has brought back to you or consolidated your negative perceptions of mathematics or the way you feel about yourself and your capability. You can work to rectify this and you are certainly not alone in doing so. Remember that all the questions above arose from the reflections made by other student teachers who felt afraid of the mathematics element of their teacher training yet were determined to overcome their difficulties in order to fulfil their aspirations.

Mathematics – Knowledge learnt from an internal relationship

Student teachers' accounts of their mathematical experiences in the first section of the reflective framework describe mathematical knowledge learnt from an external relationship with mathematics being transferred to passive learners who felt little control over their learning which was limited in depth, affecting self-esteem and confidence levels and resulting in a tendency to not want to engage in mathematical activity. The second section of the reflective framework is qualitatively different as it describes the notion that mathematics constitutes knowledge learnt from an internal relationship. Here, mathematical knowledge was described by student teachers as being gained via teacher-demonstrated methods and attempts at forming an internal relationship with mathematics through individual practice and working through schemes so that given methods could be followed to reach required 'right' answers. As previously, mathematics was perceived as an entity separate to the learner, qualitatively differentiated by the inclusion of given methods and rules as well as facts to be memorised, alongside some individual and internal relational learning. Mathematics was viewed as concerning number, but with some relevant connection to real life. Rather than giving up in the face of mathematical adversity, frustration was described of the apparent inability to understand mathematics as it was perceived to be the realm of 'logical people' with 'mathematical brains'. Hence, while mathematics was limited to knowledge as opposed to understanding, some internal and relational engagement with learning mathematics through working through schemes was described, alongside an awareness of the limitations of mathematical knowledge without understanding.

Reflection points

- Do your memories of learning mathematics include teachers demonstrating and modelling mathematical methods on the board?
- Were you then required to practise the methods individually?
- Do you recall working individually through schemes such as textbooks?
- Was there an expectation to follow the teacher's given method to reach the answer required?
- Were you introduced to methods and rules you had to then remember?
- Did your mathematics lessons mainly consist of number but with some relevance made to everyday life?
- Did mathematics frustrate you?
- Did you feel like you did not fully understand what you were doing?
- Do you think people who can do mathematics are logical and have brains that think a certain way?

In this part of the reflective framework, mathematics is described less as an external body of knowledge that has been imposed on the learner, but more as something which the learner has more engagement in as they follow methods shown to them, as opposed to the rote learning based on memorisation of the first part of the framework. As learners work individually through set schemes, there is more opportunity for them to assimilate mathematical knowledge on an internal level although learners are left feeling that, despite perhaps achieving the required correct answers, they are not really sure that they understood what was going on beyond following the rules expected.

Elements of the first and second parts of the reflective framework may resonate with you. It is not expected that you would necessarily 'fit into' any particular section. Instead consider the qualitatively different descriptions of mathematical experiences and how they can widen your awareness of your own perceptions of mathematics and how they have formed over a lifetime of different forms of mathematical activity. As you develop this reflection, consider why you feel about mathematics as you do and particularly how your mathematical understanding has developed, what teaching approaches have helped or hindered you and what approaches to learning mathematics have best suited you.

Mathematics – Understanding learnt from an internal relationship

Differing qualitatively from the second tier of the reflective framework where mathematics was perceived as knowledge learnt from an internal relationship, is this third tier where the importance of mathematical process and the notion of development of mathematical understanding are seen as necessary for everyday life. An ambivalent attitude towards mathematics is described with a social acceptance of not being good at mathematics, varying degrees of confidence, frustration at not achieving 'right' answers and the perceived elusiveness of mathematics as a structured science with rules to be followed to get answers constituted in given curriculum content to be learnt. However, an internal relative understanding constructed through social interaction involving questioning, engagement and application alongside helpful teachers using a variety of methods and resources to meet learners' needs including visual apparatus, collaboration, games, logic, vocabulary and encouragement of mathematical thinking was identified as necessary to gain understanding.

Reflection points

- When you were being taught mathematics, was an emphasis made on the importance of mathematical process?
- Were you shown different mathematical methods for the same problem as opposed to following one set method?
- Was it more important to know how to go about solving mathematical problems as opposed to necessarily getting the right answer?
- Was mathematics linked to everyday life?
- Were you encouraged to use mathematics that you knew and apply it to what you did not know?
- Do you neither really like nor dislike mathematics?
- Does your confidence in mathematics vary?
- Do you feel a sense of frustration when you cannot get the right answer?
- Do you see mathematics as a science?
- Does mathematics have its own rules to be followed in order to get to the answer?
- Did your mathematics lessons adhere to a set curriculum content?

(Continued)

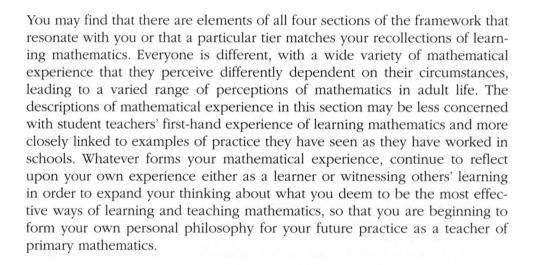

(Continued)

- Did your mathematics lessons allow you some chance to question, get involved and apply what you understood?
- Were your teachers helpful?
- Did your teachers use different methods to aid your mathematical understanding?
- Did your mathematics lessons involve the use of resources to help you learn through visual means, collaboration, playing games, using logic and developing mathematical vocabulary?
- Did your teachers encourage you to think mathematically and to express your mathematical thinking through different means?

You may find that there are elements of all four sections of the framework that resonate with you or that a particular tier matches your recollections of learning mathematics. Everyone is different, with a wide variety of mathematical experience that they perceive differently dependent on their circumstances, leading to a varied range of perceptions of mathematics in adult life. The descriptions of mathematical experience in this section may be less concerned with student teachers' first-hand experience of learning mathematics and more closely linked to examples of practice they have seen as they have worked in schools. Whatever forms your mathematical experience, continue to reflect upon your own experience either as a learner or witnessing others' learning in order to expand your thinking about what you deem to be the most effective ways of learning and teaching mathematics, so that you are beginning to form your own personal philosophy for your future practice as a teacher of primary mathematics.

Mathematics – A way of thinking

The reflective framework has begun with mathematics learning being confined to knowledge that has been passed on from an external source in an attempt to be absorbed by a passive recipient, before moving on to mathematical knowledge that is learnt with more of an internal relationship between the learner and the mathematics through attempts to work individually through given tasks, activities, methods and rules, to the third tier where the learner's mathematical understanding is being developed through a greater focus on mathematical process, the use of more varied methods of learning mathematics involving more social interaction and with higher levels of learner confidence. The fourth and final tier outlines student teachers' descriptions of their mathematical experience, either through their own learning, approaches to teaching they have witnessed or their own aspirations to teach mathematics that view mathematics not necessarily as an entity to be taught but as a way of thinking.

Mathematics is described in this final tier by student teachers as creative, as opposed to a scientific, structured body of knowledge to be learnt or a prescribed curriculum to be taught. It is viewed as the way in which children and adults understand the world around them and communicate their understanding to each other. Attitudes were presented of enjoyment and interest in mathematics, excitement in engaging in mathematics and the desire to be inspirational teachers. In so doing, accounts described the difficulties in changing perceptions of mathematics, based on prior experiences, some of which had negative associations, with aspirations to be creative, approachable, encouraging, promoting interest, fun and excitement and diagnosing children's understanding.

Awareness of curriculum requirements was acknowledged, but the approach to learning was qualitatively different through aspirations to provide learning environments that promote an internal relationship with mathematical development amongst learners, where children can question, collaborate, feel comfortable and work at their own pace, with intentions to meet children's needs through flexibility, group work, learning tasks, visual, interactive and practical activities, use of different methods, relevance and cross-curricular links. The scientific nature of mathematics was described as being facts, methods and rules that have been created by mathematicians and which can be explored by children through a flexible approach of active learning that encourages development of thinking and use of different ways of solving problems, in addition to posing problems, based on the notion that mathematics is itself a way of thinking. Difficulties in learning mathematics were described not in negative terms, but as a challenge to be embraced with a sense of fascination, for a philosophy of mathematics that represents a framework for trying to describe, understand and shape the world and that is seen as a source of stimulation and wonder. Rather than being merely relevant, mathematics was perceived as not only *essential* to everyday life and to functioning in the world, but also as a way of thinking that has been used by humans to make sense of the world and communicate understanding, to be used by children through investigation and an holistic approach.

Reflection points

- Do you perceive mathematics as creative?
- Do you think of mathematics as a way of making sense of the world and communicating human understanding?
- Is mathematical understanding a part of everything we do?
- Can mathematics be a source of wonder and stimulation for children?
- Is engaging in mathematics a challenge?
- Do you see such a challenge as a potential source of enjoyment, interest and excitement?
- Do you aspire to be an inspirational teacher of primary mathematics?
- As a teacher of primary mathematics, do you aspire to be creative, approachable, encouraging; promote interest, fun and excitement; diagnose and develop children's mathematical understanding?
- Do you hope to provide mathematical learning environments where children can question, collaborate, feel comfortable and work at their own pace?
- Do you intend to meet children's needs through flexibility, group work, learning tasks, visual, interactive and practical activities, use of different methods, relevance and cross-curricular links?
- Do you see the structured, scientific aspect of mathematics that includes accepted facts, rules and methods as having been created by mathematicians before us?
- Do you think children should explore mathematics via active learning that encourages development of thinking and use of different ways of solving problems, in addition to posing problems?
- Do you see mathematics as a way of thinking?

You may find that this final part of the framework has led you to think about not only the approaches to teaching mathematics that you experienced as a learner, but also those you may have witnessed in more recent observations and involvement in primary teaching. This in turn may have led you to think about how you want to teach mathematics and approaches you do not want to replicate if you did not yourself find them useful. It may be that you have confirmed your mathematical perceptions and are now chomping at the bit to begin your teacher training and learn more about how you can put your aspirations into practice. The rest of this book may help you prepare for that and perhaps to provide support for colleagues along the way.

If this reflection about your own experiences and aspirations for your future makes you feel that an impossible task lies ahead of you, do not worry as it is not impossible. An increasing awareness of what your mathematical perceptions are and how they may have been influenced by your past experiences is a starting point for change. You are in a position to use that increased awareness to compare your own mathematical experiences and perceptions with those of other student teachers so that you can decide on your own philosophy for learning and teaching mathematics. Having reached this stage you are then ready to identify the changes you wish to make and how to achieve them.

Reflection points

- What have you learnt about your previous mathematical experiences?
- How do these compare to the mathematical experiences of other new teachers?
- How would you describe your perceptions of mathematics?
- What, if anything, would you want to change about the way you perceive mathematics if you could?
- Go back to your previous reflections on the kind of primary mathematics teacher you aspire to be. What changes, if any, do you need to bring about in order to fulfil your aspirations?

If reflecting on your previous mathematical experience and making conscious your mathematical perceptions has been a somewhat painful experience, you may find it heartening to read the following case study. This outlines the reflections of an experienced mathematician and teacher of mathematics who you may perhaps expect to identify most closely with the top tier of the hierarchical framework. You may therefore be encouraged to learn that this is not the case for, as previously intimated, we all have different mathematical experiences, some of which were out of our control, but all of which have contributed to our mathematical perceptions. What matters is that we are aware of what these are and able to act according to what we identify as being in need of change.

Case study 📂

Faye has an Honours and a higher degree in mathematics, has taught mathematics in secondary and primary schools, lectured in mathematics at degree level and has worked within initial teacher training with student secondary and primary teachers. In engaging with the hierarchical framework for reflection, she found different periods of her learning and teaching of mathematics resonated with different tiers of the framework.

Taking her earliest memories of her own primary mathematics education, she very much identified with the lower tier of the framework. Aspects of mathematical knowledge were required to be learnt parrot-fashion, such as multiplication tables, and other areas of mathematics were dependent on practising methods, as demonstrated by teachers on the board, whereby all learners within groups completed the same tasks, although some finished earlier than others. There was some provision to meet different children's needs, with children grouped according to ability with different sets of work on the board. Faye was aware of fierce competition within the class to come top in exams, but although she found the mathematics easy and frequently got high marks, she knew she didn't really understand. She recalls in particular a feeling of dread when the weekly session of problem-solving came around. This was an opportunity to apply the largely number-based practice from daily lessons to word problems in a series of books which caused Faye to panic and get upset as she remembers she had no idea how to solve them, despite the teacher's expectation that she should be able to.

Faye's recollections of her grammar school education matched many elements of the second tier of the reflective framework. The teachers modelled examples of mathematical method on the board and then learners were expected to work individually through a series of examples in textbooks. There was an expectation to understand and very little support from the teachers for anyone brave enough to admit they didn't. Peers who did seem to do well at mathematics tended to be regarded as 'swots' and mostly played down their achievements so as not to be singled out. Endeavouring to understand from worked examples and individual progress, together with pressure from teachers, peers and parents to do well meant that a greater internal relationship between learner and mathematics was needed to try to make sense of the tasks set. This frequently took the form of looking up the answer in the back of the workbooks to try to work backwards to the question in an attempt to fill in the required method so as not to be accused of cheating. The focus was very much on gaining a set of correct answers, with teachers never seeming interested in how much pupils really understood. This led to some development of mathematical knowledge, sufficient to pass assessments to gain both 'O' and 'A' levels in mathematics, but it was a frustrating time with a constant intimation from teachers that it was never good enough.

Faye went on to study mathematics at university and her experiences remained linked to the second tier of the hierarchy as the mathematics teaching was rooted in lecture-style modelling of methods with lecturer expectations to follow up through practising examples. Faye and her peers were acutely aware of the gaps in their understanding and provided support for each other, determined in their efforts to pass their exams as opposed to much intrinsic motivation, and Faye was aware of her lack of ability to use and apply her knowledge. She could complete set tasks well, using the particular form of statistical analysis stated in an activity for example, but would not have been able, given a set of data, to know independently which form of analysis to apply.

After university, Faye went into secondary teaching, where she felt limited by what she deemed to be outmoded ways of teaching, far too similar to the ways she had been taught herself. Frustrated by the apparent lack of awareness in the schools in which she taught of recommendations being made by reports such as Cockcroft (1982), she moved to primary school teaching where she was just as dismayed by the requirement to teach using individualised textbooks with a lack of practical work, investigation and exploratory problem-solving. Her experiences at this time closely reflected the second tier of the framework until she was able to teach in a school that embraced her philosophy of children's mathematical experiences being tailored to their particular needs. Although Ofsted required her to adhere to the National Curriculum and whole-school policy to the National Numeracy Strategy, these were used only to guide the content of lessons as she had the freedom to teach in the way she thought best. Children were encouraged to ask questions; to use practical apparatus; to use visual prompts; to discuss, argue, conjecture and explain; and in so doing, experience a range of methods and approaches to decide which worked best for them in reaching mathematical understanding and confidence. Parents came into school wanting to see what happened in mathematics lessons that caused their children to talk so much at home about mathematics and to be so excited about the subject. Faye's personal philosophy therefore resonated with the final tier of the reflective framework as she encouraged children to think mathematically, to see the world through a mathematical lens in order to be able to understand and explain it and to use mathematics to make things happen.

Building on this experience, Faye moved to teach at a university where she attempted to maintain her philosophy for teaching mathematics in degree-level classrooms, but was instead met with an ethos to adhere not only to statutory curriculum but also to non-statutory guidance which was accepted and presented to student teachers with little critique. Attempts were made to

(Continued)

(Continued)

encourage student teachers to use a range of approaches, to focus on mathematical process and to use and apply their mathematical knowledge, skills and understanding, but the approaches used by some lecturers themselves did not always mirror the underlying philosophy and Faye's experience here resonated with the third tier of the reflective framework. Faye was encouraged by the teaching team to use set teaching plans which gave examples followed by opportunities for students to try out the activities for themselves, which involved social collaboration and the use of resources to meet learners' needs, including visual apparatus, collaboration, games, logic and vocabulary, but the development of autonomous mathematical thinking did not seem to permeate all learning opportunities as a somewhat didactic approach was taken by the teaching materials Faye was required to adopt and time constraints prevented learning at a deeper level.

Post-Script: Faye became disillusioned with the constraints of higher education and changed jobs to return to primary teaching where she had more autonomy and could be true to her mathematical beliefs.

As can be seen, there is a range of variation in the student teachers' accounts of their own mathematical perceptions which provided the basis of the framework. As the case study demonstrates, the framework can be used as a basis of individual reflection in order to focus on personal experiences of mathematics, to compare these with the hierarchical elements of the framework in order to analyse what constitutes effective mathematics learning and teaching and the impact that mathematical perceptions can have. The hierarchical nature of the framework does not mean judgement is placed on the student teacher engaging with such analysis if, for example, an individual realises that the lower elements of the hierarchical framework resonate more than the higher since, as the case study shows, an individual could relate to several, if not all, of the framework tiers in reflecting on past experiences that have led to current mathematical perceptions.

If your reflections resulted in you finding your own mathematical experiences linking to different elements at different times, perhaps Faye's example will encourage you to realise that this is no reflection on your own ability. Faye was able to reflect on her experience and perceptions in order to move her teaching on to match her own philosophy and values in a different arena. What is important is not what your past mathematical experiences constitute, but that you use your developing awareness of your mathematical perceptions to decide on your philosophy for learning and teaching mathematics and identify and plan changes you intend to make in order to reach your goals.

You have begun to give very careful thought to your past mathematical experiences, your mathematical perceptions, your aspirations for learning to be a teacher of mathematics and your aspirations as a future primary teacher. Further chapters in this book will focus on some of the key areas of reflection presented in this framework in order for you to identify and make any changes that you may consider necessary.

Chapter summary

In Chapter 3 you have built on your reflections upon a range of pedagogical elements pertaining to mathematical development, based on your examination of prior mathematical experience, the ways in which you were taught and have learnt mathematics, the ways in which you aspire to teach mathematics and the ways in which you hope to learn mathematics through initial teacher training. The importance of teachers being aware of their own mathematical understanding, what mathematics means to them, how they feel about it, how mathematics can be learnt and how they believe it is best taught has been explored. The chapter presents a pragmatic framework for reflecting upon past mathematical experience in a structured way with the intention of raising your awareness of previous mathematical experience and associated perceptions, and comparing this with others, in order to consider differing perspectives, identify personal perceptions, ascertain aspirations and set goals for mathematical learning and development within initial teacher training.

The hierarchical structure of mathematical perceptions arising from actual described experiences of student teachers is presented here to provide a framework for you to reflect on your own mathematical experiences, beliefs and aspirations for teaching. Consideration of the framework facilitates your development of awareness of a range of perceptions of mathematics amongst student teachers, identification of your own perceptions of mathematics within the framework, comparison of your personal perceptions of mathematics with the range of variation of mathematical perceptions presented and identification of your aspirations for learning and teaching mathematics.

4
Attitudes towards mathematics

Learning objectives

Having read this chapter you will ...

- Make conscious your feelings about and attitude towards mathematics
- Reflect on the potential reasons for you feeling the way you do
- Consider the impact your attitudes may have on the ways in which you learn and teach mathematics in the future
- Set yourself goals and think about the changes you may need to bring about in order to achieve these

Introduction

At this point you will be aware, if you were not already, that difficulties have been experienced with mathematics learning and teaching for a long time. You are not going to be able to change this overnight, but you can make a difference in your own way. By being conscious of your own mathematical perceptions, comparing them with others and beginning to identify the changes you want to make, you are in a better position to set about becoming an effective teacher of primary mathematics.

As outlined previously, a good starting point is to raise your awareness so that you can reflect and act upon your reflections, as the way in which change can be brought about lies entirely with you. What this chapter can help you with in particular is analysing your attitude towards mathematics so that you can consider further how you feel about mathematics, what has led you to feel that way, the impact your attitude could have on your future learning in initial teacher training and on your teaching in the primary classroom, so that you can set about making changes as necessary. The chapter includes a case study of a student teacher who set out on initial teacher training with a very negative attitude towards mathematics and outlines what she put in place to improve her situation.

Case study

Students embarking on training to become primary teachers are incredibly brave if they have the extreme negative emotions associated with mathematics as those whose descriptions constituted the first category of the reflective framework in Chapter 3. Carla was one such student.

She recalled early experiences of mathematics that included unfriendly teachers in her primary school who shouted at children and banged rulers and board rubbers on desks in front of them in an intimidating manner. Carla's primary school environment was one of fear as children who did not get right answers were targeted by insensitive and, at times, bullying teachers. Mathematics was a subject Carla particularly struggled with and she remembers feeling picked on in lessons.

At secondary school, Carla's teachers were less aggressive but tended to be impatient. She felt that she lagged behind as she had learnt little in the previous, hostile primary school environment but she tried hard to follow the examples that were given on the classroom board and to do her best. Carla recalls wishing that she had been able to ask questions in order to help her understand, but her teachers would get cross if they had to repeat or go over explanations. There was an expectation that the children should follow the methods shown and then reproduce them without the need for individual support and teachers didn't like children saying they didn't understand. Some teachers were unapproachable and Carla describes feeling like she was wasting the teacher's time if she asked for help.

Before beginning her teacher training, Carla had tried to catch up on her mathematics subject knowledge by buying and working through self-study guides and had paid for private tuition for further help with certain areas. Her university also provided a pre-course booster week for students who needed support in mathematics and she signed up for that. Although her extra studying had helped, Carla didn't feel she really understood mathematics, even on the occasions she got the correct answers as written in the back of her

(Continued)

(Continued)

self-study books. She never felt sure why what she had done had resulted in the correct answers and she certainly didn't feel confident in explaining methods to children when the time came for her to teach.

Carla began the booster course by shying away from offering ideas or responding to the tutor or the rest of the learning group. Given learning tasks, she would wait to see how other people would go about solving the problems before she had a go herself. Even when she got the same answers, she was convinced she had done it wrong if her methods differed from others.

As the week's course progressed, Carla began to panic less and relax more, feeling increasingly confident in asking questions of her fellow students and the tutor. She became noticeably more cheerful in engaging in the mathematics activities. When asked if she would like to discuss her progress with the tutor, she confided how apprehensive she had been to enter a mathematics classroom again after her traumatic experiences in school. Carla had begun the course with very little confidence in her mathematical ability and very worried about what the tutor and her fellow students would think of her.

The tutor asked her to explain what had helped to boost her confidence during the week. First, Carla had been relieved that she was not the only one to find mathematics so difficult and also in discovering that others had had similarly disturbing experiences learning mathematics at school. Although she had gained the mathematics qualification needed to start the initial teacher training course, she felt that she had been 'going through the motions' and that understanding mathematics was beyond her capability. However, the methods used on the course, the interaction between individual and groups sharing their ideas, approaches and concerns, the use of practical apparatus and trying out different methods to solve problems had helped Carla see that there were different ways to approach mathematics. She was grateful for the friendliness and support of the group and the encouragement to ask questions and work at her own pace.

Post-Script: Carla knew that she still had a lot to learn, but she had discovered that the mathematics of her classrooms as a school-age learner were different from the classrooms she could expect during her teacher training. Her self-esteem continued to flourish as she learnt more about mathematics education throughout her course and made conscious decisions about the teacher she wanted to be.

Attitudes towards mathematics

It is clear from talking to many student teachers, especially those interviewed for the reflective framework in Chapter 3, that varying attitudes towards mathematics exist. What is of particular concern here is that negative attitudes such as Carla's towards mathematics have been shown to affect students' learning (Townsend and Wilton, 2003). There is a distinct possibility that negative perceptions of mathematics held by student teachers can detrimentally affect learning and developing professional practice during their teacher training.

However, there is hope, not least through Carla's example, for attitudes can be worked upon and changed. Indeed, mathematical difficulties amongst student teachers have been shown to be overcome during initial teacher training (Hopkins et al., 2004). It is not expected that negative perceptions can be changed quickly; only you can establish if changes need to be made and ascertain how you might best achieve them. Carla's case study exemplifies how she was able to reflect upon her previous experiences and understand how her negative attitudes towards mathematics had been formed. She was then able to build on new and different mathematical experience to build her confidence and self-esteem. She realised that it was perhaps not mathematics itself that was problematic, but the way in which she had been introduced to it. Not all cases will be the same as Carla's, but her story may act as reassurance that it is possible to change your mindset even with extremely negative associations with mathematics at the outset.

In an attempt to identify your potential difficulties in terms of your attitude towards mathematics, therefore, let us return specifically to the framework in Chapter 3 so that you can begin to analyse how these affect your mathematical perceptions and, in turn, the impact this could have on your learning and teaching practice. The fear presented in the first part of the framework stemming from experience is demonstrated in adult life through lack of confidence and self-esteem regarding mathematics, leaving some student teachers fearful of teacher training. Nervousness, belying a desire to overcome difficulties, constitutes the second category, whereas the third section of the framework comprises actions planned for improvements identified as necessary during teacher training. The final category depicts mindfulness of what learning is needed, but differs from previous sections in terms of student teachers' excitement towards teacher training and future practice in school.

You may have found the descriptions of mathematical experience from the lower part of the reflective framework brought back similarly painful memories from your own mathematical learning. The learners who contributed to this part of the reflective framework described a sense of knowing something about mathematics, but really only what was confined to memory with very little associated understanding. This resulted in a fear of mathematics, as there was an awareness of the need to understand and yet an acute sense of failure that this was not achieved. Marianna, for instance, stated that she never liked any of her mathematics lessons at school as she used to get upset and cry. Student teachers recounted 'horrible' and 'awful' memories of learning mathematics and some, like Carla, had been afraid of both their teachers and the subject. There is a real danger here to learning, as such fear of teachers has proved to be a factor detrimental to mathematical performance (Cockburn, 1999).

The mathematics learning that student teachers recalled as 'divisive and daunting' left a legacy of feeling unable to do mathematics and a sense of stupidity, since their past experiences had created ridicule and feelings of oppression. They talked of being 'devastated' by their experiences, which they described as 'soul destroying', with pressure from teachers that left them feeling inadequate and self-conscious. As Barbara explained, the responsibility for not understanding rested firmly on their shoulders as children as she intimated that she could not speak out in her school classroom and admit to not understanding the mathematics presented or she was subjected to what she termed 'public humiliation'. Her description of her experience was that pupils who did not understand were 'made to look thick'.

Barbara was not the only one who described feeling dislike of mathematics, indicating that these feelings continued into adulthood. Such negative experiences affect motivation and certainly can have long-lasting effects on confidence. At the outset of her teacher training course Naz, for example, stated that she 'dreamed about not ever having to worry about maths again'. Some, like Robert, felt ashamed by their struggles with mathematics, describing his relationship with mathematics as 'a big black cloud hanging over' him.

Real depth of feeling was shown towards mathematics amongst these student teachers and they are not alone, as research has shown that mathematics can be 'intensely emotional' (Bibby, 2002a, p. 706), evoking 'real emotional turbulence' (Brown, 2005, p. 21). Remember that these were new student teachers and, if like them, you feel as frightened about mathematics as they did, then you are to be commended in addressing such fear in order to be able to achieve your goals.

While it could be a painful process, confronting your own thoughts about mathematics will be a worthwhile process if it helps you to take stock of your situation and decide how you can make things better. Nobody else needs to hear your thoughts and you personally do not need to feel ashamed about these for, as your reflections may have revealed, there are many factors that may have led you to feel about mathematics in this way, many of which you probably had little control over. By addressing the emotions you feel towards mathematics head-on, through recognising and being aware of them, you will be in a position to seek to overcome any negativity standing in your way.

Reflection points

- Are there, or have there been, times when having to do mathematics has scared you?
- Have your previous experiences of mathematics instilled fear in you that has stayed with you in adult life via lack of confidence and self-esteem regarding mathematics?

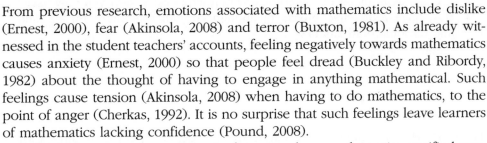

- Do you look ahead to initial teacher training with a degree of fear about the primary mathematics education involvement?
- Does it really worry you that you do not understand mathematics as much as you think you should or as much as you would like to be able to?
- Do any of your own mathematical experiences resonate with these painful memories that these new teachers describe?
- What were the reasons for you feeling that way about mathematics?
- To what extent do you still feel the same way about mathematics?
- Although you cannot change the past, how could your attitude towards mathematics be improved?
- What would you need in order to be able to change to fulfil your aspirations?
- How can you bring that change about?
- How have your reflections so far influenced your aspirations for learning and teaching mathematics?

From previous research, emotions associated with mathematics include dislike (Ernest, 2000), fear (Akinsola, 2008) and terror (Buxton, 1981). As already witnessed in the student teachers' accounts, feeling negatively towards mathematics causes anxiety (Ernest, 2000) so that people feel dread (Buckley and Ribordy, 1982) about the thought of having to engage in anything mathematical. Such feelings cause tension (Akinsola, 2008) when having to do mathematics, to the point of anger (Cherkas, 1992). It is no surprise that such feelings leave learners of mathematics lacking confidence (Pound, 2008).

Perhaps there have been times in the past where mathematics terrified you, but you now have a more comfortable relationship with it. The second level of the reflective framework of Chapter 3 indicated that some learners were aware of their limited mathematical knowledge, but instead of shying away from mathematical engagement, they attempted to internalise mathematics understanding through the learning opportunities that were presented to them. However, they talked of 'horrible teachers' and 'being taught in a horrible way from a blackboard' with learning seen as 'very off-putting'. Experiences of this type were not frightening or humiliating but learners did describe 'embarrassment at not understanding as there's only so many times you want to ask someone'. They also described feeling frustration towards mathematics as they experienced difficulties in learning that were not resolved by the teaching approaches that were used. Some described a sense that teachers expected them to understand and as such not much support was provided, thereby adding to the frustration. Such frustration with mathematics has also been witnessed amongst student teachers by Haylock (2010), who describes the attitudes some adults have towards mathematics as the 'emotional baggage' (2010, p. 5) of feeling a mathematical failure and a legacy of anxiety concerning the depth of mathematical knowledge required for teacher training.

Reflection points

- Do any of your own past mathematical experiences resonate with those described by these students?
- Does it frustrate you that you do not understand mathematics as much as you think you should or as much as you would like to be able to?
- Which of the teaching and learning approaches that you experienced would you emulate in your own practice?
- Which of the teaching and learning approaches that you experienced would you not take on board for your own practice?
- Have your previous experiences of mathematics created anxiety that has stayed with you in adult life making you nervous of mathematics?
- Do you look ahead to initial teacher training with a degree of anxiety about the primary mathematics education involvement?
- Are you determined to overcome any mathematical anxiety you may have?
- How have your reflections so far influenced your aspirations for learning and teaching mathematics?

There is a wide range of research that evidences people feeling foolish (Haylock, 2010) because of their perceived mathematical ability, and mathematics causes adults to feel bewildered (Buxton, 1981) by it. Some have described feeling ashamed (Bibby, 2002a), guilty (Cockcroft, 1982) and inadequate (Brown et al., 1999). As seen in the reflective framework, such feelings can lead to distress (Akinsola, 2008) and panic (Buxton, 1981). If you recognise yourself in these descriptions, then try not to take this as a reflection on your worth and instead recognise the contributing factors that have led to you feeling this way and that you are not the only one to have experienced this.

In the third category of the framework, learners described a better understanding of mathematics and seemed to have formed an internal relationship with mathematics. Although not particularly over-enthused by the subject, mathematics did not hold much anxiety for them and they presented varying degrees of confidence. There was, however, a certain sense of it not being 'cool' to admit to being competent with mathematics, with Marie, for example, indicating that 'I do like sitting down working out problems – it's quite sad really.'

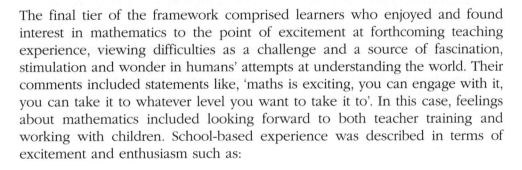

Reflection points

- Does this somewhat ambivalent attitude with mathematics resonate with you?
- What are the reasons for these feelings towards mathematics?
- Do you enjoy mathematics?
- Do you find mathematics interesting?
- Have you already identified or made changes to improve the way you think about mathematics ready for your initial teacher training course?
- In what ways could improvement be made from the perspective of the teacher you are to become, entrusted as you will be with teaching mathematics to children in the future?
- How have your reflections so far influenced your aspirations for learning and teaching mathematics?

The final tier of the framework comprised learners who enjoyed and found interest in mathematics to the point of excitement at forthcoming teaching experience, viewing difficulties as a challenge and a source of fascination, stimulation and wonder in humans' attempts at understanding the world. Their comments included statements like, 'maths is exciting, you can engage with it, you can take it to whatever level you want to take it to'. In this case, feelings about mathematics included looking forward to both teacher training and working with children. School-based experience was described in terms of excitement and enthusiasm such as:

> seeing the kids getting it I was actually – I was thinking, I remember that and yeah, and I actually did feel myself getting excited. I've observed a few lessons, maths lessons specifically, that I have felt, oh, excellent, cool, you know that's really great, that's grabbing me that.

The fourth category in the framework constitutes an enjoyment of, interest in and liking for mathematics which correlates with confidence in mathematical ability, extending to excitement at the challenge of engaging in mathematical activity, alongside fascination for the way in which mathematics allows the world to be explored and understood. It is probable, given that you have chosen to read this book, that you do not necessarily feel that your own feelings resonate with the descriptions given in the higher tier of the reflective framework, but that perhaps these are feelings you aspire to even if gaining such positivity towards the subject seems a long way off. Remember, however, that a good starting point is to ascertain what your feelings are and what changes you would really like to make, so that you can build on that growing awareness to begin to both identify a need for and work on making changes.

Reflection points

- If you really enjoy mathematics, what are the reasons for that?
- Do you find mathematics challenging, but think that it is OK to feel challenged by it?
- Do you find mathematics fascinating?
- Do you find mathematics stimulating to the brain?
- Do you find in mathematics a sense of wonder at how humans have attempted over the years to understand the mysteries of the world?
- Are you in a position to support colleagues who are not as enthused by mathematics as you are and if so how?
- If you do not really enjoy mathematics, is being able to enjoy it something you aspire to?
- What would you need in order to be able to improve your relationship with mathematics to this extent?
- Are you mindful of what you need to learn through your initial teacher training course, and excited about the prospect of learning primary mathematics education and your future practice in school?
- How have your reflections so far influenced your aspirations for learning and teaching mathematics?

Teachers have enormous influence on the children in their care; 'teachers can and do make huge differences to children's lives … indirectly through their … attitudes' (DfES, 2002b, p. 2). Thinking about this responsibility that you will have over children's learning of, and relationship with, mathematics may be daunting, but keep in mind your goal of improving your own relationship with mathematics so that you can provide quality mathematical learning experiences for the children you will teach.

It is recognised that if you 'lack confidence and dislike the subject [you] may find it difficult to work up the enthusiasm to teach mathematics in an effective manner' (Cockburn, 1999, p. 15), but your aspiration is to be a primary teacher and as such you will teach mathematics. No matter what your past experiences of mathematics have been or how you feel about the subject, you owe it to the children in your care to teach it effectively so that they have the best chance of learning mathematics confidently and with understanding. If your own recollections of learning mathematics are not all positive you can be bolstered by a determination for history not to repeat itself in your own classroom. Negative past experiences of learning mathematics can serve as a good basis of how not to teach yourself.

If your confidence is not high and you do have negative feelings towards mathematics, do not let this put you off your goal of becoming a primary teacher. It can seem like a long road lies ahead of you, and student teachers before you, like Carla, have questioned their ability to overcome their fears in order to be able to teach primary mathematics well. It is essential that teachers present a positive attitude towards the subject if this is to be encouraged in learners (Akinsola, 2008). You may have to work on how you portray your own attitudes to the children you teach, so that you are not unconsciously influencing children in a way you would not want to do.

You may be wondering at this point if it is enough to fake a positive attitude in front of children. While this is perhaps a starting point, hopefully you will gradually develop your confidence and outlook and substantiate the vibes you give off in the classroom, especially as children are very good at seeing through a mask! While it is probably just common sense and easily accepted that a positive attitude towards mathematics is beneficial to effective teaching (Mooney and Fletcher, 2003), it may alarm you to read that there are also recommendations that 'excited and enthusiastic' teachers of mathematics are needed if mathematics learning and teaching is to be improved (ACME, 2006, p. 4). If you are reading this book because you are a long way from being excited and enthusiastic about teaching mathematics, then remember what your long-term goals are and be comforted that you *are* doing something about it.

One the one hand, mathematics has been described as an unemotional subject (Paechter, 2001), yet Bibby (2002a) observed amongst teachers that attitudes towards mathematics can be highly emotional. There is no doubt amongst student teachers that emotions can run high where mathematics is concerned. While there is no assumption made that only negative attitudes exist towards mathematics, there is no doubt that there are strong perceptions and pervasive emotions associated with mathematics (Perry, 2004). If your anxiety is increasing at this point through recognition of some of the negative attitudes described, you are not alone as such negative attitudes have been recognised amongst teachers (Ernest, 1991), primary teachers (Wilkins, 2008) and student teachers (Haylock, 2010). Existing research provides practical evidence of student teachers presenting with anxiety regarding mathematics during their initial teacher training (Jackson, 2007, 2008). Indeed Briggs (2009, p. 100) stated that 'many people teaching mathematics in the early years and primary age range do not have positive feelings about the subject'. With a mind to children deserving better, this does not bode well for their chances of effective and positive mathematical learning experiences, but since you have chosen to address this issue you, at least, do not intend to continue the potential cycle of mathematical negativity being passed, however unconsciously, from teachers to learners in your own practice.

Children deserve to learn mathematics in the company of teachers who are not debilitated by negative attitudes and anxiety towards mathematics. The variation presented in the reflective framework ranges between the excited, enthusiastic teachers advocated by ACME (2006) and severely negative feelings about mathematics (Morris, 1981). Reflecting on your past experience of mathematics, establishing what your attitude towards mathematics is and analysing the reasons for the way that you feel may have been a difficult process for you, but is a way of facilitating an understanding for you of how your attitudes were formed. It can be even more alarming for those who already have an aversion to mathematics to be under the illusion that their fear is an irrational phobia (Hodges, 1983) when in fact it is far more likely that there are sound reasons for your beliefs and attitudes, based on past experiences.

Although initial teacher training providers need to be aware of the extremes of student teachers' emotions towards mathematics and endeavour to design courses accordingly, the responsibility for learning ultimately lies in your hands. Wherever you find yourself after these focused reflections on the hierarchical framework, do not be disheartened because by being aware and addressing how you feel about mathematics and comparing your perceptions with those of others, you can develop to the position where you can set yourself clear goals for the kind of teacher you aspire to be and to begin to think about what you can do to gain more positivity in your outlook towards mathematics.

The task that lies ahead is by no means to be underestimated, but negative perceptions can be altered and mathematical difficulties can be overcome during teacher training. Although such feelings are recognised as being potentially painful (Clarke, 1994), there is a clear need for you to confront any negativity you have about mathematics. Since research suggests that such emotion is learnt and can be unlearnt (Ashcraft and Kirk, 2001; Pound and Lee, 2011), it is recommended that you examine your past experience in order to identify the source of negative perceptions, and consider other aspects of mathematical perceptions within the reflective framework to set your goals and begin to address your learning needs. Perhaps your reflections have helped you identify the reasons for any negative emotions linked to mathematics. While the original circumstances leading to those negative attitudes may have been largely out of your control, you are able as an autonomous, adult learner to approach your mathematics learning with the outlook you choose and prepare to meet the needs you have identified for your learning within initial teacher training to ensure that you begin to develop your mathematical confidence with a view to teaching in the future.

Chapter summary

This chapter has focused on attitudes towards mathematics and the potential implications of these for your learning for initial teacher training and future teaching of mathematics. Negative attitudes towards mathematics amongst adults have been examined, including student teachers like yourself. While it is recognised that there is a range of attitudes towards mathematics, this chapter focuses on pervasive emotions associated with mathematics that have been documented amongst teachers and student teachers. Student teachers' perceptions of mathematics, arising from past experiences, can affect learning within teacher training and the chapter has explored ways in which negative attitudes towards mathematics have been shown to affect learning and how beliefs can affect understanding. Since teachers' attitudes affect, directly or indirectly, the way they teach and their students' learning experiences, it is important to nurture a positive attitude towards mathematics, so that you can reflect upon how you feel about mathematics and how you would like to feel about mathematics, and so that you can analyse your own experiences of learning and being taught the subject in order to establish why you feel the way you do and to identify the changes you would like to begin to make.

5
Mathematical engagement

Learning objectives

Having read this chapter you will …

- Consider your emotional and physical reactions to mathematics and how these may affect the ways in which you engage mathematically
- Reflect upon the potential implications of that on your future learning and teaching of mathematics
- Identify improvements you would like to make about the way in which you engage mathematically

Introduction

It is very clear from the theory presented so far, together with the evidence from student teachers, that there are difficulties inherent in teaching and learning mathematics and that there is a diverse range of attitudes amongst student teachers towards the subject. In the previous chapter you reflected upon your own attitudes towards mathematics, arising as they have from years of mathematical experience through everyday life and educational situations. You have also considered ways in which these attitudes may potentially affect your own learning of mathematics during and beyond your teacher training as well as the effect your attitudes can have on your future teaching.

The notion that attitudes towards mathematics can affect the way in which people engage in mathematical learning is taken forward in this chapter, with particular focus on how your perceptions of mathematics can potentially affect your mathematical engagement. The chapter begins with a case study of a student primary teacher who experiences mathematics anxiety but who has kept this hidden. Other students' experiences, together with reference to academic material, will help guide reflection on your own past mathematical experience with regard to mathematical engagement and potential implications for your future learning and teaching, so that you can raise your awareness and think about changes that you may wish to make.

Case study

Kay was a student teacher about to begin a postgraduate initial teacher training course. Prior to securing her place, she had studied to gain the equivalent of the required mathematics qualification for the course as she had not achieved this when in school some years ago. Since leaving school, Kay had married, brought up a family and was now in a position to pursue her goal of becoming a primary teacher.

Kay's memories of school were patchy. She had vague recollections of not really understanding what was going on and knew that she struggled with learning mathematics, but she thought she had blocked it all out as they were unhappy memories for her. Her story was an interesting one, as she recounted the ways in which she strove to avoid mathematics at all costs. She described the various coping strategies that she used in everyday life, which included paying by cheque or credit card for her shopping so as not to have to count out money at the supermarket check-out. She had an intense fear of not having enough money at the check-out since she struggled to estimate how much her shopping added up to as she went round the shop. When out with friends, she would offer to pay for meals with her credit card so that her friends would give her the cash for their own, so that she would not have to work out her own share and could avoid having her friends see that she couldn't mentally divide a bill or add up various items. Kay enjoyed baking but had developed her own recipes by trial and error that included cups, handfuls and splashes of ingredients as opposed to the need for anything to be measured out. When friends asked her for copies of her recipes and commented on the format, she claimed they were handed down from her grandmother.

The many coping mechanisms that Kay outlined were really very ingenious, but when this was suggested to Kay, she dismissed any claims to common sense, use of initiative and ability to problem-solve. Instead, she saw herself as a failure where mathematics was concerned. She felt completely at sea whenever mathematical activity arose and she described a feeling of rising panic at times where she knew she was going to have to perform something

(Continued)

(Continued)

mathematical in front of anyone. She was certain she would be incapable of doing it and was also convinced that people would think she was stupid.

Kay certainly felt badly of herself because of her perceived mathematical inability and it had clearly affected her self-esteem and confidence for completing many everyday tasks. While she had developed coping strategies for the most common, Kay would also avoid where she could any other potential activities that would mean her having to do mathematics. She gave examples of times where, at a family fun day, she had been asked to keep scores on a parent–child cricket match and had feigned illness to remove herself from the situation. Kay hated having to avoid such situations and hated even more having to think up excuses to extricate herself from them, but felt she had no choice.

On the occasions where mathematical situations could not be avoided, she described physical reactions that overcame her. She told of occasions where she had flushed with embarrassment, stammered, experienced palpitations, broken out into a sweat, had shaking hands and felt such panic that she could not think straight.

It had taken a lot of self-encouragement for Kay to seek support from a neighbour to help her with the mathematics learning she needed to prepare for her university's mathematics assessment for those entering initial teacher training later in life without the usual school qualification. She had found the one-to-one tuition terrifying at first, but had learnt enough to pass the test and get on to the course, but she still did not feel confident. Her next hurdle was to cope with the mathematics element of the teacher training course, which she was dreading.

Post-Script: Prior to, and during her course, Kay offered to help out voluntarily in her local primary school. While sitting in on lessons and helping individuals and small groups under the guidance of the class teacher, Kay was mesmerised by the teaching methods and resources, which were all new to her, being completely different from the way she had been taught mathematics. She found herself learning mathematics alongside the children she was helping and reported that, for the first time, she was beginning to understand and actually enjoy mathematics. Her confidence in mathematical engagement progressed to such an extent that she had told her husband she wanted to take over the household accounts and arrange to pay the bills, as she had previously had to rely on him managing the household budget.

Mathematical engagement

As in previous chapters, it is not assumed that only negative perceptions of mathematics are held by those training to be teachers, but such negative perceptions are the particular focus of this chapter, since if mathematical engagement can be affected by negative attitudes then it is important if you do have them to raise your awareness of these together with how mathematical engagement can be affected in order to improve your ability to learn and teach the subject in the future.

As you consider the lower tiers of the reflective framework in Chapter 3 you may find yourself identifying with some of the student teachers' experiences that led them to dislike being faced with mathematical involvement. The group of students whose reflections on past mathematical experiences helped to create the reflective framework of Chapter 3, together with Kay's descriptions of a lifetime of trying to avoid mathematics, very clearly exemplify student teachers with negative perceptions of mathematics that detrimentally affect their engagement. Their attitudes towards mathematics, as demonstrated in Chapter 4, range from fear, to anxiety, to frustration and ambivalence, to enjoyment and excitement.

While the previous chapter concentrated on student teachers' emotional responses to the negative attitudes that can cause anxiety, in this chapter you will examine the notion that negative perceptions of mathematics can have a further-reaching association than emotional effects on an individual as they can also manifest physically in ways that can directly affect mathematical engagement. If you are in any way anxious about mathematics, then using the reflective framework to consider your own perceptions and the impact they have on the way you engage with mathematics is a good starting point to making necessary improvements.

Although the process can be a painful one, it is useful to consider possible reasons for the way you feel about mathematics so that you can then begin to change your mindset by being aware of the contributing factors and considering what you can now, as an adult, do to make things better. For example, perhaps, like the past mathematical experiences described in the first category of the reflective framework, you feel that the way you were taught debilitated your progress in mathematical learning. Perceptions formed at school can last into adult life (Houssart, 2009) and a single humiliating incident (Ernest, 1991) or a single teacher's judgement (Perry, 2004) can form a lasting conviction of mathematical inability in a learner. Some student teachers' descriptions supported such long-lasting negative connotations with mathematics, including being ridiculed by teachers for not understanding, being made to feel stupid in front of their peers, having things thrown at them in class and objects banged aggressively on the desks in front of them and being told they would never amount to much. Charlotte, for example, was acutely aware of her teachers' potential reactions, 'If I come across something I can't do, I panic straight away because I think nobody's going to be able to teach it to me and they're going to get angry at me and I'm going to get upset.' As you analyse your past mathematical experiences, consider not only what your mathematical perceptions are but also your thoughts on how they were formed. Take heed of the recollections of some of the student teachers here, who describe their past experience in mathematics classrooms as 'frightening. He [the teacher] was really scary – he'd shout at you when you didn't know the answer' and 'horrible, really horrible. You were made to feel really stupid if you couldn't do it. I'd just sit there feeling really thick and just wanting to cry with desperation half the time.' These descriptions are also supported through a range of research whereby teachers have been documented as being unsympathetic (Briggs and Crook, 1991), showing hostile, gender-biased, uncaring, angry and unrealistic behaviour (Jackson and Leffingwell, 1999) and creating a classroom environment of hostility, impatience and insensitivity (Brady and Bowd, 2005). If you had similarly bad experiences learning mathematics, then it would be no surprise if engagement with the subject now is not something you find enjoyable.

While hostile mathematical learning environments are a possible cause of a lack of enthusiasm with mathematical engagement, there are also examples of learning expectations being a potential factor. Euan, for example, recalls mathematics teaching as being 'like a whirlwind you were stuck in and couldn't get out of. The teacher would rattle through stuff on the board – like by watching her you'd just automatically get what she was going on about, and then, whoosh, like magic you were supposed to be able to do it yourself then and if you couldn't it was your fault, there's no way she'd go over it again, you'd just get told off for not listening in the first place.' Research carried out with learners of mathematics also suggests an expectation to understand after brief explanations of concepts (Brady and Bowd, 2005) and learners feeling a nuisance in their attempts to understand (Haylock, 2010). Charlotte, for instance, describes trying to ask questions but feeling 'like I was just a pain in the neck or I was being awkward. I'm sure they thought I was doing it on purpose just to wind them up, but you just give up asking in the end.'

In such environments, teachers are seen to be correct and learners accept blame for not understanding (Miller and Mitchell, 1994), being too afraid to ask questions (Haylock, 2010), demonstrating low self-esteem (Akinsola, 2008) and embarrassment (Brady and Bowd, 2005) with the fear of 'being found out' by someone judgemental and in 'authority' (Buxton, 1981). Whatever the reasons for their perceptions of mathematics, some student teachers felt a general ineptitude towards the subject, such as Kelly who was convinced 'I can't do maths, I just can't do it. As soon as I have to do something I just got straight back to that place of fear where I just feel completely out of my depth,' and Charlotte who suggested 'my teachers told me I was hopeless at maths, so that's it, you believe them don't you? I'm hopeless at maths, it's impossible to teach me maths because I just don't understand it, so, well, that's it really.' These student teachers are not alone in their accounts, as literature clearly substantiates. Haylock

(2010, p. 5), for instance, describes learners feeling 'written off by their mathematics teachers', who, like Charlotte, can have a tendency to believe teachers who indicate they lack mathematical ability (Miller and Mitchell, 1994). If, like these examples, you also doubt your ability to do mathematics, as an adult you are now in a position to analyse why you think that and reassess your future involvement with mathematics.

Experiences of being taught mathematics leading to feelings of inadequacy have been shown to affect attitudes towards the subject (Perry, 2004), with some learners 'mentally scarred by past experiences of failure' (Suggate et al., 2006, p. 2). Rosa, for instance, was determined to overcome her fears but at the same time doubted herself, asking

> Am I kidding myself wanting to be a primary teacher when I'm such a wreck where maths is concerned? Sometimes I can't believe I've been accepted on the course then other times I think maybe it's good, you know, maybe because I struggle and really have to learn maths all over again, I'll be a good teacher because I'll be able to help kids who struggle too.

Some student teachers described bewilderment, which, incapacitating as it is in any adult faced with mathematics (Buxton, 1981), must be genuinely worrying for those who know they have to be able not only to learn more about mathematics but also to be in a position to teach it. Trudi, for example, explained the effect on her mathematical engagement, saying 'my mind just sort of goes blank', and Barbara asserted that 'I just get so confused my brain just seems to stop working; no other subject gets me like that'. If engaging in mathematics affects you similarly, then reflecting on how you feel, what has caused you to feel that way, ascertaining how you would rather feel, and planning to find ways to change this is a starting point for being able to participate successfully in the mathematics element of your teacher training.

Mathematical anxiety has been shown to cause tension (Akinsola, 2008), confusion (Kogelman and Warren, 1978) and panic (Buxton, 1981), all of which is recognised in both existing research and in the student teachers' descriptions as they talked of their circumstances at the outset of their teacher training. These affective associations with mathematics can lead to physical manifestations amongst learners which are detrimental to their involvement in mathematical activity. Physical effects on mathematical engagement have been shown to include sweating, nausea and palpitations (Krantz, 1999), churning stomach (Maxwell, 1989), difficulty breathing (Akinsola, 2008) and illness and faintness (Smith, 1997). Such concrete effects on well-being and ability to engage in mathematics were borne out in student teachers' accounts, such as that of Penny, who explained 'I just panic and feel really ill – I'm absolutely dreading having to be in a maths classroom again. It's not just not understanding and feeling thick, it's feeling so bad that you actually feel physically ill about it. But I want to be a teacher so I've got to sort this.' Perhaps such severe reactions to mathematical engagement resonate with you, and if not, awareness of the depth to which learners can suffer is valuable for any teacher of mathematics who could have such a level of anxiety amidst their class.

Several student teachers described feeling upset in mathematical situations and literature evidences learners describing uneasiness (Smith, 1997), feeling helpless and not being able to cope (Akinsola, 2008), crying while struggling to learn multiplication tables (Ambrose, 2004) and an inability to perform on tests (Smith, 1997). Physical manifestations of such circumstances are described by student teachers such as Rosa as 'it's like being put on the spot and you just can't think. I mean, you just can't think at all what's going on where the maths is concerned, but it kind of freezes your brain completely, like you've gone so blank you can't even think what day it is. It's really weird the effect maths has on me – it's not normal is it?' Her perspective is supported through research, which shows that the potential impact of mathematical anxiety upon performance can include concentration being difficult (Tobias, 1978), the ability to remember being affected (Kogelman and Warren, 1978), and an inability to think clearly (Tobias, 1978) to the extent that learners can become 'paralyzed in their thinking … and … prevented from learning' (Morris, 1981, p. 413). If you too share such experiences, it is time to prevent your past mathematical engagement affecting your aspirations for your future learning and teaching other than to add to your determination to improve the lot of both yourself and the children you will teach. You deserve better and, as an adult, you are in a position to shape your future learning of mathematics, beginning by being sure of what you need to learn and the best ways you can go about learning.

It is clear from literature (Cockcroft, 1982; Maxwell, 1989) that people with an aversion to mathematical engagement may, like Kay in the case study above, develop coping strategies. This is evident amongst the student teachers whose distress had resulted in various coping mechanisms being put into place, including: procrastination, reliance on mathematical aids such as calculators, getting someone else to do mathematics for them instead, and attempting to disguise a lack of mathematical understanding. Marianna, for example, admitted, 'I think I cheated my way through most things, thinking oh my god I've no idea what's going on here.' The answer for some student teachers was to try to avoid mathematical situations, such as Trudi, describing being faced with mathematics as 'like freezing in the headlights, so I'll just avoid it and not tell anyone I'm any good.' Evasion of mathematical engagement is substantiated by theoretical evidence; by avoiding mathematics classes (Smith, 1997), choosing to teach younger children, assuming that the mathematics required is easier

(Tobias, 1978), developing coping strategies for everyday life (Cockcroft, 1982) or copying (Maxwell, 1989) and generally avoiding it wherever possible (Brady and Bowd, 2005). It is recognised that some learners subsequently become disaffected (NACCCE, 1999), give up (Skemp, 1989) or drop out (Papert, 1980) under their assumption of mathematical inability (Metje et al., 2007). For you as a future primary school teacher, however, avoidance is not an option, since mathematics is a core primary school subject, despite Haylock and Thangata's (2007, p. 14) assertion that 'many trainees start primary teacher training courses with considerable anxiety about having to teach mathematics'. Their work suggests that problems originate from past learning experiences, and indeed, a range of research points to the educational environment as the major source of infliction of mathematical pain.

The student teachers' aspirations, as presented in the reflective framework, showed unanimous determination to become primary teachers, desire to overcome hurdles and awareness of the need to make improvements where necessary to be able to teach mathematics effectively. However, the fears of some clearly remained as they talked about their concerns for their forthcoming teacher training. Marianna, for instance, was very anxious about what would be expected of her on the course and was torn between a plan to try to hide at the back of the classroom so as not to be 'found out' and her determination to face her fears and start afresh with learning mathematics in what she anticipated would be 'new ways', as her recent experience in school as a teaching assistant had led her to realise that learning mathematics could be an entirely different experience to what she herself had witnessed in her own education. If you share such emotions about the subject, you can feel proud of yourself for your determination in seeking to overcome whatever has led you to feeling this way.

As you consider the reflective framework of Chapter 3, you may find that aspects of the lowest tier have, like Kay, caused you to avoid mathematics. The student teachers whose own reflections contributed to this framework had experienced mathematics teaching whereby an external mathematical relationship was formed through rote learning of facts to be remembered in an individual learning environment, frequently with separate seating and silence. The student teachers considered themselves, in many ways, to have an inability to engage with mathematics, as their school experiences had led them to believe that this was the case. They gave examples where teachers seemed to have given up on them and made no attempts to help them to understand – circumstances which are also reflected in literature with learners feeling 'written off' (Haylock, 2010) and teachers indicating to learners a lack of their mathematical ability (Miller and Mitchell, 1994), which did nothing to inspire them to progress mathematically. If this resonates with you, then it would be beneficial to reflect on your mathematical experiences and to analyse the potential reasons for feeling the way you do when you engage in mathematics and the extent to which it is due to your perceived 'inability'.

The exposure to an instrumental teaching environment where mathematical understanding was not achieved seemed to lead to these learners believing themselves to be at fault. On the surface, they blamed themselves for not being better at mathematics and considered what they perceived to be an elusive, external body of mathematical knowledge to be beyond their grasp. They had therefore developed a tendency to 'switch off' from mathematics, to 'give up' (Skemp, 1989), to disguise their situation, like Kay, through coping strategies (Cockcroft, 1982; Maxwell, 1989) and described a sense of there being no point trying to engage as they were sure they would never be able to do it. These were learners who had accepted the status quo, dovetailing existing theories of disaffection (NACCCE, 1999) and mathematical avoidance (Brady and Bowd, 2005). These problems, experienced both by student teachers and learners of mathematics presented in a range of research, are real and may also potentially affect you and your mathematical engagement, so it is useful to take some time to reflect upon your own position in this regard.

Reflection points

- Do you have a tendency to 'switch off' when in mathematical situations?
- Do you have a tendency to 'give up' when faced with mathematics?
- Do you have a tendency to avoid mathematical situations if you can?
- Are there coping strategies that you have developed to avoid mathematics or disguise your mathematical ability?
- To what extent do you think that you have an inability to do mathematics?
- Have you felt like teachers have given up on you in the past?
- Have you given up on yourself in this regard?
- To what extent do you think it is your fault that your mathematical ability is as it is?
- During your reflections to date, are you able to ascertain the possible reasons for the way you engage with mathematics?
- In what ways would you like to improve your engagement with mathematics?
- What would you need in order to be able to do that?
- How can it be brought about?

The depth of feeling towards mathematics that causes some student teachers to avoid mathematical situations is severe and debilitating, so if you share such negative perceptions, you are to be commended in your now facing those fears so that you can consider what can be done to turn your perceptions around and begin to believe in yourself. Mathematics is really not beyond you – it has just escaped your grasp until now!

Perhaps you can see yourself in such descriptions of wanting to avoid engaging in mathematics or maybe your own mathematical experiences were not so severe as to cause real fear, but were such that you were left feeling anxious about mathematics and so, while not deliberately avoiding mathematical situations, you are nevertheless aware of a lack of mathematical understanding.

Working through the reflective framework of Chapter 3 you may identify with the second tier where student teachers were not fearful of mathematics, but were nevertheless acutely aware of their lack of mathematical understanding which frustrated them and caused them anxiety. While they were not tempted to avoid mathematics, instead they worried about not being better at it. Feroza, for instance, indicated self-expectation that she should be better at mathematics, stating that 'if you're put on the spot to do it, I think, as an adult, I don't know, I expect that I feel like I should be able to do it.' These students described past experiences of attempts to remember rules without knowledge of how and why they work, previously identified amongst learners by Davis (2001).

Whereas student teachers in the lower part of the reflective framework had recounted expectations of them memorising mathematical facts, the student recollections forming the second tier of the framework were of having to memorise rules and procedures, an approach to mathematics teaching that has been seen through other studies of learners (Akinsola, 2008; Boaler, 1997; Boaler and Greeno, 2000; Kyriakides, 2009). These student teachers recalled that they were required to follow a teacher's method, usually via a whole-class demonstration on a board, or methods provided in textbooks, which they then had to reproduce with various similar examples. They indicated the lack of mathematical engagement that they perceived they had experienced in school, such as Brian's recollection of being 'shown how it's done on the board and then work through the books and it's not like, it's not particularly like, it's not particularly engaging. It's basically watching somebody do it and not doing it yourself.' Such recollections were accompanied by the restriction of getting more involved in the mathematical learning process when learners wanted to, with Euan, for example, explaining 'there's the reluctance to ask the same question twice. If they've explained it to you once and you don't quite get it then it's I can't ask again because it's already been explained' together with student teachers recounting the lack of support they got from their teachers, such as Katya who recalled 'you're always the person that's asking the questions so in the end I just didn't ask any. That's the attitude she gave, I had real trouble with it, because she'd literally actually walk away with impatience.' They suggest an element of internally related learning through individual engagement with tasks, but this is limited to mechanical use, as also identified through research by Lampert (1990), since the rules and procedures were not necessarily understood, a result that has also been identified in literature (Grootenboer, 2008; Haylock, 2010; Nunes and Bryant, 1996). Because they were reliant on memory instead of understanding the rules they tried to use, their mathematical engagement was affected as they describe 'going through the motions', in that they completed the tasks their teachers set them, but did not really feel they had understood or fully engaged with what was going on.

The student teachers' descriptions of their mathematical engagement in the second tier of the reflective framework outline a lack of enjoyment, interaction and use of practical resources, as described in schools by Foss and Kleinsasser (2001). The expectation to follow the strategies of the teacher and the structure of the examples provided were regarded as unhelpful. Concurrent with Brady and Bowd's (2005) work, these students critique their mathematical experiences in relation to whether mathematical difficulties are inherent or due to teaching styles. They displayed a clear willingness to engage mathematically through desires or attempts to question teachers, who were unapproachable, impatient and disinterested, as also evidenced in Haylock's (2010) observations of learners who were too afraid to ask questions, but were left feeling that they had not fully engaged mathematically. There was awareness of specific areas of mathematics causing difficulty and they had begun to analyse the ways in which they were taught, identifying limitations in terms of lack of diagnosis of learning mathematics, provision for different learners' needs and teaching for understanding. While these are all pedagogical approaches that have also been analysed in respect of effective mathematics learning and teaching (Brown et al., 1999), the student teachers also suggested various alternative approaches which they thought might have enhanced their mathematical engagement. By analysing the ways in which you were taught mathematics, you can both ascertain what was helpful to your learning and what may have prevented you from fully engaging in mathematics.

Perhaps, like these student teachers, you have not been tempted to give up or switch off from mathematics, but instead wish that you had the chance to improve your mathematical ability. If so, it is good that you are taking steps to do this and taking responsibility for improving your confidence in engaging in mathematics as an adult. As you reflect on past experience you may gain a better understanding both of what led you to feel the way you do about mathematics as well as to analyse the kind of mathematical engagement that would have been beneficial for you. In so doing, you can begin to form a philosophy for the way you aspire to teach mathematics as well as plan ahead for your teacher training and consider how best you think you can learn, or re-learn, mathematics.

Reflection points

- To what extent do you feel anxious about engaging in mathematical activity?
- Have you ever felt embarrassed, ashamed or humiliated when engaging in mathematical activity?
- If so, what were the reasons for feeling like that?
- To what extent does engaging in mathematical activity cause you frustration?
- When you are involved in mathematical activity do you frequently feel like you do not really understand?
- Did your past mathematical learning involve trying to remember rules?
- Did your past mathematical learning involve trying to follow a given method that was demonstrated to you?
- To what extent did you understand the mathematical rules and procedures that you used?
- What opportunities were available for you to ask questions and for support?
- What approaches were used by your teachers to help you to understand mathematics?
- To what extent do you enjoy mathematics?
- What teaching approaches do you think are helpful to aiding learners' understanding of mathematics?

As you train to teach, you will also have recent experiences of mathematical engagement to draw on, either from everyday life or perhaps, like Marianna, observations and involvement in school classrooms through your work or voluntary experience for your teacher training course. As you recognise the ways in which mathematics can be taught and learnt effectively, your ongoing reflections may resonate with the third section of the reflective framework as you expand your mathematical awareness.

You may find that you identify with this third category of the reflective framework of Chapter 3. These were student teachers who recalled enjoying mathematics and who were happy to engage in mathematical activity, giving examples from their past experiences of learning mathematics or recent observations in primary schools that they deemed helpful and had begun to identify elements of what they considered to be effective practice, including having children talk to each other about mathematics, using resources and, as Sian suggested, 'bringing things much more to life to focus on and to visualise and to work with and to help understand stuff'. Positive elements of mathematics teaching and learning that they identified included collaborative learning, as advocated by Von Glaserfeld (1990), which enables group engagement with mathematical activity, bringing different explanations to the learning group. Such approaches to mathematical engagement form the kind of social community that Vygotsky's (1978) work espoused where there are opportunities to communicate and reach shared meaning. Student teachers had begun to think ahead about what they needed to address for their own teaching, such as Suzanne indicating that 'the one thing that worries [me] the most, especially in terms of me teaching maths, is that if I understand how to do something, I will show a child how to do it, but then if they don't understand, then I'm not sure I can think of another way of saying it, another way of getting the same point across' alongside reflections on what they aimed to put in place to make improvements, such as Katiana suggesting 'I'm going to have to really practise my maths. I think I learn better doing a problem and like, you know, trying to work it out rather than just writing it out and memorising'. As part of this engagement, student teachers indicated an associated development of mathematical vocabulary (Wilson, 2009) as part of developing mathematical communication. Concurrent with Lee's research (2006), there was engagement via the use of visual apparatus and practical work as advocated by Brown (2000), including games that helped learning through concrete hands-on manipulation (Edwards, 1998) and puzzles to engage logic and reasoning skills. Perhaps your own experience of learning mathematics or the observations you have made in school resonate with engagement of this nature and you have begun to consider the value that such approaches can provide.

These were early days, as the student teachers were due to start their teacher training but their awareness and reflections were useful in thinking about future learning needs. As you reflect on, and using the framework analyse, your own experiences you will be able to set goals for your own learning of mathematics in teacher training and also for the kind of teacher of mathematics you wish to become.

Reflection points

- Do you enjoy mathematics?
- What teaching approaches do you intend to use in order to help children enjoy engaging in mathematical activity?
- In what ways can collaborative learning aid mathematical engagement?
- How can this collaborative engagement aid mathematical learning and understanding?

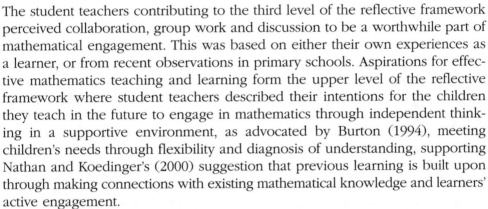

- What teaching approaches do you intend to use in order to provide collaborative mathematical engagement for children?
- What do you need to do in order to be able to provide these kinds of mathematical learning opportunities for children?

The student teachers contributing to the third level of the reflective framework perceived collaboration, group work and discussion to be a worthwhile part of mathematical engagement. This was based on either their own experiences as a learner, or from recent observations in primary schools. Aspirations for effective mathematics teaching and learning form the upper level of the reflective framework where student teachers described their intentions for the children they teach in the future to engage in mathematics through independent thinking in a supportive environment, as advocated by Burton (1994), meeting children's needs through flexibility and diagnosis of understanding, supporting Nathan and Koedinger's (2000) suggestion that previous learning is built upon through making connections with existing mathematical knowledge and learners' active engagement.

The socially constructive elements of learning and teaching that were identified as good practice in the third level of the framework were described in the fourth level of the framework as approaches student teachers recommended utilising, in addition to planned use of differentiated learning opportunities. Active mathematical engagement was espoused through interaction with aspirations expressed of 'engaging in mathematical process through active thinking', which according to Bottle (2005), can aid mathematical understanding, as well as encouragement for children to question, as advocated by Pound and Lee (2011) as a crucial element of developing mathematical reasoning. Student teachers were beginning to form their own philosophy for teaching and learning mathematics, such as Finn suggesting that 'it's always better for children to be encouraged to try and work out how to do it themselves first rather than being spoon fed, you know, like encouraging an active mind, proactive thinking, rather than just sitting back and being told how to do things'. Collaborative working was espoused where children can describe and discuss their ideas, such as the suggestion that mathematics

> should be taught creatively, using loads of different resources, group work, individual work, games, visual aids, and like, using as many different resources

as you can. I think they should be encouraged to discover things for themselves rather than just teaching them this is how you do it … getting them to
explore something for themselves … not sitting them down with a book and
getting them to learn a set way.

Such practice is recommended by Anghileri (1995), whereby children have the
opportunity to make sense of their own and others' reasoning and develop
communication skills and mathematical vocabulary. Research literature supports that these aspects of mathematics teaching and learning can help the
construction of understanding through relational engagement and development
of mathematical thinking (Desforges and Cockburn, 1987; Skemp, 2002). The
highest level of the reflective framework presents mathematics as a way of
thinking, with engagement being a natural part of social activity as opposed to
imposed teaching or an expectation to learn by transmission or adherence to
a set curriculum. Mathematics perceived as a way of thinking is one of many
ways that people observe, explore and communicate what they make sense of
as they interact in the world.

The student teachers had clearly begun to think about the processes they
had gone through in learning mathematics and had begun to compare their
own experience with what they saw happening in primary school classrooms.
This focus on mathematical process is further exemplified in the top section
of the reflective framework where they described their intentions to foster an
internal relationship with mathematics in learners through viewing mathematics, not as an external entity to be taught, but as a form of understanding to be
constructed creatively. Their aspirations for their future teaching were exemplified in Kora's statement that she wanted 'the children to find it exciting and a
challenge, because if you understand the challenge is there to learn from, it can
be a joy and that applies to all different levels, at all different subjects'. As you
develop your understanding of the ways in which you yourself engage with
mathematics, you will be able to consider the extent to which you agree with
these student descriptions of mathematics in the higher tier of the framework.
Subsequent chapters will return to this notion of mathematical engagement as
a creative, active process to help your understanding further.

You may already be in a position to emulate the descriptions of a teacher
of mathematics fitting the top tier of the framework and may be reassured that
you feel confident and motivated to fully engage with the mathematics element
of your teacher training. Your reflections may also motivate you to support
colleagues who may be less enthusiastic. If so, the framework may help you
to gain a deeper understanding of their position and how you can help them,
whether during teacher training or once you are a practising teacher and perhaps leading mathematics within your school and able to provide CPD opportunities for colleagues.

Perhaps you do not feel you actually have that confidence to engage mathematically as presented in the upper tier of the reflective framework, but your reflections lead you to set aims for your learning during teacher training and to identify both where you wish to be and some of the hurdles you may need to overcome in order to teach effectively. It may initially seem a far-off goal, but raising your awareness of the ways in which you engage in mathematics is a starting point for you to make plans for the future.

Reflection points

- Do you have aspirations to teach mathematics through support, interaction, collaboration, group work, discussion, description, idea sharing, flexibility, diagnosis of understanding, differentiation, sense-making, communication and development of mathematical vocabulary?
- Why do you think these approaches will be effective for mathematics learning?
- In what ways do you think children's independent mathematical thinking is important for their learning?
- Do you believe that previous learning is built upon through making connections with existing mathematical knowledge and learners' active engagement with mathematics and if so, why?
- Do you believe that it is important for children to ask mathematical questions and if so, why?
- How can children develop mathematical reasoning?
- How can mathematical understanding be constructed?
- What do you understand by the term 'mathematical thinking'?
- What do you think is meant by the term 'relational engagement' with regard to mathematics?

As is so often the case with learning, you may find at this stage that you are raising more questions that you are answering. That is good! You are actively reflecting, not just on your own mathematical experiences, but also on those of other student teachers and considering the range of variation in mathematical engagement pertinent to your future learning and teaching goals. Throughout this chapter you have considered variation in mathematical engagement ranging from an external relationship with memorisation of mathematical facts leading learners to switch off and avoid mathematical situations, internal memorisation of rules by learners aware of a lack of understanding and in need of alternative teaching approaches to aid mathematical understanding, experienced mathematical engagement through an internal relationship with mathematics through interaction and use of learning materials leading to mathematical understanding, and espoused practice for the latter. While this range of reflective components arose from student teachers' descriptions of their mathematical perceptions, it is evident that these elements of mathematics teaching and learning practice are also supported by research and theory. By reading this you should be raising your awareness of different levels of mathematical engagement and considering the kind of teaching approaches you aspire to adopt, and identifying aspects of personal development that you need to address.

In this chapter you have read student teachers' responses and a range of theory, which supports the notion that negative mathematical perceptions from past experience have far-reaching consequences. If you recognise yourself in any of the student teachers' descriptions, you can take comfort from the fact you are not alone in having any anxieties, and that, by identifying your own position on the reflective framework you can ascertain your current perceptions and set goals for where you would like to be. If, initially, you felt that your apparent mathematical ability was your own fault and something inherent that means you are incapable of understanding mathematics, then look again at some of the student teachers' experiences and research discussed in this chapter. By reflecting on past experience you may recall particular instances that may have led to the formation of your current feelings about mathematics which may be potentially detrimental to your involvement in anything mathematical. While you set goals for becoming an effective teacher, do not let any past negative experiences put you off or convince you of your mathematical inability. Instead, use them to form a personal philosophy that includes the kind of teacher you are determined you will *not* turn into.

In reflecting on the framework you may recognise, as did Faye in the case study of Chapter 3, that you identify with elements across the various stages and although you may not confidently place yourself in the final tier, you aspire to teach flexibly and creatively and to change your mindset from one that may harbour niggling anxieties to one that sees mathematics as a creative discipline where children can learn through actively thinking and doing in order to make sense of the world in ways that suit them. Your aspirations for teaching may not match your own previous experience of learning and being taught mathematics, but you have begun to form your own teaching philosophy as well as focusing on how your engagement with mathematics may need to change. As you will be profoundly aware, there is no quick fix to reaching such a goal, but you have made the first steps by using the reflective framework to identify your own perspective on mathematical engagement. Negative past experiences can be replaced with positivity, as long as you are aware of your preconceptions and are in a position to reflect upon the changes you want to bring about.

Chapter summary

Whether you have established that you may have negative perceptions of mathematics that could affect your learning, or whether you are aware of colleagues who may be in this position that you wish to support, consideration is needed of how mathematical engagement can be affected by negative attitudes. This chapter has used student teacher reflections and existing research literature to demonstrate that negative perceptions of mathematics are not confined to emotional associations, since there are also apparent physical effects on mathematical engagement. Various techniques are employed by learners in such situations, including avoidance and coping strategies. However, avoidance is not an option if you are to be a primary teacher and coping strategies are not enough if you are to provide the children in your care with the mathematical learning opportunities they deserve and if you do not want to repeat any poor teaching approaches you yourself experienced. If your confidence with mathematics is not high, then you are assured that there are other student teachers who carry the emotional baggage of mathematics anxiety. Through pragmatic reflection you can address difficulties, for which subsequent chapters will guide you further.

6
Mathematics subject knowledge

Learning objectives

Having read this chapter you will ...

- Reflect on the way you were taught mathematics and the ways in which this developed your understanding
- Consider surface and deep approaches to learning and teaching mathematics that can result in fragmented or cohesive conceptions
- Think about the ways you aspire to teach mathematics
- Identify your needs within teacher training to develop the approaches to learning mathematics you ascertain are most effective

Introduction

In this chapter, you will build on your reflections so far to unpick your understanding of mathematics on the premise that this is unique to an individual, based as it is on prior experience. By reflecting on the effectiveness of experienced pedagogy, you can begin to identify changes that you may need to make in order to develop your personal mathematics knowledge, as the quality of your teaching is likely to be affected by your mathematical understanding. Indeed, subject knowledge is crucial for effective teaching but it is also recognised that this is not necessarily straightforward. As well as examining previous student teachers' experiences and theoretical underpinning, the chapter includes a case study of a student primary teacher whose difficulties with mathematics subject knowledge has affected his progress with the QTS numeracy skills test. Throughout the chapter there are opportunities for reflection to enable you to ascertain the need for mathematics subject knowledge development and how this can be brought about.

Case study

Jonathan was a student primary teacher struggling with the required QTS numeracy skills test. He sought help from a mathematics tutor and reported he was unable to carry out the mental maths questions in the time given. He displayed obvious mathematics anxiety and a lack of confidence in his ability. Conversations with Jonathan revealed that he was keen to train to become a primary teacher but felt that his subject knowledge would let him down as he was sure that he was no good at mathematics. Attempting practice questions for the numeracy skills test had exacerbated his worries and he described feelings of panic as he tried to work out mental maths problems against the clock.

It was quickly apparent that Jonathan's difficulties were not due to a lack of mathematical ability, but a lack of subject knowledge. He was trying to work out the problems in his head by using written calculation methods as these were the only ways he knew to try to find answers. This was not working because he really needed pen and paper to complete the algorithms and could not keep the various numbers in his head to be able to work out solutions mentally using these methods.

His tutor therefore set about working with him on mental mathematics, beginning with basic tasks that used visual and practical apparatus to help his conceptual understanding so that he was able to work mentally with increasingly complex problems. Although Jonathan was able to understand, he initially questioned the tutor's decision to begin with the basic number work as he did not see the relevance to what he was working on and the kinds of questions on the numeracy skills test. He did, however, stick with it as he did recognise that the maths he was working on would be useful for his future teaching.

As the sessions progressed, Jonathan began to make connections between the basic number work and his developing understanding of how numbers were made up and how various operations could be made with numbers in ways that were different to those he had previously learnt. He developed ways of calculating mentally and realised both how these were different from but also connected to the written methods he was already aware of. As well as

(Continued)

(Continued)

developing his understanding, his confidence began to grow and he realised he was enjoying working on the mathematics. He found himself making up numbers to multiply and divide in his head when he was stuck in traffic or could not sleep and became increasingly adept at calculating mentally.

The preparatory work led to Jonathan being able to take different approaches to the test questions. Instead of trying to apply written methods without pen and paper, he was able to apply the new mental methods that he had learnt. The most valuable aspect of his learning, however, was that he realised he was not hopeless at mathematics as he had first surmised. Jonathan recognised that his initial difficulties were not due to a lack of aptitude but a lack of knowledge as he had never learnt to work mentally with mathematics in this way until this point.

Post-Script: Jonathan passed both his QTS Numeracy Skills Test and his initial teacher training course. He learnt a lot on his course but finds that he learns more about mathematics every day as he works alongside his class of Key Stage 2 children. He has found that daily mental maths sessions help his own speed and accuracy as well as the children's. Although he is aware that he has to work at mathematics, he now has the confidence to plan ahead for his lessons and prepare in advance as he knows he is capable of developing the expertise he needs to be able to teach and that he does not lack aptitude, but does need to develop his experience and continue to learn.

Importance of mathematics subject knowledge

There would be little argument against an assertion that teachers need mathematics subject knowledge if they are to understand the subject sufficiently to be able to teach it. If you are on an initial teacher training course then you have demonstrated sufficient subject knowledge through the qualifications needed to be admitted to the course and to pass the QTS numeracy skills tests. However, whatever tests may have been passed, assumptions cannot be made that a level of mathematical knowledge is sufficient to be able to teach well (Goulding et al., 2002) since knowledge learnt for the purpose of passing examinations does not necessarily equate to confident and secure mathematical knowledge needed to be able to teach the subject (McNamara, 1994). You have most probably chosen to read this book because you are aware that, having jumped through the hoops to get on your teacher training course, you now need to increase your confidence in understanding mathematics sufficient to be able to teach it effectively.

As Smith (2004) has argued, there is a range of knowledge needed by teachers of mathematics, including pedagogical knowledge, and for this, underlying subject knowledge is essential. While your teacher training will guide you through pedagogical development and give you experience of teaching mathematics, research supports the notion that deep mathematics subject knowledge needs to underpin this (Goulding et al., 2002).

You will know from earlier chapters that you are not alone in wanting to address development of your mathematics subject knowledge. Teachers' understanding of mathematics has been an issue raised by many over several years and is not confined to the UK (MacNab and Payne, 2003), with international studies having raised concern about the quality of teachers' mathematical knowledge affecting the proficiency of teaching (Chapman, 2007). Neither are such concerns new, since some time ago Alexander et al. (1992) raised concerns in the UK about teachers' subject knowledge, their report contributing to a stronger emphasis on this within initial teacher training providers' requirements, with teachers' standards documentation (DfES, 2002b) stating that teachers should have secure subject knowledge and understanding, and current standards require that new teachers should 'have a secure knowledge and understanding of their subjects/curriculum areas and related pedagogy to enable them to teach effectively' (TDA, 2007, p. 9).

Mathematics subject knowledge has been identified in the UK as 'one of the main differences between the most and least effective … mathematics lessons' (Ofsted, 2005, p. 14), with 'weaknesses in teachers' subject knowledge [continuing] to detract from the quality of teaching' (Ofsted, 2005, p. 14). Evidence was provided by ACME (2006) of teachers, including headteachers, lacking confidence in mathematics subject knowledge. It is surely uncontestable that 'teachers require a sound understanding of the mathematical concepts which they teach and an appreciation of how children think and learn' (Cockburn, 1999, p. 3), and that new teachers need 'to be fully competent and confident about your own mathematics subject knowledge, skills and understanding' (Mooney et al., 2009, p. 69) but achieving this is no simple matter.

While it is recognised that improving mathematical knowledge is a valued component of teacher training (Goulding et al., 2002), it is crucial to not limit this knowledge to a superficial level, as teachers need a deep understanding of mathematics to include 'how it interconnects within the subject and how it relates to applications outside it' (ACME, 2006, p. 6). According to Fennema and Franke (1992, p. 151), 'when a teacher has a conceptual understanding of mathematics, it influences classroom instruction in a positive way', yet research suggests that conceptual understanding needed for effective teaching can be lacking (Mewborn, 2001). However, despite the legacy of difficulties encountered with mathematics teaching and learning, do not be disheartened as there is a range of evidence to show that student teachers' ability to teach mathematics can be improved through initial teacher training (Brown et al., 1999; Carré and Ernest, 1993; Goulding et al., 2002; Hopkins et al., 2004) and you have made a constructive start by beginning to reflect on your own feelings towards mathematics and your level of engagement with the subject.

Reflection points

- How confident did you feel meeting the mathematics entry requirements for your initial teacher training course?
- To what extent do you feel prepared for teaching mathematics?
- Are there particular aspects of mathematics that you feel confident about?
- Are there particular aspects of mathematics that you need to develop further?
- What is your interpretation of the notion of 'secure' knowledge and understanding as required in the Teachers' Standards?

Framework for reflection

This book is not intended to develop your mathematics subject knowledge *per se*, but you will find others that are written specifically for that purpose (Haylock, 2010). Instead, this chapter will guide you through reflecting on your own level of subject knowledge so that you can ascertain what you may need to develop for your goals of primary teaching. You may find, as did Jonathan in the case study above, that as you widen your understanding of how you feel about mathematics, based on your reflections from Chapter 4 and the ways in which you engage with mathematics as considered in Chapter 5, you are able to identify what your underlying difficulties might be with the subject. By increasing your awareness of your personal mathematical knowledge, you can plan to make changes in your approaches to engagement and in your thinking, and as you see improvement your confidence will also develop.

If you began this chapter doubting your ability as a mathematician, Jonathan's case study may encourage you to find out where your difficulties lie; in his case it was a lack of experience that he struggled with as opposed to a lack of aptitude. The reflective framework of Chapter 3 may also be useful to you in analysing your subject knowledge.

The lower tier of the framework describes student teachers whose knowledge of mathematics was limited to what was learnt from an external relationship with the subject as mathematical experience focused on memorising facts to be recalled. Such knowledge is characterised by knowing without necessarily having underlying understanding and can be found in learners who lacked confidence in and enjoyment of mathematics to the extent that their perceived lack of knowledge and ability cause them to fear mathematical engagement.

In contrast, the second level of the framework outlines mathematical knowledge that has more grounding than remembering and recalling facts, as learners describe more of an internal relationship with the subject as they attempt to follow methods provided by teachers or textbooks and individual practice working through examples. However, student teachers suggested this too was limiting in terms of their confidence and understanding as it was dependent on following given methods to reach required answers and they were aware of the lack of depth of understanding as rules and procedures were presented to them to regurgitate.

The third level of the reflective framework, however, demonstrates means by which learners developed mathematical understanding by a more in-depth internal relationship with mathematics as learning focused more on the process of mathematics. Although reaching correct answers was a goal, there was more emphasis on the ways in which learners worked to find such answers, with different approaches taken as opposed to following one set method provided by the teacher or the textbook. In so doing, learners were also encouraged to apply what they understood to new mathematical situations in order to develop knowledge further and apply this to everyday life.

These descriptions of learning included expressions of enjoyment and confidence in working mathematically. Such attitudes were stronger in the final level of the framework where student teachers presented with interest and excitement about mathematics. Here, mathematics was described not so much as a subject to be taught and learnt, but as a means of understanding the world and as such, as a way of thinking, mathematics being developed by an individual as their understanding of the world progresses. Rather than a structured curriculum to be followed in a classroom, mathematics was seen as a communication device and a way of making sense and use of what is around us. For example, in knowing what time to get up, estimating the amount of water to put in the kettle, gathering information from the data displayed on the television news about a current political campaign, mentally calculating the length of journey to work compared to the petrol left in the tank, spatial awareness of being able to park the car and counting correct change for the parking meter. As people's everyday lives become more complex, their mathematical knowledge develops accordingly, whether this be a child's everyday play or a scientist's calculations necessary for sending spacecraft to take readings from a comet. Mathematics is an internal and relative experience unique to the individual but the school experience to develop this in a more structured way can be via social and interactive learning approaches that are creative and based on an understanding of process as opposed to surface learning of facts and methods.

There is a clear need for new teachers to 'confront the nature of their own mathematical understanding' (MacNab and Payne, 2003, p. 67) but there are indications that little research has been carried out in higher education with regard to subject matter and its relation to students' learning (Prosser et al., 2005, p. 139) and, according to Beswick (2007), research has been limited in its scope for use in improving mathematics education. Some exceptions are Bibby (2002b), who looked at teacher identity in relation to mathematical beliefs, Mji's (2003) South African study linking mathematical conceptions to learning, and investigation by Gullberga et al. (2008) of prospective teachers' conceptions about pupils' understanding of science and mathematics. To address this, this chapter builds on research conducted with student teachers whose accounts underpin the reflective framework. As you have discovered in Chapter 4, negative attitudes towards mathematics have been shown to affect students' learning (Townsend and Wilton, 2003) and beliefs about a subject can affect understanding and can impede learning (Hofer and Pintrich, 2002). It is purported that if new teachers 'lack confidence and dislike the subject they may find it difficult to work up the enthusiasm to teach mathematics in an effective manner' (Cockburn, 1999, p. 15). Hence there is a need for you to determine how confident you feel with your mathematics subject knowledge and to raise your awareness through honest reflection to determine what you can do to make any necessary changes.

In the 1970s, approaches to learning were studied and differentiation made between surface and deep approaches, the former constituting a quantitative conception about learning that is superficial and the latter involving students who 'have a deep idea, or qualitative conception, about learning' (Cano, 2005, p. 206). Experiences outlined in the reflective framework of teaching by transmission where students have learnt mathematical facts and rules without conceptual understanding and the ability to make connections to apply to problem-solving situations, is an example of a 'teacher-focused' (Trigwell et al., 2005, p. 352) and 'surface' approach (Prosser et al., 2005). In contrast, a 'deep' approach would endeavour to develop conceptual change and be 'student-focused' (Trigwell et al. 2005, p. 352) where students 'engage with what is being learnt in a way that leads to a personal and meaningful understanding' (2005, p. 351) and have 'awareness of and control over their own learning processes' (Biggs, 1987, p. 5). By determining the ways in which you have been taught mathematics and ascertaining the approaches you feel would have been helpful to you, you will be in a better position to decide the kind of teacher of mathematics you aspire to be and plan ahead for developing your mathematics subject knowledge through your teacher training in ways that suit you best.

Reflection points

- To what extent has your previous mathematics learning been reliant on memory?
- What value do you place on teaching mathematics by rote?
- To what extent has your previous mathematics learning been reliant on copying given rules and methods?
- What value do you place on teaching mathematics by rule and method following?
- To what extent has your previous mathematics learning focused on finding different approaches to apply to seeking solutions to mathematical problems?
- What value do you place on teaching mathematics by introducing a range of methods and developing use and application of existing mathematical knowledge?
- To what extent have you considered mathematics to be a way of thinking by which we make sense of the world to reach an understanding of phenomena and use as a means of communication?
- How would this latter perception of mathematics learning affect the way in which mathematics might be taught in the primary school?

Mathematical knowledge through memorisation and recall

If any of your previous mathematical experience resonates with the lower tier of the reflective framework, then it is worth examining how much of your mathematical knowledge is based on facts that you have learnt together with the understanding that underpins those facts. Take Joe, for instance, who learnt his multiplication tables at an early age and is confident in his recall of these multiplication facts. He was surprised when he began his career as a teaching assistant to find that some children with whom he was working found it difficult to remember multiplication facts and were also unable to apply what they knew to different circumstances. As he gained experience working alongside their new teacher, he learnt different approaches to learning multiplication and witnessed the use of visual and practical resources that helped the children to understand more about the numbers they were working with.

He realised that they were not actually memorising abstract multiplication facts but recalling, with increasing speed, things they knew and understood about numbers. Instead of trying to remembers that 'eight 7s are 56', because they understood that 7 multiplied by 8 meant eight lots of 7, and that by doubling 7 they had two lots of 7, doubling that gave them four lots of 7 and doubling again gave them eight lots of 7 they were first carrying out quick calculations in their heads of 7, 14, 28, 56 to get the answer then later with further experience were able to recall this without the need to work it out. If they later forgot, they had the means to quickly work it out and also apply their understanding of doubling to other problems.

Although at first Joe questioned the justification for taking so much classroom time to work on the various aspects of mathematics that the teacher introduced, given that he himself had been taught multiplication facts by rote and that this had served him well, he came to recognise that the time was well spent as children not only came to know their multiplication tables, they also understood what they were recalling and had the means to apply their understanding to work out things they did not instantly know the answer to.

Joe was fortunate in that he was able to remember mathematical facts and was confident in applying his knowledge to new situations, but as his experience showed, this is not the case for all learners. Student teachers also describe previous experiences of learning by rote and their teachers expecting them to remember various mathematical facts such as formulae, which they were acutely aware that they did not understand. As demonstrated in Chapter 4, this led to some being convinced that they were no good at mathematics, resulting in some of them giving up and developing the strategies shown in Chapter 5 where they would procrastinate, rely on others, try to disguise their perceived lack of ability and avoid mathematical situations wherever possible. The legacy of their experiences had followed them into adult life with their confidence and attitude towards mathematics detrimentally affected, such that some approached their forthcoming teacher training with fear.

This lowest tier of the reflective framework depicts learners who have experienced a dualist approach to mathematics teaching constituting memorisation of externally given facts, limiting mathematical knowledge to recall, which contributes to perceptions of mathematics as being a difficult subject owing to learners' lack of understanding, and this has been demonstrated in research (Pound, 2008). Rote learning, practice and repetition can, as in Joe's case, enable mathematical facts to 'sink in' and be absorbed (Ambrose, 2004; Wong, 2002), but the question is whether 'knowing' something without deep understanding gives learners confidence in their mathematical ability, whether such knowledge can be remembered without the associated understanding and the extent to which such knowledge can be applied to different circumstances as may be needed.

Although government guidance (DfE, 2013) supports memorisation of mathematical facts, student teachers' experiences described here raise concerns regarding the difference between recall of externally presented facts and recall of mathematical knowledge with which the learner has previously internally engaged to reach understanding. It is worth reflecting on mathematical facts that you are able to recall and to ascertain the extent to which you understand those facts. In so doing, you can analyse the value of children reaching a deep understanding of mathematical facts and consider what the implications may be for your own future learning and teaching.

Reflection points

- Think about some mathematical knowledge that you know, e.g. 2 × 2.
- Analyse how you actually know it.
- How could you prove your answer to be correct?
- How could you explain it to a child who does not yet know?
- Can you identify some mathematical knowledge that you know but cannot explain how you know?
- Try explaining it to yourself or to a friend.
- How would you teach it to a child?

Mathematical knowledge through following rules and methods

Perhaps your previous mathematical experience involved some following of rules and methods, as described by student teachers within the second tier of the reflective framework. They recalled being taught mathematics by means of demonstration, by teachers via the classroom board or via textbooks, worksheets or cards. While this involved some degree of developing knowledge as the learners engaged with the given methods in order to reproduce them as shown and using mathematical rules as given, there was still a lack of understanding intimated by the student teachers.

They describe their teachers presenting a single method to be used uniformly by the class which was then reproduced by learners in a series of similar examples, which increased in difficulty. Finn gives a concrete example as she described being given a procedure to copy from the board that everybody was expected to follow and practise regardless of whether they understood what they were doing and now says 'if I was asked to work out even like long division or multiplication, I'd have to look up how to do it' as she is now aware that she never really understood the procedures she was copying or why they worked. Reflections such as these are supported in research literature; Alexander and Flutter (2009, p. 26), for instance, suggest a need for a 'a consistent focus on children understanding mathematics they are doing rather than just regurgitating rote learnt rules'.

Such regurgitation was evident amongst student teachers represented by the second tier of the reflective framework since it was apparent that their mathematical experiences had involved applying rules and procedures without necessarily understanding how or why. Marie, for instance, commented that she was expected to follow the teacher's way of carrying out a procedure or it was considered wrong. Without understanding the given methods, learners appeared to forget what they had learnt, with Sue, for example, stating that 'I used to forget the way I was supposed to work things out. Sometimes I found that I could do certain sums, but I didn't necessarily understand why I do things that way.' Even those who were quite confident in their ability to reach the 'right' answers were aware of their limitations in understanding. Lizzie recalled learning statistics and getting top marks in her exams but that, upon leaving school, she had no confidence to pursue a career as a statistician as she had no idea which statistical tests to apply to different types of data, since her learning had involved very little mathematical thinking on her part aside from applying given statistical tests. Fhea had similarly limiting experiences as she felt she was taught in 'a very narrow way'. Since becoming a teacher she is now aware of the lack of diagnosis from her own teachers with regard to how she and her peers learnt and that there was very little provision of differing learners' needs, also supported by Barbara's comment that 'there was no special educational needs. It was just a case of sink or swim. Well, I sank.' Some of these recollections relate to aspects of a Platonist perspective (Ernest, 1989), where learners had some opportunity to 'discover' mathematics as it was provided by teachers via working through given examples. However, while there was some degree of active learning and teacher interest in learners' mathematical thinking, an emphasis on process was not transparent and was not actively encouraged by other approaches, such as open-ended tasks, to encourage more autonomous mathematical thinking to develop their understanding (Oxford and Anderson, 1995).

Student teachers described not being able to remember the mathematics they learnt at school because they don't believe they really understood it. Sian, for example, says, 'I'm always jotting words down in maths, thinking I haven't got a clue what that is. I'll look it up. You do forget, you know. Words keep cropping up and you think, what the heck is that?' Naz gives a specific example regarding the angles of a triangle. Working within an initial teacher training classroom, she said, 'I knew it was 180° as soon as I was told it again, but facts have slipped my memory. I'm sure if someone back then had shown me that if you rip the corners off and stick them together they always fit on a straight line it would have made perfect sense to me and I wouldn't have to remember it then because I do know that a straight line is 180° … I've remembered that!' As student teachers gained experience both within teacher training and school classrooms, they talked about their observations of children working practically and showing understanding of what they were doing instead of being expected to remember things that were told to them. Toni remarked that elements of mathematics that she uses frequently, such as time, did not cause her difficulties, saying that 'I've forgotten all those things that I'm going to need to know again. There's lots of things that I know I've forgotten the rules of and I need to relearn them because you don't use them.' Her comments suggest that there was a range of mathematics that she had once learnt but subsequently forgotten, indicating that it was the memorisation of rules that was the focus of her learning as opposed to understanding processes and learning how to find things out she did not know. Such recollections of mathematical experiences describe procedures taught in isolation (Anghileri, 1995), and, while some mathematical knowledge including facts, rules and methods was acquired, these were reliant on memory, suggesting what Mji (2003) terms 'limited, fragmented understanding'.

Such surface approaches to teaching and learning have been shown to be detrimental to learners' perceptions of their mathematical ability and the notion as intimated by the student teachers in this case of 'falling behind' (Shodahl and Diers, 1984), as a set body of mathematical knowledge was passively received through teacher demonstration (Ernest, 2000). Look back at your own experience of learning mathematics and the approaches taken that were helpful to your understanding of the mathematical rules and methods to which you were introduced.

Reflection points

- Can you identify some mathematical knowledge that you know but cannot explain how you know? E.g. 420 × 20
- How do you find an answer?
- How can you explain your method to someone who does not know how to work it out?
- How much of your explanation makes sense?
- Imagine explaining it to a friend who keeps asking 'why?'
- How convincing is your explanation?
- Analyse what mathematical knowledge is needed to be able to fully understand the method you have used.
- What would a child need to learn before they could fully understand what you have done … place value? … partitioning? … factorising? … commutativity? … doubling? … multiples?
- To what extent does your experience of learning and teaching mathematics facilitate the learner to understand mathematical procedures as opposed to copying the teacher's method to get an answer?

Mathematics – Knowledge with understanding

Perhaps you recognise that some of your previous learning experiences have left you unable to remember facts, rules or procedures because you did not really understand them at the time. Maybe, like Jonathan in the case study you are able to identify changes you would like to make in order to understand mathematics with more confidence.

The student teachers of the third level of the framework had begun to identify aspects of mathematics teaching that either helped them develop their subject knowledge or observations of children's mathematical understanding being developed from current experience in schools. The recommendations they outlined for practice included that mathematical learning should be associated with real life so that it makes more sense to children, that making connections with various aspects of mathematics and with other learning is useful, that a variety of methods should be used for teaching and that there should be more autonomy in their use, with Marie suggesting, for instance, that 'you should be able to find your own way of working something out, rather than saying that's the way you do it, do it like that'. What the student teachers describe here is mathematics pedagogy that focuses on process rather than simply producing correct answers (Mikusa and Lewellen, 1999). They indicate a need for an emphasis on development of mathematical thinking and facilitation of children's internal relationship with mathematics as they relate their mathematics learning to their everyday lives and to other aspects of their learning.

They also identified that mathematics should be taught more inclusively with differentiation for learning and understanding, for as Barbara suggested, 'there should be different levels and different abilities for every child. If a child is struggling with something, take him back a level. If they're not understanding it, don't move on to the next level.' They very much believed that children should be able to seek understanding through asking questions, and certainly without ridicule. Contrary to her own learning experiences, Melissa remarked on the teaching she had recently observed where the teacher 'didn't explain it to you like you were stupid or like you had to do it at the front of the class. There were some people who were fantastic at maths and some who struggled and I saw how she helped them, she never once belittled them and I thought that was fantastic.' The student teachers' experiences led them to believe that children's difficulties should be diagnosed and differentiation put in place for learners' needs, with a focus on mathematical understanding using a variety of methods to aid development, the importance of teachers' awareness of learners' existing understanding being an approach recognised in the literature (O'Sullivan et al., 2005).

Developing mathematics subject knowledge was seen in this level of the framework as focused on mathematical understanding and the need for children to practically engage with mathematics, apply their knowledge to different situations and for children to focus on process as opposed to 'being hung up' on getting a right answer. Student teachers advocated a need for teachers to diagnose children's mathematical thinking, such as Fhea's recollection of her own learning where she was 'encouraged to develop the ways you set out your problem solving and helped to follow the flow of the problem, or the process you were using and I suppose then it was helpful to the teacher to follow what you've done, so they could then in theory help you see where you'd gone wrong.' Recording mathematics as a way of supporting the learner's thinking processes is recognised here, in addition to teachers understanding that process, and suggestion of learner autonomy in having a choice of mathematical strategies (Pound and Lee, 2011).

Descriptions of mathematical learning here are consistent with constructivist theory (Bruner, 1966), whereby mathematical knowledge is constructed through active engagement, mirroring elements of a purist view (Ernest, 1991) where mathematical process and learners' development through construction of understanding are emphasised within a supportive environment. By examining your own mathematical experiences, either as a learner yourself or examples of teaching you have observed, you can reflect on the extent to which your own learning mirrors that which is described by student teachers in the third level of the framework and how this matches your own aspirations for teaching primary mathematics.

Reflection points

- Make up a multiplication problem – as complicated as you like, e.g. 2.28×7.6
- How would you work this out?
- How would you explain to someone else how you did it?
- How can you justify your method to be sure it makes sense to the other person?
- How could you do it differently if the other person did not understand?
- How does your approach link to the method you used previously to work out 420×20?
- What knowledge and skills have you used to apply to this more complicated calculation?
- In your experience, are children encouraged to use a range of mathematical strategies?

(Continued)

(Continued)

- Are they expected to 'discover' strategies for themselves, are they taught a range of strategies, or is there a combination of the two?
- In your experience, are children encouraged to make use of a range of strategies depending on how they make sense of the mathematical problem or are they required to follow the teacher's suggested strategy?
- To what extent are their learning experiences passive?
- To what extent are their learning experiences active?
- How much value do you place on children being engaged in mathematical process as opposed to solely concentrating on resulting in a right answer?
- How can children be encouraged to develop their mathematical thinking skills?
- How can teachers recognise how children are thinking mathematically?
- How much active engagement was there in your own mathematical learning opportunities?
- To what extent do you 'think mathematically' as opposed to applying facts, rules and procedures that you know will work?
- To what extent do you think you need to develop your mathematical thinking?
- How do you expect to go about doing that?

Mathematics – Knowledge and understanding related to the way an individual thinks about the world

As the reflective framework demonstrates, there is a difference between being able to remember mathematical facts, rules and procedures and remembering them alongside understanding of what they mean, how they could be worked out if instant recall was not possible, and how they can be used in different circumstances. The final part of the framework builds on this notion of children achieving mathematical understanding to apply to questions that are provided, but it also forms a basis of children's curiosity to also ask the questions.

Starting from birth, children gradually develop their understanding as they make sense of what is around them. Part of their understanding is verbal, using language to communicate and learn, or pictorial and diagrammatic; in fact there are many ways in which humans gain understanding, mathematics being just one of the mechanisms we can make use of. In other words, mathematics is the name we give to one of the means by which humans over the centuries have sought to make sense of the world and communicate their understanding in a particular way. How we think about the world and understand is unique to an individual and as such the way we think mathematically is part of that understanding.

To gain mathematics subject knowledge is therefore dependent on the way we think because it actually *is* part of the way we think. It can be very difficult therefore to remember mathematical facts we have been told if we do not first understand them. Without understanding we do not really have in-depth knowledge. For example, I know that Einstein evolved a theory of relativity and I could also quote his associated formula, but I have no idea what the formula or his theory means and so I have very little understanding and those facts are useless to me. Fortunately my life does not depend on having any understanding of the theory of relativity, whereas my life would be incredibly limited if I had no mathematical knowledge.

Similarly, it is very difficult to be shown a mathematical procedure and to be required to both copy it and remember it at a later date if you were not able to understand what was happening as it is very likely to be forgotten and is not likely to inspire you with confidence as a mathematician. This is because you are not engaging as a mathematician, you are instead copying someone else's knowledge of how to solve a problem instead of making sense of it in a way that is appropriate for the way you think and understand.

If your reflections have led you to question the way that you have been taught and to wonder about the limitations of your mathematical understanding, then, like Brenda found on her teacher training course, 'once you've learnt something it's very hard to relearn it a different way' as she began to be introduced to concepts and different ways of working mathematically that were new to her. However, although this might not be an easy process, it is doable, as Sian found, remarking that 'if you don't sort of shut it off and think it is prescribed and that there is just one end result … it's getting yourself into that mindset if you've not been used to that with your background and how you've learnt and how you see maths to be'. Indeed, Daniel commented at the end of a mathematics subject knowledge booster course prior to teacher training that 'I wanted to change my mindset and I believe I have done that now and I feel a lot more confident. I'm not fazed over it any more.'

The students of the final tier of the reflective framework outlined their teaching aims expressing a desire to diagnose children's understanding, encourage independent thinking and provide active learning opportunities for children using different approaches, such as Suzanne's suggestion that 'you've got to have things that engage them and get them to think about it in the different ways. I would love to develop a way in which it was constantly active and moving and just different approaches.' They described their aspirations for children to be able to question and collaborate without fear of 'getting things wrong' and where they are able to work at their own level of achievement, with Sue for instance advocating that 'children understand before I move on and don't make them aware of that's the lower ability group. If everyone knows which one's the best group, you're Group 4, you feel devastated. Not putting children on the spot as well to answer questions – not like picking on people and making them feel really ridiculous like they did with me.' Katiana sums up the desired focus on mathematical process that arises from a child's thinking, expressing her aim to 'make sure that children understand how they get to the answer. The approach might be different for every child so they can come to an understanding of the answer.'

These descriptions of mathematics as a way of thinking encompass ideas of children involved in pattern seeking (Anghileri, 1995) and active engagement, including: playing, experimenting, noticing, describing, showing, articulating, testing, convincing, consolidating, developing new situations and contexts (Delaney, 2010). These are non-dualist learning opportunities for pedagogy that engages with interactive and creative practice (Anghileri, 1995) to facilitate children's internal relationship with mathematical learning through questioning, collaboration, practical activity, use of different strategies and development of mathematical thinking. Intentions for practice are described in terms of mathematical engagement to develop relational understanding through active development with a focus on mathematical process, linking to a non-dualist notion of forming mathematical understanding through doing (Atkinson, 1992). Such approaches to teaching promote learning opportunities where children can gain understanding of their world and use mathematics as a way of thinking as opposed to a prescribed body of knowledge to be taught.

Although mathematics teaching and learning is structured in England via a prescribed and statutory National Curriculum and hence there is a set body of knowledge to be taught, the pedagogy described by student teachers here is one which seeks to provide experiences for children that, while adhering to statutory requirements, are planned and presented in such a way that the development of their thinking is paramount as they extend their own individual mathematical understanding concurrent with their stage of development through their natural curiosity and inquisitiveness to make sense of the world.

Reflection points

- To what extent have you questioned what you have learnt mathematically and how you have learnt it?
- To what extent will you welcome children questioning what they experience around them, what they do not know, what they want to know, what they think they know and how they know?

- In what ways do you need to develop your own mathematics subject knowledge to be in a position to nurture children's curiosity?
- How can you go about making improvements in your mathematics subject knowledge?
- To what extent have the teaching approaches you have experienced affected your mathematics learning?
- To what extent do you think a surface approach was taken?
- To what extent do you think a deep approach was taken?
- What do you think are the reasons for any improvement in mathematics subject knowledge that you have identified?
- Were these external or were you fully responsible?
- To what extent can you now take control of your mathematics learning to achieve what you want to?
- To what extent do your approaches to learning need to change in order to further develop your mathematics subject knowledge?
- What do you need to change?
- How do you plan to instigate change?

Links between experienced mathematics and mathematics subject knowledge

Actually developing your mathematics subject knowledge is something that can come later as you identify your particular needs and how to address them. There is pedagogical knowledge needed in order to be able to teach, alongside subject knowledge, but the way you think about mathematics needs unpicking if either, or both, of these are to be developed. Indeed, Silverman and Thompson (2008) suggest that there is limited knowledge about mathematical knowledge itself in terms of what teachers need and how it can be developed!

Your past mathematical experiences can lead to the adoption of a learnt response to mathematical engagement dependent on your familiarity with mathematics as an accumulation of facts passively received, or with mathematics as an active construction of conceptual understanding (Hofer and Pintrich, 2002). There are therefore potential implications for your teacher training related to your prior experiences of being taught mathematics with regard to the pedagogy you experienced both as a learner yourself together with your experiences in classrooms more recently as an observer.

As the reflective framework demonstrates, perceptions of learning vary related to prior experiences (Prosser and Trigwell, 1999) and there is a link between your perceptions of mathematics and your approaches to learning. Reflection on these can be used to analyse the way you learn and have learnt, and the way you intend to learn mathematics. For mathematics to be taught effectively, teachers need to be aware of how mathematics is learnt (Speer, 2005) as they may tend to teach in the way that they themselves were taught (Wilkins, 2008). 'Fragmented' conceptions, such as mathematics as numbers, rules and formulae, applied to solve problems, lead to a surface approach to learning (reproducing parts), whereas 'cohesive' conceptions, such as mathematics as a complex logical system and way of thinking used to solve complex problems and providing insight for understanding the world, lead to a deep approach to learning (Prosser et al., 1998).

An instrumental approach, where mathematics is experienced as a teacher-led externally imposed body of knowledge (Trigwell et al., 2005), is likely to lead to a surface approach to learning (Cano, 2005). The contrasting deep approach to learning mathematics focuses on the learner (Trigwell et al., 2005) and is dependent on the non-dualist perspective of engagement with phenomena in order to create personal meaning and understanding. There is therefore a need for you to consider your previous learning experiences of mathematics and identify your expectations of your teacher training. If an instrumental experience of being taught mathematics has led you to take a surface approach to your own learning, change will be necessary in order for deep learning to be facilitated.

Chapter summary

This chapter builds on previous chapters where you have reflected upon past mathematical experience, thinking about the ways in which you were taught and what helped you to learn. Here you have been encouraged to consider mathematical understanding being unique to an individual and linked to the effectiveness of experienced pedagogy. The quality of your own future learning and teaching is likely to be affected by your mathematical understanding. Subject knowledge is crucial for effective mathematics teaching but this is not necessarily straightforward. In engaging with the reflective framework you have been able to compare your own levels of mathematics subject knowledge with those of other student teachers so that you can begin to identify your aims for future practice. You have been able to consider your previous mathematics learning in terms of surface and deep approaches to teaching and learning, and the extent to which your own experiences have led to fragmented or cohesive conceptions, and the implications this may have for your future learning and teaching practice.

7
Beliefs about mathematics

Learning objectives

Having read this chapter you will ...

- Make conscious your beliefs about mathematics
- Begin to question and challenge assumptions based on prior experience
- Reflect upon your beliefs in consideration of the kind of teacher of mathematics you intend to be
- Think about how your mathematical beliefs influence the way you learn mathematics
- Consider changes you need to make in order to prepare to meet your aspirations for learning and teaching mathematics

Introduction

So far you have considered your past experiences to raise your awareness of how you feel about mathematics, the extent to which your engagement with mathematics is affected and have begun to analyse the impact on your subject knowledge and what you need to do in readiness for your future teaching career. As you have identified your own perceptions, compared them with those of other student teachers via the reflective framework and begun to form your own philosophy about how mathematics can be taught and learnt effectively, you will have been acting on your mathematical beliefs. This chapter will guide you through further analysis of what you believe about mathematics so that you can add these beliefs to your considerations of the kind of teacher you aspire to be and plan ahead to make any changes that you determine may be necessary. Beginning with a case study of a practising teacher whose confidence in mathematics was improved through self-study and a change of perspective, the chapter uses the reflective framework of Chapter 3 with relevant academic literature to consider varying beliefs that are associated with mathematics teaching and learning so that you can compare your own with those of others and consider potential implications for your own practice.

Case study

Dawn was a Foundation Stage teacher who had felt great relief to come out of her teacher training course unscathed and to have passed the mathematics elements as it was a subject she shied away from wherever possible. It had always been her goal to teach, but she was comfortable in her Reception classroom, where she felt she could easily cope with the requirements for teaching.

Dawn's son had recently begun secondary school and was rapidly reaching the stage where she could no longer assist him with his homework and he had brought home some particularly challenging problems on percentages. With the aid of his textbook and her sketchy memories they muddled through together by applying rules of multiplying by numerators, dividing by denominators then dividing by 100, until they reached the more challenging questions that asked for the original price of an item, given the sale price and the percentage the original had been reduced by. At this point her son was losing what little interest he had started with and was beginning to get frustrated. Dawn was beginning to feel the familiar rising panic that she knew well from her own school days. It seemed the best idea to set aside the homework before tempers frayed.

Rescue came in the shape of a neighbour who was looking for the owner of a cat discovered in her garden shed. The cat conversation turned into a cup of tea and the neighbour's observation of the discarded maths books. Fortuitously, the neighbour was a primary teacher more than happy to help. Expecting to glaze over in minutes, Dawn and her son politely gathered round the dining table to anticipate getting lost once more in a maze of numerators, denominators and random multiplication or division by 100. Half an hour and a sheet of torn-off wall-paper covered in doodles and diagrams later, Dawn and her son found themselves playing a game of dividing by ten, halving, doubling and discovering a completely different way of looking at percentages. Another half an hour later of cutting up various shapes from a discarded cornflakes packet to represent original amounts decreased by various percentages, they were able to answer all the homework questions but one.

Signs of teenage rebellion and adult dismay began to re-emerge until, left to discuss the question while the neighbour answered a call on her mobile, they triumphantly announced to her that the question was impossible, giving as it did an answer that didn't make sense (it in fact resulted in the answer being a fraction of a sweet, which didn't make any sense). Not only had they confidently answered what had seemed impossible questions, they had just as confidently found a question for which there wasn't actually a sensible answer within the context. Dawn's son liked the idea of being able to tell his teacher the homework had a 'duff' question in it, the neighbour went off to return the cat to the grateful owner who had telephoned her and Dawn was left wondering if in fact it wasn't that she was so rubbish at maths after all and maybe just that she was looking at it the wrong way and she just needed a different teacher.

Post-Script: Dawn employed the neighbour to tutor her son periodically in mathematics and she sat in on the sessions, learning different approaches to mathematics that she had never encountered at school herself. When her headteacher proposed that she move into Key Stage 1 teaching the following academic year, she did so with confidence. With continued private tuition, she feels the potential prospect of teaching Key Stage 2 in the future is no longer beyond her.

Potential impact of beliefs on learning mathematics

Past experiences will have led you to hold specific beliefs about the nature of mathematics. These beliefs may be conscious or otherwise and the guided reflection in this chapter is intended to raise your awareness of them, and for you to compare them with a range of student teachers' beliefs and to question and analyse your beliefs in order to develop your personal philosophy for teaching and learning mathematics.

It is likely that you have never given much thought to what mathematics is and what you believe about mathematics teaching and learning, as it is something we have all grown up with. We have all been taught mathematics via different approaches and we have all learnt mathematics with varying degrees of success. It is a core requirement of our school education and as such perhaps is not open to much question as there is no getting away from it as learners. However, now that you are going to be in a position not only to continue your learning of mathematics, but also to teach the subject yourself, reflecting on your beliefs is an important part of forming your own personal philosophy that will shape your future practice.

As touched on in previous chapters, the hierarchical levels of the reflective framework in Chapter 3 present a range of beliefs shared by student teachers that encompass mathematics being perceived as an external entity to be trans-ferred from teachers to passive learners through the expectation of producing correct answers and for mathematics to be perceived as a set body of rules and methods that can be demonstrated by teachers and copied by learners in order to reach correct answers by following the correct procedures, much like Dawn's experience as evidenced in the case study. Mathematics can be seen as something that learners engage with in order to form an internal relationship with the subject through teaching approaches that foster a process of using and applying existing knowledge to gain further understanding and this can be nurtured through active, social, practical approaches to teaching and learning. Dawn's experience of being introduced to a different approach to teaching led her to perceive different ways of learning mathematics, and both she and her son benefited from this. For some, mathematics is perceived less as a subject to be taught and more a way of thinking, whereby the learner experiences an ongoing internal relationship with how they think and question so that teaching approaches are flexible in order for learning to be a creative process through exploration and investigation.

Reflection points

- What is mathematics?
- How difficult was it to answer that question?
- What is unique about mathematics that distinguishes it from other subjects?
- What is shared with mathematics and other subjects?

Framework for reflection

Alongside the recollections of learning mathematics recounted by student teach-ers whose comments formed the first part of the reflective framework, were perceptions of mathematics confined to involving numbers. Their accounts described memorisation of given mathematical knowledge so as to be able to recall, with a limited use of wider aspects of mathematics. Similarly limited was the development of mathematical vocabulary, which student teachers like Ray described as being 'beyond comprehension' with Euan likening mathematics to 'a secret code that I don't understand'. There seemed to be an emphasis within their experienced teaching approaches that expected a correct answer and their accounts very much echoed Finn's notion that in mathematics 'there's a right and wrong answer'. Robert, for instance, recalls 'when I was taught maths many years ago, it was all about getting the right answer. A series of numbers that didn't always seem to make sense and I wasn't sure why I was studying it.' These descriptions are of a limited view of mathematics restricted to number and the notion that there are either right or there are wrong answers in mathematics, a perception that has been recognised in research (Haylock and Thangata, 2007).

Motivation for learning mathematics taught this way is limited to an expectation of provision of required answers to closed questions (Boaler and Greeno, 2000). In the case study, Dawn and her son tackled the homework questions in this way, believing there to be correct answers and both trying to remember what they were 'supposed' to do in order to find them. Since they could not remember, they did not get very far. Mathematical beliefs from this perspective limit learning to finding what are believed to be correct answers that already exist and which are known already by the teacher (Lampert, 1990). The expectations by both teacher and learner therefore lead to concentration on the goal of giving the correct answer (Cockburn, 1999; Cross, 2009), with the behavioural reward of getting the answer right (Skinner, 1954).

Such approaches to teaching are associated with the attitudes towards mathematics outlined in Chapter 4 and the level of engagement in Chapter 5 as well as development of mathematical knowledge in Chapter 6, since the evident expectations can lead learners to believe they ought to be able to provide correct answers, and if they cannot, then inevitably they consider themselves to be no good at mathematics. Student teachers described 'getting left behind', perceiving that they had to keep up with others as opposed to learning at their own level. This competitive element between peers has also been recognised in research literature (Boaler and Greeno, 2000). Part of the competition also involved the element of time as student teachers described a perceived need for mathematics to be carried out at speed, a belief that has also been noted in research (Bibby, 2002b). In this lower tier of the framework, student teachers described mathematics as something they believed they ought to be better at, resulting in shame at not meeting expectations (Cockcroft, 1982). Rather than questioning the approaches to teaching, they tended to take the blame as learners for not being able to follow what their teachers presented to them (Miller and Mitchell, 1994), believing mathematics to be beyond their comprehension. The feelings of embarrassment, humiliation, stupidity and fear demonstrated in Chapter 4 were associated with their beliefs regarding not being able to produce the right answers that were expected. Unsurprisingly this can result in distress and such reactions have also been evidenced in research amongst learners of mathematics (Akinsola, 2008), alongside a perception of being a nuisance to teachers when their expectations were not met (Haylock, 2010).

Elements of this first part of the reflective framework may resonate with some of your own experiences. Take a moment to reflect on whether this is the case and consider the value of such approaches to teaching that you experienced.

Reflection points

- Do you believe mathematics involves numbers and that it can be taught by rote and learnt by memorisation?
- Was your earlier definition of mathematics related only to number?
- What other aspects of mathematics might there be?
- Do all the aspects of mathematics you have listed link back to numbers?
- In what way is mathematics a form of language?
- Does mathematics always involve correct answers? Why?
- To what extent has your learning of mathematics been motivated by an expectation that you should produce the right answer?
- Does mathematics have to be carried out quickly? Why?
- As a learner of mathematics, do you feel you have to keep up with everyone else and if so why?

In the second tier of the reflective framework, student teachers' descriptions also constitute mathematics perceived as mainly consisting of numbers with the same requirement to get the right answers, the difference being that they had methods to follow to get those answers instead of relying on memory. Student teachers described these answers being produced by following teacher-given rules and procedures that were demonstrated in a short, hurried manner and not necessarily understood (Brady and Bowd, 2005), or presented in textbooks constituting received knowledge (Boaler, 2002) from the source chosen by the teacher.

The emphasis seemed to be on completing tasks as opposed to working with understanding. Part of their lack of understanding was being able to use mathematical language in attempting to make sense of problems. Robert, for instance, recalled that, 'it was more about getting the task accomplished, rather than understanding how the maths worked. It was just, have you got it all written down in your exercise book and ticked, rather than knowing how it worked.' They also expressed confusion at their teachers' expectations for learners to present neat mathematical recording, evidenced also within research (Boaler and Greeno, 2000) linking the pedagogical approach to Ofsted's (2005) observations of teachers emphasising recording at the expense of mathematical reasoning. These learners were acutely aware that they did not fully understand and recognised inadequacies in learning mathematics through the teaching approaches that they experienced, suggesting that they might have understood more had they been encouraged to engage more in their learning, which could also have been more interesting and fun.

Despite attempted internalisation through individual working, there was an expectation to use the teacher's demonstrated strategy and there was a belief that a 'correct' method also had to be used in order to get the correct answer. As Julie commented, 'you had to use her method or it was wrong, even if you got the answer right. Just downright weird.' Expectations of using a particular method were also recognised in Bibby's research (2002b). This notion is exemplified in the case study, where Dawn and her son tried to remember a method of working out percentages that they had been shown. Since it did not make sense to them they struggled to remember it and encountered further difficulties when these limited methods had to be applied to different questions. The single method frequently used by the teacher is described by Boaler and Greeno (2000) as 'knowing the tricks', where there is a lack of flexibility in strategies, as outlined by Schuck (2002), and the danger of what Burton (1994) terms 'learner dependency', as autonomous use of a variety of methods is not encouraged.

In these terms, mathematics is therefore presented as facts, rules and methods to be demonstrated and followed in order for the learner to follow a correct method to find the correct solution. Looking back at your own experiences of learning, it is worth reflecting on the approaches to teaching that were used and also to analyse the teaching you observe in current classrooms to consider whether mathematics is perceived by teachers and learners in this way.

Reflection points

- Do you believe mathematics involves numbers to which correct methods must be applied in order to get correct answers?
- To what extent does the teaching you have witnessed expect the learner to follow a demonstrated method and then use the method to find answers?
- In your own learning experiences and in observed recent practice, how much emphasis is put on ensuring that learners understand methods that are presented?
- Should mathematical recording be expected to be neatly set out in a particular way? Why?

(Continued)

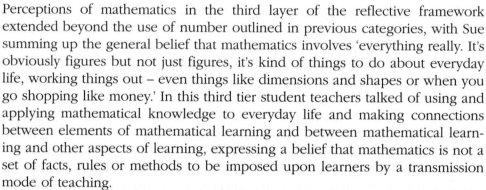

(Continued)

- To what extent do teaching approaches that you have witnessed, both in the past and more recently, focus on children's reasoning as they work on mathematical solutions?
- To what extent do teachers teach a range of strategies?
- To what extent are children encouraged to develop and use their own strategies?

Perceptions of mathematics in the third layer of the reflective framework extended beyond the use of number outlined in previous categories, with Sue summing up the general belief that mathematics involves 'everything really. It's obviously figures but not just figures, it's kind of things to do about everyday life, working things out – even things like dimensions and shapes or when you go shopping like money.' In this third tier student teachers talked of using and applying mathematical knowledge to everyday life and making connections between elements of mathematical learning and between mathematical learning and other aspects of learning, expressing a belief that mathematics is not a set of facts, rules or methods to be imposed upon learners by a transmission mode of teaching.

Although student teachers in the third tier describe using mathematical facts, rules and methods, their experiences of learning, both from their own education and the practice they observe in current classrooms, involved more internal engagement on the part of the learners who were encouraged to take a more active role in their learning through discussion, play, practical and investigative work. They described current observations of teachers who were more helpful than they recalled their own to be, as well as encouraging of children to work at their own level and speed, making diagnoses of their difficulties so that they were on hand to intervene as necessary. Learners were encouraged to make cross-curricular links, question, discuss, explore practically, work collaboratively and develop relational understanding.

Instead of reliance on one particular method, student teachers gave examples of current practice and from their own learning where a variety of approaches were used to aid understanding, with Marie for example recalling that her teacher 'used to show us all different ways and then say we could use whichever one was the best. In fact I think he's one of the reasons that I do love maths now. He always used to say – look I don't mind how you get the answer as long I can see how.' Marie and other student teachers recounted a focus on mathematical process, with less worry about getting the answer correct, as understanding what to do was considered more important than a minor error resulting in the wrong answer, even though the overall goal was to be accurate. Their descriptions of experience indicated a belief that mathematics is a process, which may involve the use and application of known facts, rules and methods, as a means by which children can develop their understanding through an internal relationship with the phenomena around them through a range of learning opportunities provided by the teacher.

There was hence a variation from the pursuit of right answers via reproduction of recalled facts or the following of given rules and procedures, as an internal relationship was formed between mathematics and learner through active engagement in order to reach an understanding of how answers were reached and the processes involved. Dawn witnessed this when a different approach was taken to teaching her and her son what percentages actually meant, how they could be worked out, how they linked to fractions, decimals, ratios and proportions and how visual, practical resources could be used to physically model what they were trying to work with in the abstract.

Despite such flexible approaches being advocated by student teachers in the third tier of the reflective framework, their view of curriculum was a structured one of mathematical material that had to be taught as a statutory requirement and that this body of mathematical knowledge formed a science made up of mathematical facts, rules and procedures. In defining mathematics as a science, they expressed beliefs that indicated mathematics was not, in itself, creative, which was in contrast to the creative ways in which they aspired to teach the subject. Suzanne, for instance, summarised this in saying

> there are definite answers in mathematics, and a definite way to get to that answer so you've got to learn rules to get through it, because it's a science, you have to follow the rules. Whereas with more arty subjects like English or history it's more dynamic isn't it? I mean your opinion is your opinion and it's neither right or wrong as long as you've got evidence to back it up, whereas with maths, it's very rigid. You can't be creative, because if you can't follow those rules or you don't understand those rules, the whole subject is blanked off then and you can't do it.

Mathematical process was explained as understanding, using and applying associated facts, rules and procedures and as such regarded as separate to the 'arts' and hence not for the creatively minded. With this in mind, they indicated a belief that there are good reasons for someone not to be very good at mathematics, and as such, in contrast to those who feared or worried about mathematics and avoided it, these student teachers perceived social acceptability in admitting to not being good at mathematics.

There is an inherent difference in the mathematical beliefs indicated by student teachers' contributions in this third tier of the reflective framework as there is greater emphasis on mathematics being perceived as related to everyday life and learnt through a variety of teaching approaches that guide children through the application of their mathematical knowledge of rules and methods that are scientific, via an active learning process. Based on your own experiences of learning mathematics and your experiences of current teaching practice in schools, take a moment to reflect on this perspective of mathematics to clarify your own perceptions in this regard.

Reflection points

- Do you believe that mathematics is not just what is on the school curriculum but should be linked to everyday life?
- To what extent have you experienced mathematics being used and applied in lessons?
- In your experience, how relevant are the mathematical contexts to the children?
- Do you believe learning mathematics should be an active process? If so, what does that look like in practice?
- Should children be introduced to a range of strategies and given choices to decide how to go about developing their mathematical understanding?
- Is the answer more important than the process or is the process more important than the answer? Why?
- Do you believe that mathematics is a science as opposed to being a creative subject? Why?

In the upper tier of the framework, student teachers describe a more relational view of learning whereby the focus is on mathematics being used as a tool and a way of thinking and a means by which phenomena are made sense of and understood. Children have an innate sense of curiosity and can develop more sophisticated ways of understanding, articulating and communicating that understanding through mathematics with its vocabulary and agreed rules. It is the way in which the children engage with the subject that is important to their learning rather than the expectation that the subject will be taught to them by means of absorption or copying. Their inquisitive nature can therefore be encouraged as they develop understanding of phenomena through the use of mathematics both for the practical uses that are necessary in everyday life but also for no other reasons than intrinsic enjoyment and stimulation.

Although mathematical rules were recognised as scientific, these student teachers also saw mathematics as creative, both because mathematicians before them had been creative in their establishment of rules, proofs and methods, but also in the way they advocated that learning mathematics through exploration, investigation, problem-solving and questioning were all the result of creative minds. Sue, for example, suggested that

> maths is a science because there are these theories and you use your logic, but you can teach it in a creative way, so it's kind of like you've got your right answer but there can be different ways of working it out and that can actually be quite exciting and fun to see what you can find, and see how other people have done it differently – that's really interesting.

Similarly, they believed teaching mathematics to be a creative process as they advocated teachers making diagnoses of children's needs and finding ways to facilitate the development of their mathematical and independent thinking. Katiana, for instance, advocated concentrating on mathematical processes in order to 'make sure that children understand how they get to the answer, and the approach might be different for every child so they can come to an understanding of the answer their way'. Finn articulated this by suggesting that

> it's always better for children to be encouraged to try and work out how to do it themselves first rather than being spoon fed. You need to get them thinking and plan your lessons so that you are encouraging an active mind, proactive thinking – rather than just sitting back and being told how to do things.

They expressed their aspirations for their own teaching, such as Leona's idea that 'it should be taught creatively, using loads of different resources, group work, individual work, games, visual aids, and like, using as many different resources as you can.' Their focus was 'the actual doing of maths' for children to explore and discover their own mathematical meanings, described by Sally as 'they should be encouraged to discover things for themselves rather than just teaching them this is how you do it – getting them to explore something for themselves, not sitting them down with a book and getting them to learn a set way'. For some student teachers, like Euan, their mathematical beliefs had changed from those originally based on their own mathematical learning experiences. He expressed a desire to

> make it more accessible to people and less scary, so for me personally it was, it was something that has a definite structure and this is what you

need to do and you cannot stray outside that and as soon as you don't understand the structure, you feel like you've got it wrong. I think if it's taught in that more creative way of, you know, when you're writing a story and there's never necessarily a right or wrong way to do it and it needs to have that element of creativity within in as well as being able to kind of rigidly teach those basics. So there are things you've got to learn and then use, but then the way you use what you know is up to you – you should be free to do what makes sense to you instead of having to try and follow something that's just way above your head.

As such they also demonstrated creativity themselves in acknowledging and challenging some of their past mathematical experiences and their determination and success in changing their belief systems as they learnt more about mathematics through their teacher training.

In this category mathematical perceptions differ from the facts, methods and rules that learners found difficult to understand through transference teaching and mechanical learning, to the belief that although that framework of shared facts, methods and rules exists and forms a requirement of teaching via statutory curriculum, it is necessary for children to learn through opportunities to think for themselves, discover and create their own unique meaning. As such, teaching approaches can be creative, children can be encouraged to be creative in their thinking and mathematics in itself is creative in the sense of finding ways of answering questions and making sense of the world.

Such belief systems corresponded with student teachers' attitudes towards mathematics, with Stuart, for example, stating that

I feel like the shackles have been taken off. I was so hung up before on maths being this thing that you had to get right and had to do right or it was wrong if even the answer was right – I was so confused. But now I feel like I can do my own thing – I look at maths problems now and think to myself, right, what do I know and how can I use that to work something out? I mean, I'm actually thinking now, not just staring at the page trying to remember what I'm supposed to be doing. This is going to sound daft, but it's almost like an adventure, you know, what's going to happen, am I going to be able to do this, but before I'd've been really bothered if I couldn't. Now, I just think, oh OK, not this time, I need some help – you know, instead of automatically feeling thick. It's like a revelation – maths is hard sometimes and that's OK! Wow!

Kora summed up this notion in saying that she was really excited to set out on her teaching career with her aim to ensure that children were not afraid to either question, nor to get things wrong and there was general agreement that children should be able to work at their own pace for, as Leona, suggested 'everyone's got a chance of being good at maths – it's a case of what's good for them, it's nothing to do with where anybody else is up to.' Barry remarked that he'd noticed teachers telling children that it didn't matter if they got the wrong answer, which jarred for him initially as he pointed out

> at first I was thinking, of course it matters if you get the wrong answer, the whole point of maths is to get it right. I mean you can't get your numbers wrong if you're a banker, or your distances wrong if you're an astronautical engineer, or whatever. I never understood this idea that oh you do your workings out but we don't care if you don't get the answer right. You think, hang on, maths is a science, it either works or it doesn't. In real life if you make a mistake you're making it with money and it costs you so there's no room for error. It's only recently where I've suddenly understood that what the maths teachers were trying to do was to see if you know what you're doing. You might put a 1 instead of a 2, but you can correct it later, the main thing is to see if the kid understands what's going on and the right answer can come later.

While student teachers in this upper tier of the reflective framework recognised the value in children learning mathematics facts, rules and methods and their ability to use and apply these to different circumstances, their focus was less on curriculum content and more on finding ways of teaching that enabled children to ask their own questions and find their own answers. For Gina, mathematics is 'all about logical thinking and reasoning – a way of making sense of the world and operating'. They believed mathematics to be a tool for thinking and reasoning, rather than the starting point in itself, so that children could make sense of the world through the means of mathematics rather than learning mathematics for mathematics sake. While they recognised the significance of learning mathematics, with Naz, for instance, stating that 'it's a way of helping children get by in the world, I can see that it's absolutely essential they're good at it', they regarded it less as a separate curriculum subject, but as a way of thinking to add to other ways that children came to understand the world, summed up by Marianna, who suggested 'it needs to be like the early years for everything … all over the place … go with the flow – that's the way the world is'.

Mathematics is described here as having agreed facts, methods and rules that are tested and agreed by a mathematical community, but alongside the ideology of learning mathematics creatively there is the philosophical notion of mathematics as a way of thinking, with children following in the footsteps of creative-thinking mathematicians. Barry, for example, remarked that 'it's weird that most of our great philosophers were mathematicians as well'. With a focus on mathematical thinking, developed at a child's own pace, these student teachers believed mathematics to be a challenge, but one that could be enjoyable, with a sense of satisfaction for achievements made. Diane summed this up with her statement that it is 'stimulating and fascinating how it all works out, like in nature and things like that. I can feel a sense of wonder about maths.' Despite recognising that mathematics can be difficult sometimes, these student teachers met the challenge with confidence, its 'mindblowing' nature being a source of interest as opposed to being something to cause anxiety, with Barry saying that 'it nearly made my brain pop. What really spurred me on was how good the Greeks were. If you take Pythagoras and think what he came up with – you know, a real intellectual and Euclid inventing all that stuff. I found that really interesting.'

The scientific nature of mathematics is described here as being facts, methods and rules that have been created by mathematicians and which can be explored by children through a creative approach of active learning that encourages development of thinking and use of different ways of solving problems, in addition to posing problems, based on the notion that mathematics is itself a way of thinking. Rather than being merely relevant to everyday life, mathematics is believed to be essential to functioning in the world, and viewed as a way of thinking that has been used by humans to make sense of the world and communicate understanding, to be used by children through investigation, and a holistic approach and to be enjoyed for its intrinsic nature of interest. Difficulties in learning mathematics are described not in negative terms, but as a challenge to be embraced with a sense of fascination for a philosophy of mathematics that represents a framework for trying to describe, understand and shape the world and that its very mystery, rather than being perceived with anxiety, is a source of stimulation and wonder. Instead of viewing science as a structure for adherence to be used and applied, the final tier of the reflective framework depicts the creative nature of science and mathematics providing a means to understand the world, whereby learners create personal meaning (Trigwell et al., 2005). The mathematical belief is one of creative process, based on the relationship between phenomena and the experiencer, the meaning being subsequently created, constituting the mathematical understanding of the individual as inherent human need for sense-making. It is thus considered a process of question-posing and problem-solving that focuses on the child's understanding (Ernest, 1989; Kuhs and Ball, 1986) based on personal construction of mathematical knowledge and dependent on relational learning (Skemp, 1989). In indicating the desire to encourage children to question, there is intimation of an element of problem posing, practice advocated by Pound (2008) and considered an essential element of learning as problems are reformulated and generated in the problem-solving process (Brown and Walter, 2005). Pedagogical practice is espoused that encourages exploration and investigation, with children working in a creative rather than a structured way in order to access personal meaning, indicating the development of mathematical thinking as solutions are sought to problems (Pound, 1999). The use of different strategies is advocated as an approach that can facilitate construction of meaning and understanding as connections are made, patterns spotted and relationships recognised (Pound, 2008).

Reflection points

- Returning to the question posed at the beginning of this chapter, what is mathematics?
- How can you harness children's natural curiosity to help them learn more about their world using mathematics as a tool?
- How can you meet the requirements of a set curriculum whilst ensuring that children gain a deep and relational understanding and develop their ways of thinking mathematically?
- In what ways is mathematics a creative subject?
- How can you approach teaching to ensure children get opportunities to make connections between everyday phenomena, mathematics and other subjects on the curriculum?
- Can you see mathematics as a challenge to be embraced instead of feared?

Relationality between the subject of mathematics and the learner

Research and the accounts of student teachers in the reflective framework clearly suggest the existence of negative attitudes towards mathematics and as you have determined in previous chapters, there may be physical effects caused by such negativity. Learners' past experiences of mathematics have been shown to shape perceptions of the subject itself. Beliefs about the nature of mathematics are linked to attitudes (Swars et al., 2009) and these in turn affect 'the way we learn mathematics, the way we teach it, and will affect the way the children we teach view mathematics' (Ernest, 2000, p. 4).

In considering your mathematical learning during your teacher training it is crucial to explore various beliefs concerning the nature of mathematics and associated pedagogical perceptions of teaching and learning mathematics. It is evident in this chapter that beliefs about mathematics are varied amongst student teachers and it is hoped that their recounted experiences have aided your own reflections on your beliefs. The perception of mathematics as an external entity to be endured in the pursuit of right answers is a limited view that could potentially be repeated in practice as well as limiting future learning. The perception that right answers are produced by correct procedures limits the potential for relational mathematical understanding using a range of strategies and autonomous thinking. Mathematics can be viewed as a subject that learners engage with to form an internal relationship via a mathematical process of enquiry, which in a confined way can be viewed as non-creative, bound by facts and rules, and therefore limited in terms of autonomous mathematical thinking relational to the individual. In contrast, mathematics can also be viewed as a creative process through which individuals make sense of phenomena by questioning, exploring and investigating where the relationality between the learner and the subject is key to learning. Throughout the varying beliefs held by student teachers, there are hence two distinct concepts which are interesting to consider in relation to the way we may think about mathematics.

The first is a dualist perspective, where mathematics is viewed as existing in its own right, as a separate entity seen as a body of information to be taught and learnt. From a teaching perspective, mathematics is therefore seen as a set curriculum of mathematical knowledge which can be imposed upon a learner as an 'external body of truth' (MacNab and Payne, 2003). This concept of mathematics supports a belief that it is a phenomenon that exists to be explored separately from human perception since the reality of the world and an individual's understanding of it are separate. That is to say, there are two separate entities involved – the subject of mathematics and the human who is learning the subject of mathematics.

At first glance, that perhaps seems to be a sensible concept as we know mathematics exists as a set curriculum in school. Consider therefore, an alternative belief system. A non-dualist perception is one where mathematics does not exist separate from the human as mathematics is a human concept in itself. That is to say, there are phenomena that we experience which we then interpret and those interpretations utilise a range of means by which we make sense of them, understand them and communicate this understanding. The phenomenon is not mathematics, but rather mathematics is the means by which we understand the phenomena through human interpretation and way of thinking by which we make sense of our world.

Take, for example, a nautilus shell, which is a naturally formed phenomenon that exists in its own right. It needs us to observe it and perceive that the shell constitutes a pattern. We can describe and re-create the pattern, giving it the name of a spiral and applying a sequence of numbers to be able to graphically reproduce the pattern accurately, applying a factor to re-create it on a larger or smaller scale, to be able to communicate our aesthetic interpretation and scientific measurement of the pattern, to utilise the pattern in art or for practical purposes such as a stairway, the list is endless, but all involves interpretation, sense-making and meaning derived from the original existing phenomena. In so doing we use a way of thinking that we have come to call mathematics and we extend our understanding of the phenomenon encountered, out of interest, for pleasure or to make use of what is learnt for a future purpose.

As a learner therefore, what is important is the relationship you have with the subject, as opposed to the subject itself. Mathematical understanding is entirely your own and not the same as anybody else's, as the relationship you have with the subject is what forms *your* understanding. Nobody else can make you understand something. Learning facts because you are told they are correct does not mean you understand them. Following other people's methods does not necessarily mean you understand them. What is important is that you use the way you think to make sense of phenomena, and reaching understanding is unique to the relationship between yourself and the subject.

In other words, learning is dependent on the individual's relationship between themselves and what is learnt (Marton, 1986) and so your mathematical understanding is dependent on the relationship between yourself and the phenomena you experience. The 'subject' of mathematics, rather than being something that exists in its own right separate from human interpretation is in fact as 'man-made as polystyrene' (Owen, 1987, p. 17) because it has been devised over the centuries based on interpretations of phenomena. We are therefore not discovering mathematics for the first time when we develop our mathematical understanding as the subject has been created already by mathematicians before us, but for us to understand as individuals we can use this created subject and relate to it in our own way in order to develop our own understanding. By using teaching approaches that facilitate children asking questions and exploring their world, we are in some part modelling that discovery for them to reach their own relational understanding. This non-dualist perception views mathematics as a conceptualisation where 'our world is a real world, but it is a described world, a world experienced by humans' (Marton and Booth, 1997, p. 113), involving the ways in which individuals interact with phenomena.

Epistemologically, the opposing perspectives have potential implications for learning and teaching mathematics. A dualist perception of mathematics teaches by instruction and transmission of facts, explanation and practice of procedural method and can lead to recalled and mechanical mathematical knowledge as opposed to relational understanding. In contrast, the non-dualist perception is one whereby mathematical understanding is created through teachers' facilitating active engagement with hands-on, practical, contextual problem-solving and posing so that learners are engaged interactively in a process that encourages them to make sense in their own way of phenomena by questioning and seeking solutions that relate to their own way of thinking to reach mathematical understanding.

A non-dualist perspective of mathematics is that it is a creation, based on the way individuals relate to phenomena, where mathematics does not exist without us, since mathematics *is* a human perception created of understanding as phenomena are interpreted. Hence, learning mathematically involves a qualitative experience dependent on the interpretations learners put on their experiences based on the 'internal relationship between the experiencer and the experienced' (Marton and Booth, 1997, p. 113). The creation of mathematics is formulated by humans in their attempts to understand their world, to communicate their understanding and work with what is around them, as well as for intrinsic enjoyment and challenge, and its makeup is the social construction of ideas arising from interest, activity and practical need (Thompson, 1992). This man-made perception of mathematics is one where problems are posed and solutions sought (Szydlik et al., 2003) and involves an active process (Hersh, 1986) whereby mathematical activity is crucial for learners to engage in problem-solving to reason, think, apply, discover, invent, communicate, test and critically reflect (Cockcroft, 1982) and enjoy the challenge and wonder that mathematical engagement and awareness can bring.

Humans have always sought to understand the world around them, to utilise the resources of their environment and to communicate in a variety of ways through the spoken word and symbols. Humankind hence created the discipline of mathematics to be passed on and learnt in order to be used by all in the understanding, utilisation and communication of the world around them. Hence, naturally occurring phenomena were understood through the sharing of a created phenomenon, and therein lie epistemological difficulties. As demonstrated in this chapter, learning mathematics is not straightforward in the sense that what began as a creation became a discipline of instruction, the learner's understanding thus being dependent on another's teaching, and the last century documents the inadequacy of mathematical learning via various permutations of this process.

By considering student teachers' differing experiences as presented in the reflective framework of Chapter 3, you can think about your own experiences and how these have led to your own beliefs about mathematics so that you can make conscious perceptions that may have lain dormant until now. Through this reflection you can both identify your beliefs and compare them with those of others so that you can question and challenge approaches to mathematics teaching and learning in readiness for your future learning and teaching. In previous chapters, you have reflected upon the hierarchical framework and the different ways in which student teachers recount their mathematical experiences regarding how they feel, how they engage with mathematics and their level of subject knowledge. Now take some time to consider how your reflections link to your beliefs about mathematics.

Reflection points

- To what extent have you previously thought about what mathematics is?
- Given the presentation of opposing perspectives of beliefs about the nature of mathematics above, how do your own experiences link to your beliefs about the subject as born from the ways in which you have learnt mathematics and observed approaches of mathematics teaching either as a learner yourself or more recently in preparation for your teacher training course?
- To what extent are your beliefs about mathematics consistent with mathematics being a set body of knowledge externally imposed, by transference, to passive learners?
- To what extent are your beliefs about mathematics consistent with the perception that relationality, between learner and subject, is key to learning and hence developing an understanding of phenomena through mathematics?
- How do you think your beliefs may affect your learning of mathematics?

Chapter summary

Building on your prior reflections on the ways in which you engage with mathematics and your mathematical knowledge, this chapter has sought to delve deeper to analyse the belief system that underpins these. By reflecting on your own experiences and comparing these to a hierarchical framework of student teachers' reflections, it is intended that you have started to unpick what you understand mathematics to be, how your beliefs are linked to your past experiences, and to perhaps challenge some of your assumptions. Mathematics is not necessarily an easy subject to learn, as was clearly seen in Chapter 1, but it is probably no less difficult than learning a language or a science or an art, because mathematics is a language, it is a science but it is also an art, depending on how it is perceived. Perhaps the most valuable belief can be that, although it is not easy, mathematics is not impossible to learn and is certainly not something to be afraid of. By challenging your insecurities, just as student teachers who took part in these reflections did, you can tackle any issues you may have with mathematics in order that you make the most of your teacher training and early teaching experiences. You may not have found all the answers yet, but stick with it as subsequent chapters will continue to explore your developing philosophy of teaching and learning mathematics.

8
The relevance of mathematics

Learning objectives

Having read this chapter you will …

- Consider your perceptions of the relevance of mathematics
- Ascertain your reasons for learning and teaching mathematics
- Reflect on extrinsic and intrinsic motivation for learning mathematics
- Identify how your perceptions may affect the way you learn and teach mathematics
- Think about how statutory curriculum content can be taught in accordance with your developing philosophy for mathematics teaching and learning

In reading the previous chapter, you will have reflected upon your beliefs about mathematics as based on your past experiences and how you feel about mathematics, how you engage with it and how you develop your mathematical knowledge. Linked to those beliefs are the ways you perceive mathematics to be relevant, which have the potential to influence the way you learn mathematics and also how you will teach it.

This chapter explores the notion of the relevance of mathematics so that you can continue to raise your awareness of your mathematical perceptions, compare them with those of student teachers within the reflective framework of Chapter 3 and consider potential implications for your future teaching. Alongside academic discussion, there are examples provided from student teachers' reflections as well as a case study of a primary teacher on a mathematics specialism course.

Case study

Rosie, with several years' teaching experience was put forward by her head-teacher for specialist mathematics training. Although she was considered to be the best for the role, she personally did not feel very confident but was willing to give it a go. She thought herself quite adept at mathematics but not as knowledgeable in terms of teaching it and it was not a subject that really inspired her with much enthusiasm.

On the course, participants were asked to fill in reflective diaries, which began with thinking about what mathematics meant to them. For Rosie, it was a subject that was taught in school, differing from some other aspects of learning in that it was a core subject. She had always seen the point of mathematics being statutory in schools as, alongside literacy, it was necessary for children to learn to be numerate and literate to cope in everyday life and to be employable.

Later, course participants were asked to pick an activity they had been involved in over the weekend and, using various elements of National Curriculum mathematics, to ascertain the aspects of mathematics that their activity had involved. Rosie sat in front of a blank piece of paper as she thought about the enjoyable Sunday morning she had spent on her yard caring for her horse, but could not match the activities she had been involved in with anything mathematical.

In contrast, Richard, who was seated next to her, had spent the weekend mending his garden wall with his father, who was a bricklayer. He was compiling a whole list of mathematical involvement that included: laying the bricks equally spaced; elements of shape in terms of tessellating cuboid bricks; measurement as they had worked out the length and height of the wall plus the materials to complete the building; number as they had used ratio and proportions of the sand, cement and lime required for the mortar; apparently a great deal of problem-solving as there was a tricky bit around a tree to navigate; communication as Richard had worked alongside his dad; logic as they worked out the formation of building the wall and the use of equipment such as a spirit level for checking the wall was vertical and the brick courses horizontal. Richard only seemed to be stuck in thinking about how their activity had used data handling until he had realised that had happened prior to the building when his dad had priced up the materials using various catalogues and lists from the builders' merchants.

Mesmerised, Rosie began to see her horse-related activity in a different light as she realised she had been mixing up buckets of feed for the week using number and proportion for the combination of linseed and chop that her horse had for morning feed, with a different mix including pony nuts for her night-time feed; estimation as she examined her existing stock of hay to decide whether there was enough for the rest of the week or whether she would need to order more; spatial estimation as she figured out whether there was room in the barn to be able to store a large load of hay, which would work out cheaper; measurement as she positioned her new dressage letters in the correct order on her paddock; shape as she devised some new exercise routines around the paddock to strengthen her horse's leg after injury; and at a simple level, she wondered if she had engaged in data handling as she had tidied out her shelves, categorising her various cleaning, feeding and medicinal products on to different shelves.

She was reminded of being back at school when she recollected spending most of her time in maths wondering 'if she was doing it right' but as the rest of the group shared some of their ideas, it began to amaze her that there was so much maths involved in every different activity that people had been considering. One lady had spent a considerable amount of her time at the weekend writing reports and had solely focused her reflection on the chair she had sat on as she had thought about the mathematics that had been involved in her choosing the size of chair to purchase to fit into the space in her tiny study, in somebody having used shape and measurement to design the chair, and even the maths that had been necessary way back in the manufacturing process and prior to that in the petro-chemical industry to make the plastic in the first place. Although this level of detail seemed over the top, Rosie found it fascinating to think about things she had previously taken for granted.

At the end of a day of various mathematical tasks, participants were asked to revisit their thoughts on what mathematics meant to them. Rosie doodled in her reflective diary images of horses and brick walls and office chairs with her mind spinning. The tutor asked her if she was OK and as Rosie explained that what she was thinking now was too complicated to write down in her diary, the tutor suggested she try to articulate it out loud. Since Rosie was now convinced that there were no worries about 'getting it wrong' she felt comfortable sharing with the class that:

'I started out thinking maths was something you have to learn at school and that's OK because you need it. If you don't get some sort of qualification in maths you are limited in the jobs you can get – I mean, I remember really trying with my maths GCSE for instance because I needed it to get into teacher training later on.

'But ... looking at Richard with his wall really made me think and I realised that actually we use maths all the time. I don't think we realise we use maths all the time, but if you really think about it, we do – I mean everything, there isn't anything I can actually think of that doesn't or hasn't involved some sort of maths, even Maisie's chair – it's crazy!

'So, it's got me thinking that I get why it's such an important part of what we teach in school, you know, it's not just so we can pass exams and get

(Continued)

(Continued)

qualifications that get us to where we want to be jobs-wise, we actually need it for everyday life. I can see why it's good for the kids if we try and get them working with maths in real life contexts so that they can see the point of it, you know, that maths is useful.

'But ... there's something else and this is what I haven't really got my head round yet – I've been using maths all this time and I didn't really know I was, but it's not that I've been using the maths I've learnt and applying it to what I need to do like the curriculum says we teach, it's more a case of it's just there. I'm not making sense, I know, but it's not that I've learnt maths and then I'm using what I've learnt, it's more that I'm using maths and that's what I just do – you know, it's just what we do so that we kind of function and do the stuff we want to do. Maths is kind of there in the background, well no, not in the background, it's like it's part of us, no not part of us, part of the way we think – that's it, it's the way that we think when we need to figure something out. So I suppose what I'm saying is, it's not so much the subject that we start with, I think we do maths as part of how we just live and do stuff and so what we teach in school is just taking that a stage further so we've got more at our fingertips to kind of understand more. I'm going to have to go away and think about this as it's blowing my mind, I'm going to drive myself demented now being conscious of all the maths I'm doing all the time!

Post-Script: Rosie's tutor and fellow participants understood what she was trying to articulate and went on to think in more detail not only about the implementation of the mathematics curriculum in their respective schools but also how they and others thought about mathematics and the impact that had on their teaching. Rosie returned to her role in school as mathematics curriculum leader with far more confidence and enthusiasm, ready to share some of the course activities with her colleagues.

Framework for reflection

At the lowest tier of the reflective framework from Chapter 3 some student teachers' past experiences indicated mathematics was very much teacher-led and something they had to endure under duress. The perception was that mathematics was imposed upon learners from which they described 'having no escape'. It was viewed that mathematics was something that was 'done' to them as opposed to them having choices and they questioned the 'point' of learning it other than to meet teachers' expectations.

Mathematics therefore had very little relevance to them as learners and as an externally imposed entity was difficult to relate to. Gina, for example, explained that the lack of application to anything that was real to her affected her understanding, saying that 'things that I felt that at the time didn't apply to anything, I struggled with'. Some student teachers' recollections were hence of having very little interest in mathematics alongside minimal personal motivation. This lack of stimulation was accompanied by perceptions of pressure imposed upon them by teachers in their expectations of right answers, exacerbated by added pressure, for example from their parents, to do better in the subject.

What they presented here was the perception of mathematics as a separate entity external to the learner and as such a lack of connection with the subject that meant it had little relevance to their lives. The relevance of mathematics to them was limited therefore in terms of real life (Bottle, 2005) and their experience of teaching approaches was constrained further by a lack of connection made with other aspects of mathematics (Hopkins et al., 1999) and other than meeting expectations of others.

Take a moment to reflect upon the extent to which your past experiences may resonate with the descriptions.

Reflection points

- To what extent did you perceive mathematics as something you just had to get on with at school?
- Did you experience any pressure placed on you to learn mathematics and if so by whom and how did this affect your learning?
- How relevant did you feel mathematics was to your everyday life when you were at school?
- What impact does this have on you with regard to the kind of teacher you want to be?
- What approaches to teaching would help children recognise the relevance of learning mathematics?

We have seen learners here who struggled to see the relevance of mathematics and whose motivation to engage in the subject was externally driven by teachers and parents. In the second level of the reflective framework, student teachers described feeling frustrated at their awareness that their mathematical learning was constricted, recollecting that at school they wanted to understand yet knew that they did not. They demonstrated a more intrinsic motivation to complete tasks alongside the recognition that their learning opportunities could have had more relevance to their everyday lives, remarking that had teachers helped them see more connection to life, it would have at least been more interesting.

This desire to try to learn indicates an intrinsic and internally driven motivation, but they too described external pressure placed on them by not only teachers and parents, but also each other. Feroza, for example, described the comparisons that were made between peers as she explained, 'I thought everyone else was a little bit better than me, maybe some people were struggling with it, but it never felt like that, it always felt like everyone else was much more confident than I was.' There were also recollections of competition between peers with Sue explaining that 'you wanted to be ahead, you wanted to be with all the other people because it was so competitive you used to think but they're on Book 5 why aren't I there? There was even a Book 0. I always thought that was wrong. It was terrible and it was so competitive because you'd be thinking I'm not anywhere near there but at least I'm better than so and so, and this person. It was quite nasty really.' These pressures were exacerbated also by a desire to 'fit in' with Robert, for instance, stating that 'I think in some cases you're made to feel that you've got to be better at maths, which is probably a societal thing. It's really important, like you have to be literate and be numerate, but if you can't do one of them it's like having three wheels on the wagon.'

These student teachers regarded that they learnt a basic knowledge of mathematics, mainly confined to number with some recognition of real-life applications, but one of the reasons they recalled for learning mathematics was to pass tests and examinations. This is similar to Rosie's views in the case study that mathematics has a purpose in life, particularly for gaining qualifications that are needed in adult life. However, without the associated understanding of what they were taught, student teachers indicated awareness of limitations in that once that purpose was fulfilled, it could be forgotten, with Feroza, for example, commenting that 'you used to learn it and do it in tests and think, well I'll never need that again, so I'd just let it fall out of my head'.

The teaching approaches, constituted of set rules, procedures, content, tasks and mathematical ability, described by these student teachers led to some internal connections being made between mathematics and real life, an element of mathematical learning identified as important in literature (Atkinson, 1992; Boaler, 1997; Nunes and Bryant, 1996), but these were limited by the level of understanding to fulfilling a purpose of passing tests. There was some recognition of mathematics being relevant, in the sense of doing the best they could to keep up with others at school, which in adulthood has extended to specific goals for their teaching such as being able to meet a range of children's needs and provide accountability for parents. These descriptions of experience of mathematics lacking purpose are borne out by theory (Bottle, 2005;

Hopkins et al., 1999; Romber and Kaput, 1999) and has been shown to contribute to difficulties in learning mathematics (Pound, 2008). It is therefore something to consider as you think about how your own learning may have been and may be affected in the future by your own previous learning experiences.

Reflection points

- Looking back at your previous experiences of learning mathematics, what motivated you to learn?
- Was there competition between peers in your mathematics classes?
- What are the benefits and/or drawbacks of such competition?
- To what extent was your motivation for learning mathematics driven by assessment?
- How much of what you learnt for exams stayed with you once the assessments were over?
- Why do you think mathematics should be learnt and taught?

In the third tier of the reflective framework student teachers indicated that mathematics learning has a purpose and application to everyday life. This view is, however, not wholly straightforward, as the real world application of mathematics has proved an area of difficulty within primary education, as shown by the integration of the use and application of mathematics into the revised National Curriculum (DfEE, 1999a) from its separate section of the original version, and by the recommendation of government guidance (DCSF, 2008) of more emphasis on using and applying mathematics being needed. Although the new National Curriculum in England (DfE, 2013, p. 9) states that pupils should be taught to apply various aspects of mathematics, there is little emphasis on this aspect of teaching mathematics.

There are potential implications in consideration of the value of using and applying mathematics in terms of making connections between aspects of mathematical learning, applying existing mathematical understanding to new situations and to the application of mathematical understanding to other areas of learning and life. This is especially so regarding the difference between the use and application of externally imposed knowledge that is recalled with a lack of understanding and children building on internally related understanding as it is applied to new phenomena.

The content of the mathematics lessons described by student teachers in the third tier of the framework related to what children do in their normal lives, as for example, considered by Rosie in the case study and as described by student teacher Sue when she defined mathematics as 'everything really. It's obviously figures but not just figures, it's kind of things to do about everyday life, working things out – even things like dimensions and shapes or when you go shopping like money'. Whereas, previously, awareness was demonstrated of the relevance of mathematics to everyday life, these descriptions of student teachers' experience made specific reference to how mathematics is applied to everyday life including home, family, work and social lives. Their accounts included an understanding of how *different* aspects of mathematics have relevance in life involving a range of uses of number through estimation, money, measurement, time, length, distance, mass, capacity, conversion, shape, percentages, comparison, angle, logic and trigonometry, although this is not an exhaustive list. A perceived usefulness of mathematics was described as essential, with aspirations for mathematics to have relevance for children, for cross-curricular connections to be made and school-based mathematical activity to be linked to children's real life as advocated by Anghileri (1995).

As they discussed their beliefs surrounding how mathematics should be taught, they talked about teachers 'bringing things much more to life for me to focus on and to visualise and to work with and the teacher started to make me understand stuff'. They described making mathematics relevant to children's lives in terms of playing mathematical games, with Suzanne remarking that the teacher would 'have things like dice that he would get out, and you'd have to roll a number to make the sums and little games'; hands-on learning experiences such as Brenda's observations of 'the most successful lessons I've witnessed in maths are the ones where the children have had to weigh things themselves and work it out and count things, so the learning is more concrete'; with practical situations such as Gina's experience of lessons that were 'more practical in that you were given scenarios using your logic and reasoning, that tends to be logical puzzles and I quite enjoyed them – that sunk in', accompanied by discussion and collaboration amongst children. As they outlined the ways in which approaches to teaching were more relevant to how children act in their normal lives, they talked about developing their mathematical thinking, an example being Katya's observation of 'showing how you can break things down, pull it apart and then put them all together and you've got an answer kind of thing' as well as relating their mathematical learning across different school subjects, exemplified for instance by Sian as she talked of 'incorporating all the communication skills and speaking and listening skills and it works cross-curricular really doesn't it really, yeah, but they're incorporating so many different aspects of learning into it that it just makes it more alive'.

Rather than being based on competition, student teachers described children being encouraged 'to do their own thing', trying out different approaches to solving mathematical problems, investigating, exploring and not worrying about 'doing it right'. There was a promotion of intrinsic motivation for mathematical learning and relevance to what the children understood, as student teachers described an active quest for mathematical understanding through an internal relationship involving questioning, engagement and application. To some extent what the student teachers described was curriculum-bound as the starting point for them was to meet the needs of what had to be taught, with Sian describing mathematics, for instance as 'a means to an end rather than something that's creative'. While described methods were positive in terms of relevance, there was a degree of external motivation by the need to adhere to an externally imposed curriculum. Hence the usefulness of mathematics (Hickman and Alexander, 1998; Mason, 2000) was recognised, its relevance described and links made between mathematics and other school curricular areas, but these perceptions of mathematical relevance raise questions about the extent to which the curriculum drives learning opportunities.

There is value, therefore, in taking time to consider what relevance you place on teaching and learning mathematics in terms of its use and application to everyday life and of curriculum requirements that you will be expected to teach in the primary school.

Reflection points

- In what ways do you think mathematics is relevant to everyday life?
- In what ways do you see children using and applying mathematics in different contexts?
- In what ways do you use and apply your mathematical understanding to aspects of your life?
- Consider your most recent observations of mathematics teaching and learning –

  o In what ways can mathematical learning opportunities match children's natural way of being and thinking, e.g. through play?
  o How relevant is the content of children's mathematical learning opportunities to their everyday lives?
  o How confidently do children use and apply their mathematical understanding to their learning?
  o To what extent do you see children making connections between different areas of mathematics?
  o To what extent do you see children making connections between mathematics and other school subjects?

In contrast to mathematics being relevant in terms of what has to be done to please teachers or parents, or to compete with peers, or to fulfil curriculum requirements, students teachers in the final level of the reflective framework see its relevance as being a natural part of everyone's being in that it is a way of thinking and a way in which we interpret and operate within our lives, and is hence ubiquitous. Rosie came to recognise this notion of mathematics given time to think about the ways in which mathematics was part of her everyday thinking, but it is probably not something we are in the habit of consciously thinking about. Amongst students teachers in the fourth tier of the reflective framework, mathematics was recognised as an essential element of our thinking, explained by Marie in terms of 'if you didn't have maths everything would collapse. Everything is based on maths and people just don't realise; even like in the library all the codes, it's all mathematical isn't it?' and regarded as part of normal thinking, for instance, by Fhea who suggested 'You can make more informed decisions. You know, can you afford it? Is it right thing to do? It's just so limited if you close your mind to that subject, it affects so many other things', and similarly relevant to children in that, as Naz suggested, 'it's a way of helping children get by in the world, I can see that it's absolutely essential they're good at it'.

Since mathematics is incorporated into everything that we do and encounter and as we are constantly experiencing and placing understanding on everything around us, it is an intrinsic part of life, whether subconscious or otherwise. As such, it does not need a specific purpose for learning or for us to function within our world, despite these being recognised as important elements of mathematical knowledge, because it is just part of our being and hence mathematics can be engaged with at a personal level and for no reason other than an intrinsic source of stimulation, interest and enjoyment. Indeed, as well as stating that mathematics is necessary for everyday life, including future employment, the new National Curriculum for England specifically advocates that mathematics 'provides a foundation for understanding the world, the ability to reason mathematically, an appreciation of the beauty and power of mathematics, and a sense of enjoyment and curiosity about the subject' (DfE, 2013, p. 99). Student teachers exemplified this through their descriptions of excitement in mathematical engagement on a personal level, such as Sian's comments that 'maths is exciting, you can engage with it, you can take it to whatever level you want to take it to' and they talked of their aspirations for teaching in order that children can relate to their world by developing their mathematical thinking through teachers being approachable, encouraging children to question, promoting interest, enjoyment, fun and excitement in learning mathematics and to aid children's confidence in working at their own level and inspiring them to engage mathematically.

Although mathematics was recognised as being difficult at times, it was considered that the challenge can be enjoyable with a sense of satisfaction for achievement. Student teachers' accounts described the desire for children to also enjoy this challenge, with Kora for instance saying, 'I want the children to find it exciting and a challenge, because if you understand the challenge is there to learn from, it can be a joy and that applies to all different levels'. Its mysterious nature was therefore embraced as stimulating, and, for Diane, 'fascinating how it all works out, like in nature and things like that. There's a sense of wonder about maths.' Rather than this sense of awe being a cause of anxiety, these student teachers considered the challenges posed as something to enjoy, owing to the interest in using mathematics to make sense of things.

Student teachers in the final tier of the framework perceived a need to utilise the curriculum to benefit learning as opposed to the curriculum being the key driver. While literature suggests the relevance for mathematical development in the primary school as a forerunner for future learning, in that Rose (DCSF, 2009, p. 10) suggested 'the curriculum that primary children are offered must enable them to enjoy this unique stage of childhood, inspire learning and develop the essential knowledge, skills and understanding which are the building blocks for secondary education and later life', these student teachers saw a more fundamental purpose for developing mathematically aside from the set curriculum. Although they accepted that the statutory curriculum has to be taught, they perceived the real purpose of learning mathematics as being an intrinsic part of children's autonomous thinking as they constantly make sense of the phenomena around them and use mathematics as a tool to extend their understanding. This notion of mathematics as a tool is supported in theory in its provision of language and the means by which to conduct research, development and industrial and social development (Smith, 2004).

In the final tier of the reflective framework, mathematics was seen to be relevant as an essential means by which we make sense of the world and such a perception was met with confidence, enjoyment and interest with student teachers showing real excitement in engaging in mathematics and their desire to be inspirational teachers. Rather than being relevant to everyday life, mathematics was perceived as essential to functioning in the world, and a way of thinking used to understand the world and communicate that understanding. This was echoed by ACME (2006, p. 13) when it purported that mathematical development has relevance for its own sake, advocating debate 'about the purposes of primary mathematics that explicitly acknowledges that educational experiences should be valuable and engaging in their own right'. Accounts described difficulties inherent in teaching through the barriers that may be faced, but these were described not in negative terms, but as challenges to be embraced with a sense of fascination.

Reflection points

- Can you think of any parts of everyday life that do not in some way have relevance to the way you think mathematically?
- How conscious are you of the ways in which you use your mathematical understanding?
- In what ways do the challenge and mystery of mathematics inspire you?
- To what extent do you aspire to enthuse and inspire children to learn and enjoy mathematics?
- How could a statutory curriculum be taught creatively in order to both meet children's development needs and harness their innate curiosity?
- Why do you think mathematics is represented in the statutory curriculum as a separate subject?
- In your experience, is mathematics taught discretely in the primary school?
- What are your thoughts on that?

You have been encouraged in this chapter to consider student teachers' experience of mathematics having been imposed upon them, leading them to see the subject as quite pointless and with only vague associations with real life. It is intended that you can use your reflections to compare this against your own experiences, alongside considering the implications this could have on the way you now perceive and learn mathematics.

Within the reflective framework, student teachers described mathematics as being relevant in order to pass examinations but that there could be a tendency to forget what was learnt if this was not accompanied by a deep understanding. You have been encouraged to consider the extent to which you understand the mathematics you have been taught alongside your perceptions of the purpose for learning mathematics.

A perception arising from student teachers' reflections in the framework is that the curriculum is not the starting point as mathematics, instead of being a body of knowledge to be taught, it is actually relevant in terms of it being a tool and a means by which to interpret the world and hence perceived as an intrinsic and non-dualist relationship that individuals use to develop their understanding.

The student teachers' reflections certainly suggest a need for perceptions of mathematical irrelevance, based on past experiences of mathematics limited to acquiring knowledge to be challenged. From a non-dualist perspective, mathematics cannot be seen as irrelevant since it exists only as a conceptualisation brought about by human attempts to make sense of what is relevant to their desire to understand.

As you will have gathered from previous chapters, you are neither alone in your concerns about mathematics teaching and learning, nor in probably being puzzled about what ensures effective teaching and learning. The variation of perceptions presented here raise a curriculum-related paradox in the descriptions of mathematical content, learnt in a non-dualist environment, originating from a curriculum perceived to be a structure of facts, rules and procedures (Koshy et al., 2000) to be learnt in a linear form (Oxford, 1990). Although this content need not be imposed upon learners in a dualist transmission mode, its origins are a dualist prescribed curriculum, also contested as such within theory by Brown et al. (2007) and Hughes (1999). In addition to a perceived structure of a body of knowledge to be learnt, the current statutory curriculum (DfE, 2013) is presented in Piagetian (1953) stages that are age-related, and despite purporting that these are guidance, previous use of such age-related guidance in the shape of the National Numeracy Strategy (DfEE, 1999b) were shown to result in a push to work through objectives and hence support a dualist notion of fixed mathematical ability (Clemson and Clemson, 1994; Haylock, 2010; Pound and Lee, 2011).

According to Alexander and Flutter (2009, p. 14), a large and growing proportion of primary teachers have known no other world than the National Curriculum and they suggest that 'discussion of subjects has become entangled with a distinctly ill-informed discourse about the nature of knowledge. A subject is merely a named conceptual or organisational component of the curriculum. It can mean anything we want it to mean.' It is crucial, therefore, that you establish what mathematics as a school-taught subject means to you so that you can form your own teaching philosophy. In terms of the relevance of mathematics, if its purpose is an intrinsic way of thinking then perhaps your aspirations for teaching resonate with Rose's (DCSF, 2009, p. 28) assertion that 'an important objective of primary education is to instil in children a love of learning for its own sake'. If adherence to a prescribed curriculum is unavoidable, then there is a need to reflect upon ways in which this content can be approached via non-dualist learning experiences that provide opportunities for development of relational understanding.

You may at this point be wondering how you are expected to find definitive answers if the many educators who have come before you have not yet found them. What you can do is consider these theories so that you can decide for yourself what your teaching goals are and be in a better position to put your beliefs into practice, based on careful analysis and informed choices. With a clear philosophy you can begin to develop your ability to teach in the way that you aspire but also make contributions when qualified to whole-school decisions on approaches to mathematics teaching and learning, especially since colleagues may not share your perceptions (Briggs, 2009). Since indications from research are that schools have a tendency to accept and conform to government guidance (Andrews, 2007), and teachers having been described as 'curriculum deliverers' (Pound and Lee, 2011), it will take confidence to critique and challenge in such an arena (Haylock, 2010). If your goal is for non-dualist practice, you may find this is shared by others in terms of achieving mathematical understanding, but the true nature of relational understanding is dependent on perceiving mathematics as a creative process that can be fluid and continually changing and developing (Orton, 1994b; White and Gunstone, 1992). However, despite the dualist nature of a prescribed curriculum, it can be taught in a creative, non-dualist, non-instrumental way which provides opportunity for children to question (Pound, 2008), make connections (Suggate et al., 2006), construct understanding (Haylock, 2010) and pose and solve meaningful problems (Schifter and Twomey Fosnot, 1993).

You need to find a balance between acceptance of government-directed and statutory curriculum with intimation of the promotion of creative practice (DfE, 2013) and the indication from government of 'allowing' (DfE, 2010, p. 10) schools to make decisions regarding *how* to teach, in consideration of pedagogical autonomy as befits their mathematical perceptions.

Chapter summary

In this chapter you have considered a range of perceptions of mathematical relevance ranging from a statutory subject to be taught as a school expectation, for the purpose of passing exams for future employment, a subject that can be used and applied to real life for its everyday utility and as an intrinsic way of thinking that acts as a tool to help us make sense of phenomena. You have been encouraged to think about the impact your own perceptions may have on your future learning and teaching of mathematics, particularly with regard to statutory curriculum requirements where mathematics is presented as a school subject consisting of content to be taught.

9
Mathematicians

Learning objectives

Having read this chapter you will ...

- Establish the ways in which you see yourself as a mathematician
- Reflect upon your mathematical perceptions that determine your definition of what it is to be a mathematician
- Consider the effect this may have on the way you learn and teach mathematics
- Identify potential changes that you wish to make in accordance with your developing philosophy for the kind of teacher you want to be

---

In Chapter 8 you considered your beliefs about the relevance of mathematics and in previous chapters you have also thought about where the difficulties may lie in teaching and learning mathematics, the attitudes you and other people have towards mathematics, how these may affect both engagement in mathematical activity and mathematical knowledge alongside your beliefs about the nature of mathematics itself. In this chapter, you will be encouraged to draw together these reflections to consider the extent to which you see yourself as a mathematician and how this affects the way you approach learning and teaching mathematics. As in other chapters, the reflective framework of Chapter 3 will be used so that you can consider other student teachers' reflections relating to how they see themselves as mathematicians in order that you can compare your perceptions with others' ideas and begin to consciously ascertain the way you see yourself in this light. The chapter begins with a case study of a student teacher at the end of her initial teacher training as she describes part of the journey she has experienced on her course. References to academic literature accompany the discussion in this chapter so that you can reflect in depth on your own situation to think ahead to your own training and analyse what you need to develop during that time.

Case study

Josie had completed her first year of mathematics teaching in a secondary school in the North West of England. Here she reflects on some of her experience and concerns in discussion with a colleague:

Being a maths teacher seems to have a certain level of kudos – that's been a real surprise to me. I took maths at uni because I liked it and thought I'd be sure of a job, but I'm amazed how many people seem to think I'm clever just because my subject is maths. It's quite embarrassing really, because I am so not! I've now taken to telling people I work at a school when I meet them, rather than telling them I'm a teacher because they are sure to ask me what my subject is and then they seem to be put off further conversation – they say things like 'Ooh you must be really clever' and then move away. It's quite disconcerting!

The really sad thing though, is that most of them add, 'I could never do maths at school, I hated it.' I should look at that with a statistical head on when I say 'most' people say that, but they do – the majority of people do! It's very rare that anyone says 'That's interesting, maths was always my favourite subject at school.' Some of them are obviously good at maths though so I don't know where they get this idea that they can't do it. I mean, one guy recently was doing some work at my house and while he was telling me he couldn't do maths he was mixing concrete having worked out how much he needed to underpin our gable end wall which was looking dodgy and before that he'd erected some scaffolding so he could work on the stonework. When I chatted to him about the volume he'd estimated for the amount of concrete he needed, the proportions for mixing it and that the structure of the scaffolding used Pythagoras, he said to me, 'That's not maths, luv – that's just what I do every day.'

It was funny in a way but then it got me thinking. I thought I'd really enjoy teaching maths and I was really excited when I got this job, but I've spent the year really feeling like I'm banging my head against a brick wall. The first years aren't so bad as they are still enthusiastic from primary school but, well, I don't know what's happened since then to the rest of them but most of the kids I'm teaching really aren't interested. Some work hard and they want to get a good result in their exams and in their last year a lot of them try really hard because they know they need a C grade to get into the job or the course they want to move on to. But the majority of the time I can feel all the enthusiasm I have for the subject getting sucked out of me. It's so sad, but I'm not sure what the answer is.

I mean, you've got the kids who do it because they think they have to for their grades and you've got the ones who are just compliant and do what they're told anyway. But the rest of them are just switched off most of the time – it's like trying to get blood out of a stone every day. Where's the enjoyment? I've tried linking what they are doing to real life but it's not their real life is it? They say to me, 'Yeah, Miss, I can see how ships use these angles to know where they are going but when am I ever going to be in charge of a ship, Miss?' It's the same for areas of patios, or proportions of paint, or trigonometry for drainage, or volumes of concrete, or Pythag for scaffolding! I see their point so I don't think the real-life connection really works for this age of kids.

I want them to just enjoy maths for the sake of it. I think they see maths as something they have to do and not something that people would want to do. They can see there is a real-life point to it, but unless it's their own real life then it's not interesting. I'd like to get away from the whole, 'We do maths because ….' thing. I want them to just want to do maths because it's fun or it's interesting or because it's a challenge and it feels good to beat it! If I can get them enthused like that I'm hoping they will start to feel like maths is for them.

We had some spare time at the end of a lesson the other day before lunch because something had happened in the school kitchen, so just to see what they'd come up with I asked them to sketch their idea of a mathematician. Nearly every sketch was a geeky looking type, all wore glasses and most had mad hair, and some even wore white lab coats. When I asked if they thought they were mathematicians themselves they thought it was hilarious. One lad said, 'Even if I was, Miss, I wouldn't admit it would I?' These kids really don't identify with maths and I'm going to raise it at our next staff meeting to see if we can look at the way we teach it to see how we can get these kids more engaged.

Post-Script: Josie gave the matter more thought and came back with:

I'm thinking that, even at this age, these kids like playing – you know, solving stuff to get to the next level on computer games, stuff like that. I'm thinking that if I can set problems up as games where they've to get to the next level that maybe that's a real-life application for them and they can see more of a point to trying it out and being up for the challenge. I don't know if my Head of Department is going to be up for it and I'm going to end up with a shedload of work to do, but I'd like to give it a go.

In the first tier of the reflective framework of Chapter 3, there were student teachers who, just like many of Josie's pupils, did not perceive themselves to be mathematicians at all. Mathematics itself was something to be avoided wherever possible as they felt they did not and could not understand it to the extent that fear about engaging with mathematical activity was described. They recollected not feeling encouraged by their teachers as though the teachers themselves considered that they were, as Robert recalled, 'no good at maths so we might as well not bother really'. There was a certain acceptance of the status quo in the classroom as students like Naz indicated that they would not be challenged if 'we kept our heads down', which in some cases led learners to give up, such as Daniel who explained 'there was just no point – there were a few of us who just had no idea what was going on, but the teacher didn't bother spending time with us explaining stuff. It was like we were a lost cause, written off – we couldn't do it so we thought we never would, really.' These experiences appeared to lead to a lack of identification with mathematics and in turn a lack of self-identification as mathematicians. Mathematics was a subject other people could do and these learners could not and as such they did not consider themselves to be mathematicians in any shape or form.

It is interesting to note that, despite a range of research indicating a gender-related perception of mathematics (Brady and Bowd, 2005; Cooper and Robinson, 1989; Furner and Duffy; 2002; McVarish, 2008; Tobias, 1978), this was not a factor raised by the student teachers involved in forming the reflective framework. Their experiences did not refer at all to any indication that 'boys might be better than girls' at mathematics. However, these student teachers did not identify on a personal level with mathematics, considering it instead to be the domain of other people who 'can do it', concurring with the findings of research into mathematics that found people confining mathematics to the realm of the clever (Sowder, 2001) and the intellectual and gifted (McVarish, 2008). This was exemplified by Toni, who recalled that 'it seemed to be the clever people who got it, you know, the ones who didn't seem to mind being the swots', with Robert recalling that 'the kids who were really into maths just seemed a bit weird' and Marie reflecting that 'I suppose you think of mathematicians as being kind of nerdy don't you?'

Adding to the disassociation with mathematics was the notion that it involved its own incomprehensible language, described for instance by Daniel as 'a secret code I don't understand', further exemplified by perceptions of the nature of mathematics itself, as recalled by Toni as being something that had to be 'done right' so that you could 'get it right', with Barry defining this as having nowhere to hide: 'what switches me off, you have nowhere to hide with maths. You can either do it or you can't. That's the big scary thing with maths – you either have to get it right or everybody's looking at you. That's for me why maths always has been scary for me, there's no room for error.' Such notions of mathematics being beyond some learners led them to disengage and lack motivation for learning, and to consider that they could not be regarded as mathematicians. Instead, for them, mathematicians seem to stand apart from the rest of society as elite. Surprisingly, practising teachers have also professed uncertainty as to whether they believe themselves to be mathematicians (Battista, 1999). Perhaps your own thoughts resonate with some of these descriptions. Take a moment to reflect at this stage how you identify yourself in terms of being a mathematician.

Reflection points

- How do you define a 'mathematician'?
- How do you describe people who are good at mathematics?
- To what extent do you consider yourself to be a mathematician?
- Why?
- How were you encouraged to see yourself as a mathematician when you were at school?

In the reflective framework, student teachers described passive learning of a set curriculum by rote in the lowest tier and a limited internal engagement with mathematical process through following given methods in the second tier. They all described experiences that were confined to being presented with a body of mathematical knowledge that learners were required to learn and practise via regurgitation, resulting in a lack of confidence and negative attitudes that did not leave the learners considering themselves to be mathematicians. However, as opposed to thinking mathematicians were clever, weird, somewhat geeky people, the student teachers constituting the second layer of the reflective framework described a need to have a particularly mathematical and logical brain to be able to do mathematics, which in their reckonings ruled them out as being or becoming mathematicians themselves. Just as Josie experienced from her account in the case study, mathematics is evidently not a subject with which a lot of people associate confidently.

It was also suggested that this kind of mathematical brain was inherited, with Feroza, for instance, suggesting that 'well, my mum was always useless at maths and my sister is too so I think it runs in the family, you know'. Indeed, Fhea was concerned that her own perceived inability at mathematics was going to be repeated in her sons, saying that 'I'm not sure, as my boys seem to be doing OK but I do worry about history repeating itself. I don't want them to have to go through what I went through with maths at school.' This notion that mathematical aptitude is a result of genetics has been discussed in literature (Haylock, 2010; Haylock and Thangata, 2007), alongside perceptions amongst learners that mathematicians are blessed with logical mathematical brains (Furner and Duffy, 2002; Schuck, 2002) dependent on logic (Frank, 1990), in contrast, as seen in Chapter 8, to creativity.

These student teachers demonstrated awareness that they did not fully understand mathematics although they did work to try to be better, but these efforts seemed to be clouded by a belief that it was probably beyond their reach as they did not see themselves as having a natural proclivity to the subject. Take a moment to think back to your own learning and how you felt about yourself as a learner of mathematics and the perceptions you now have of yourself as a mathematician.

Reflection points

- Do you think that people who are good at mathematics have a 'mathematical' and/or 'logical' brain?
- Why?
- Do you believe that way of thinking is biologically determined or can it be developed?
- To what extent were you encouraged to think 'mathematically' when you were at school?

From the third level of the reflective framework we see student teachers who are more confident in their mathematical ability and so did not describe the subject as being out of their reach, but there were indications, from Katya for instance, that some people 'have to work harder at it than others'. They mused over whether that was due to natural ability or the learning experiences they had had. Instead of expressing the belief that those who can do mathematics have a 'mathematical brain', student teachers included in this tier talked of mathematics itself having a particular logic. Euan, for example, stated 'there are some people who are, kind of, a lot more creative brains and struggle to understand the processes, the mechanical processes behind maths … maths tends to be very structured and very kind of stage orientated', implying that the subject lends itself to people who think in a structured and mechanical fashion as opposed to creatively. Similar responses from other student teachers indicated that, rather than those who struggle with mathematics lacking some particular genetic or biological disposition, the subject is elusive to them because of its scientific nature and structure, which in turn, they suggested, means that people who are naturally creative are unlikely to also be mathematicians.

You may recall responses from student teachers in previous chapters where they described feeling shame and embarrassment at their perceived inability to be able to do mathematics. However, what we see in this case, as these student teachers described their perceptions of the differences between logical, scientific, process-orientated mathematicians and creative non-mathematicians, is a degree of social acceptance to admitting to not being able to do mathematics because ostensibly this was due to external factors as opposed to any blame being placed on the learner. Just as Josie identified in the case study, there appears to be a societal acceptance of 'not being able to do mathematics', a notion also raised amongst learners in academic literature (Haylock, 2010; Lockhead, 1990; Pound and Lee, 2011).

It is worth at this point considering the role of the statutory curriculum since these student teachers also appeared to struggle somewhat with their aspirations for approaches to teaching and the requirements of the prescribed curriculum, which in itself was structured. From their experiences of being taught and from their more recent observations of teaching, they described a logical set of age-related objectives based on scientific principles which in themselves they did not associate with creativity, even though they espoused that mathematics should be taught creatively.

In considering your beliefs about what it is to be a mathematician, take a moment to reflect both on your perceptions of the nature of mathematics and the approaches to teaching mathematics that you advocate to think further about how you can encourage children to think of themselves as confident mathematicians.

Reflection points

- Do you think it is socially acceptable to admit to being no good at mathematics?
- Why?
- How do you feel about that?
- Do you think mathematical development is exclusively reliant on natural ability?
- Why?

(Continued)

(Continued)

- In what ways do you perceive mathematics to be logical?
- In what ways do you perceive mathematics to be structured?
- In what ways do you perceive mathematics to be mechanical?
- In what ways do you perceive mathematics to be creative?
- In what ways do you perceive mathematics to be scientific?
- In what ways do you perceive mathematics to be an art?

By reflecting upon the range of perceptions that student teachers shared you can consider different views of mathematics, some of which you may not have consciously considered before. It was evident from some of the student teachers' recollections of their past mathematical experiences that they believed mathematics to be a science rather than an art or a creative subject. There were therefore student teachers who, in thinking of themselves as creative with a disposition towards 'arty' subjects as opposed to the 'sciences' did not consider themselves to be mathematicians. Having given considerable thought to your views of mathematics so far, in now reflecting upon yourself as a mathematician, it might be interesting to consider how 'art' is defined as 'practical skills, or its application, guided by principles' (Chambers, 2003, p. 79). Mathematics can hence be defined as an art in terms of the scientific structure constituting its facts, rules and proofs that make up its principles, having been created by mathematicians and subsequently applied in creative ways by mathematicians using their practical skills. Perhaps then, mathematics can be seen as both a science and an art. Either way requires creativity in terms of how an individual uses mathematics to develop understanding, dependent on relationality with mathematical principles.

It is an interesting paradox that student teachers on the one hand considered mathematicians to think in a logical, structured and process-orientated way and yet also advocated creative pedagogy through the use of discussion, play, hands-on apparatus, investigations and so on. Perhaps it is more a case of mathematics being an art whereby the mathematician uses practical mathematical skills and application based on mathematical principles, in creative and interactive ways in order to develop individual mathematical thinking, individual relationality with mathematics, individual understanding as they play, explore, question, investigate, discuss and collaborate together. Indeed, student teachers in the final layer of the reflective framework not only described their espoused pedagogy as creative but expressed beliefs that mathematics itself is creative in that it both stems from its creation within the human mind and is a creative means by which an individual can think and understand. They explained that since they regarded mathematics as a way of thinking and since everything we do involves us making sense of that which surrounds us, then we naturally think mathematically and are naturally creative as we ask questions and seek to find solutions, and that we are all, therefore, mathematicians.

Although they recognised that aspects of mathematics including rules, proofs and processes were tried and trusted ways of seeking solutions, these were created by mathematicians and in seeking to reach our own understanding either through our own means or applying the theorem of another, we naturally use creative means to think and make our own sense of what we are trying to understand and communicate. Since mathematics has been created by mathematicians before us it raises the question of 'discovery' learning, in that one way of approaching mathematics learning is for teachers to facilitate children finding their own ways of doing mathematics and exploring their own processes to find solutions. You might be thinking that to sit back and wait for children to discover things themselves could take up even more of your precious contact time with them in mathematics lessons and hence you might ascertain there is a need to ensure children have the time and freedom to think, but also to ensure that your teaching approach guides them in what you think is a worthwhile direction. The pedagogical perception here is that, although a body of mathematics exists in terms of what has already been discovered, its 'rediscovery' by children can be brought about, not by viewing mathematics as a known entity to be found, but as an internal relationship between the child and phenomena via creative as opposed to instrumental means as they bring about their own mathematical meaning, the organisation of which in practice is a fine balancing act.

Just as in the case study Josie was keen to find a way for her pupils to engage with and enjoy learning mathematics and see a purpose for it beyond doing what they needed to pass exams, the upper tier of the reflective framework included students' expressed aspirations to be teachers who encouraged children to enjoy being mathematicians. They described wanting to facilitate children to ask questions, seek solutions and to have the opportunity to play and explore their own ways of understanding through various mathematical means as opposed to following given rules and methods. While advocating a range of creative activity to teach mathematics in order to extend the means by which learners can continue to develop their mathematics understanding, knowledge, skills, aptitudes and perhaps attitudes, they recognised the need for a statutory curriculum and the expectation upon them as teachers to implement it, and talked of finding ways in which this could be approached creatively.

They questioned, for instance, age-related objectives which, although stated to be guidance, they saw in practice as being tightly adhered to, with children being moved on to aspects of mathematics without prior understanding and teachers worrying about 'not getting through the syllabus'. Jonathan, for instance, had sat in on a staff meeting to see how the teachers across a primary school planned for the year:

> The various year group teachers used these objectives as a starting point so it was really interesting to see what you base the lesson planning on as I had wondered where that all came from and I was relieved it was already there for us and that we just needed to know where the kids were up to. But that was the problem. I realised they were just going with the majority of the year group to decide where to start from and I was sat there thinking but what about the ones who are beyond that or the ones who aren't ready for it yet? I know we'll find out more about this thing called differentiation on the teacher training course but it all seems a bit of a minefield to me – I really don't get it yet, you know, how you match your teaching to what the kids are actually ready for.

They also expressed concern about their observations of teachers who had demonstrated particular methods of calculating which children had found difficult to understand at the expense of using other methods that were as efficient but made more sense to them. Annie, for example, described observations in a group of children she sat with in pre-ITT experience:

> I was watching this little lad work out some really quite complicated multiplications. He'd do them, get the answer, then rub out all his calculation and write it up the way the teacher had shown him on the board. He got everything right and the teacher seemed to be pleased that he could do it. When I spoke to him afterwards I asked him why he did it like that and he said he didn't get what the teacher was doing but he knew he could find the answer and figure out how to write it down so she'd get what she wanted to see. He seemed to do that all the time and I couldn't help thinking it showed real initiative. I did wonder if it actually showed he understood more than the teacher really thought but I didn't want to open a can of worms by saying anything!

Phil contributed to this as he reflected on the time aspect of teaching, saying that: 'it seems to me that there's just not enough time to get through everything in lessons – like there's this push to cover everything in the curriculum. Wouldn't it be great if kids actually had time to think and explain how they were thinking so that we could see what they saw? How else do you know if they understand it if they don't get the chance to talk about it or the teacher doesn't have time to watch them mess about in maths?'

These student teachers therefore perceived that, although they could espouse practical and creative ways of teaching mathematics, actually ensuring that teaching was creative and flexible enough to meet a range of children's varying needs while also working towards a statutory curriculum was not going to be straightforward. According to them, we are all mathematicians, but as such need to learn at our own pace and hence the role of the teacher is crucial in facilitating creative learning, and creative application of a statutory curriculum so that children's needs are met.

These accounts reflected a non-dualist way of viewing mathematics, seeing it not as a transmitted body of knowledge but as a relational conceptualisation, whereby everyone is a mathematician since everyone makes personal sense and meaning from their surroundings. They saw their job as a teacher involving figuring out how they could help children do that in practice. Their perception was that everyone is a mathematician, and that mathematics is a framework created for the purpose of understanding, making use of and communicating within the world. Their role as a teacher of mathematicians recognised both a statutory curriculum and a set of mathematics facts, rules and procedures, regarded as the result of what Marton and Booth (1997) term our 'described world'. In other words, mathematics is not to be memorised without understanding, not to be followed without understanding, and not to be presented without learner engagement leading to understanding.

Reflection points

- What recent experience do you have of children developing as mathematicians?
- If mathematics is a way of thinking, in what ways do we think mathematically?
- What is this way of thinking dependent on?
- How can you help children develop their mathematical thinking?
- What do you need to develop in order to meet your aspirations for helping children develop as mathematicians?

In terms of student teachers perceiving themselves as mathematicians, the reflective framework varies from a non-creative view of mathematics ranging from a focus on correct answers, through use of correct procedures, to rules and procedures being followed as content adheres to a prescribed structure contrasted with the perception of mathematics being creative, based on a creative process that is individual to the learner's relationality. This contrast is an interesting one to consider as you ascertain the extent to which you deem yourself to be a mathematician, to define what you perceive a mathematician to be and how you want to encourage children to be mathematicians. The contrasting creative and non-creative mathematical perceptions can be analysed in terms of the dualist pedagogy you might have experienced and compared with a non-dualist approach whereby the focus for mathematical development is on the relationship between the learner and the created discipline of mathematics.

It is apparent within the reflective framework that non-creative perceptions of mathematics are associated with it being a difficult subject to learn, a notion that Pound (2008) and Cockcroft (1982) have shown has been the case. It is hoped that you have found it helpful, if perhaps at times painful, to look back on your own experiences of being taught and learning mathematics and your more recent experiences of observing mathematics being taught in today's primary schools, so that you reflect on the way you see yourself as a mathematician and to set yourself goals for the future.

There is clear demonstration here of the problems that some student teachers faced, which you may find resonate with your own experiences. You may also be working alongside colleagues in the future who have similar difficulties and can use your help. If you are working through this book because of your own concerns about mathematics then you are certainly not alone in your worries since existing research has witnessed a degree of discomfort, if not fear, in learners of mathematics, apparently stemming from a perceived need to give the correct answers (Cockburn, 1999; Cross, 2009; Haylock and Thangata, 2007) that are expected by the teacher (Lampert, 1990), which in turn seem to stem from experience of an instrumental pedagogy (Ernest, 1989) of teaching by transmission to passive learners (Desforges and Cockburn, 1987; Ernest, 2000; Howell, 2002; Ofsted, 2008), where facts are expected to be memorised and recalled (Ambrose, 2004; DfES, 2003a; Wong, 2002), to closed questions, written neatly (Boaler and Greeno, 2000; Ofsted, 2005) and produced quickly (Bibby, 2002b). Such approaches to teaching are far removed from encouraging learners to see themselves as mathematicians and to be confident in their mathematical ability. The student teachers' accounts here link to an experienced dualist pedagogy based on mathematics as a structured and non-creative external, known, set body of facts to be imposed upon learners which does not lead to mathematical understanding and which lacks an internal relationship that might enable creative thinking and process, and does not encourage learners to think of themselves as mathematicians.

In contrast, the perception of mathematics being creative reflects a non-dualist pedagogy, which seeks to encourage learning through active engagement that facilitates relational understanding of phenomena whereby learners make mathematical meaning. Such an approach does not view mathematics as a separate entity but as a human creation, as we engage with, make sense of and communicate meaning of phenomena through mathematical thinking and doing. This approach is based on the premise that mathematical understanding can only be brought about by the relationship between learner and phenomenon via active engagement in order to be able to make personal mathematical meaning. Despite there being both an active and an interactive and socially collaborative element to learning, the development of understanding through the discipline of mathematics is inherently individual, based as it is on the individual's relationship with mathematics and as such we are all indeed mathematicians in our own way.

As you have read in previous chapters, the student teachers constituting the final tier of the reflective framework described interest, enjoyment, stimulation and wonder at mathematics, involving both pleasure in engaging in mathematical activity, but also enjoyment of the challenge of figuring out complex concepts and problems and the 'mind-blowing' nature of the world and how we try to make sense of it. This creative nature of mathematical engagement is associated with inherent pleasure, corresponding to a purist perspective (Ernest, 1991) of the intrinsically creative roots of mathematics formed by the inventors of the past (Dawson and Trivett, 1981). Alongside their confidence in engaging in mathematics, they identified themselves as being mathematicians as a natural part of what they do.

It is useful therefore for you to consider not only the extent to which you identify yourself as a mathematician but also how you encourage children to be mathematicians instead of memorisers and rule-followers. As you establish your aspirations for teaching and form your teaching philosophy, you can consider what your mathematics learning environment will look like. Will it resemble the disheartened, passive receivers of transmitted knowledge as described by some student teachers or will it be an active, lively, participatory environment where children get a chance to both think individually and share ideas with each other?

Learners can be encouraged to engage mathematically through socially constructing their own mathematical understanding, with mathematics viewed as subjective, to be created in the learner's consciousness, and reconstructed as learning develops. In such a learning environment, interaction can enable learners to engage with opportunities to internalise mathematical ideas through action, and as part of a social community to share meaning (Vygotsky, 1978). Children can be encouraged and build their experience and confidence in asking questions, which is a natural part of being a child. However, it needs a confident mathematics teacher to give children free rein to question the mathematics, each other and the teacher as well (O'Sullivan et al., 2005). Social construction is further supported as children are encouraged to collaborate, the benefits being the presentation of their different ideas, explanations and articulation of their mathematical thinking to the group (Von Glaserfeld, 1990), which enables individual and collective understanding (Burton, 1994) in both verbal and recorded forms (Floyd, 1981), with facilitation of ideas being introduced by the teacher within the group (Burton, 1994). Active engagement in a socially supportive environment enables learners to observe, play, experiment, explore, investigate, ask questions, pose problems, seek solutions, look for patterns (Pound, 2008); it also facilitates development of describing, articulating, explaining, discussing, drawing, writing, using symbols and mathematical vocabulary to express what children come to understand from abstract mathematical concepts. Vocabulary can gradually be developed and refined (Wilson, 2009) and different strategies shared and introduced (Pound and Lee, 2011).

However, as suggested here and as purported in theory (Boaler, 2009), a level of mathematical understanding and confidence is needed for a teacher to be open to such questioning and interactive engagement and therefore your level of confidence as a mathematician is crucial.

Reflection points

- Are you open to children questioning what they are learning?
- Will you encourage children to question each other?
- Would you feel comfortable with children questioning you?
- Do you feel like you have to have all the answers?
- Is it your experience of mathematics that it both has to be right and it has to be carried out correctly?
- Is it acceptable for you and your learners to learn together?
- What kind of preparation will you need to do in advance of your lessons?
- Who will there be for you to ask your own questions of, if you are unsure?

As established in Chapter 4, you will influence practice in your classroom (Cross, 2009) through your attitudes (DfES, 2002b) about mathematics and it is important that you clarify your perceptions of mathematicians and where necessary set about increasing your self-confidence as a mathematician. Aligned with your past mathematical experience, and corresponding to research findings, a lack of self-recognition as mathematicians can be compounded by debilitating lack of confidence (Pound, 2008) and self-esteem (Akinsola, 2008), detrimental comparison of yourself with others (Boaler and Greeno, 2000), considering mathematicians to be clever (McVarish, 2008; Sowder, 2001) leading to feelings of inadequacy (Cockcroft, 1982), perceiving a lack of mathematical ability (Metje et al., 2007) in yourself and self-blame (Miller and Mitchell, 1994) for this. Your critical self-evaluation, however difficult, is needed for you to analyse whether your own past learning experiences facilitated relational understanding and whether hostile teachers (Brady and Bowd, 2005; Briggs and Crook, 1991; Jackson and Leffingwell, 1999), teachers' judgements (Haylock, 2010; Miller and Mitchell, 1994; Perry, 2004) and humiliating incidents (Ernest, 1991) might have been contributory factors. Whatever your past experiences, as an adult you are now in a position to make changes, beginning with reflection to ascertain your current situation and to plan ahead.

Since feelings of inadequacy have been shown to affect attitudes towards mathematics (Perry, 2004) it is important that you identify and address your relationship with mathematics. This will be by no means straightforward, but the first step in improving a situation can be to ensure self-awareness (Gattegno, 1971) of what is to be dealt with and plan to make changes – on the premise that mathematics anxiety is learnt and as such can be unlearnt. Any learner engaging in an internal relationship with phenomena to make sense and meaning, and hence develop mathematical understanding unique to themselves, is, by definition, a mathematician. Hence, we are all mathematicians since we all make meaning of that which we experience.

Chapter summary

In this chapter you have considered a range of student teachers' perceptions of what it is to be a mathematician, from limiting mathematicians to perceptions of cleverness, logical aptitude and being scientific to a recognition that, since mathematical development is the relational understanding of that which surrounds us, we all engage in mathematical thinking and process and are thereby all mathematicians. Since that process is creative, we are, by nature, creative mathematicians. The chapter has used student teachers' recollections of their own experiences in order that you can compare and contrast your own beliefs as based on your own experiences, in conjunction with theoretical evidence from research, so that you can consider what it means to be a mathematician and to establish the extent to which you think you are one. Student teachers' accounts here have enabled you to consider that a lack of personal association with mathematics can reflect an external relationship with mathematics that has limited development of mathematical knowledge. Perceptions of mathematical ability being dependent on genetics and the ability to be logical also indicates limited development of mathematical knowledge. Also suggested is the notion of mathematics being based on science, not being regarded as creative, and mathematicians therefore not being regarded as creative. Alongside assumptions made about factors contributing to lack of mathematical ability, it is deemed socially acceptable to not understand mathematics, since the causes are out of the learner's control. This range of perceptions of mathematicians potentially has implications for your own learning and the message given to children if limitations are placed on mathematical learning, in contrast to everyone being considered a mathematician, where mathematics is recognised as an integral part of everyone's everyday lives and constituted of a creative conceptualisation of surrounding phenomena.

10
Philosophy for mathematics learning and teaching

Learning objectives

Having read this chapter you will ...

- Draw together your reflections on prior mathematical experience and make conscious your beliefs based on consideration of contrasting perspectives
- Determine approaches to learning and teaching mathematics which you think are effective
- Make explicit your personal philosophy for learning and teaching mathematics, based on your aspirations for the future
- Ascertain your personal learning needs for teacher training

Throughout this book you have reflected upon various aspects of mathematics teaching and learning from a personal perspective based on your mathematical experiences, thinking about how these have shaped your current perceptions. By reading about the experiences and perceptions of other student teachers, you may have been able to recognise some perceptions that may have been subconsciously held as well as consider a range of mathematical perceptions in order to compare and contrast these with your own.

So far you have compared your own mathematical experiences and perceptions with those of other student teachers whose accounts have constituted the reflective framework and academic theory has been used to consider the range of perceptions held. This chapter focuses on the contrasting perspectives that have been considered throughout the book, offering you the opportunity to draw together your reflections to firm up your personal teaching philosophy, based on your beliefs about approaches to learning mathematics.

Case study 📁

Martin was on the first year of an undergraduate QTS programme. Here he reflects upon a task set in his primary mathematics education course:

I was quite confident about teaching mathematics when I started the initial teacher training course as I'd always been quite good at maths at school, but it turned out to be really interesting. I realised, from the general education studies course, that maybe I shouldn't be feeling so confident as I decided I was actually what they call an 'unconscious incompetent'. I'd gone into this class and was working with a group of kids thinking I could show them what to do and they'd get it – I was sure that's how I'd learnt at school, but it quickly unravelled as they had no idea what I was talking about. Our course tutors were great though – they taught us that maybe I shouldn't be doing all the talking anyway, the kids should, and that if I used practical resources it could help them understand the concepts.

We were given an assessed item which involved making a maths resource and using it with a group of kids to analyse how it helped them learn. I was really struggling with that at first as my friends had made things like bingo games and loop cards, but I'd tried using those and figured out that although the kids enjoyed using them because they were playing games, they weren't really teaching them anything; they were just practising what they already knew really. You know, there was one lad who didn't know his multiplication facts, so there wasn't much point him playing the number bingo game this student had him involved in because if he didn't know the answer, the resource had no way of helping him figure it out.

I decided the best thing to do was to start with the children rather than thinking of a great resource. My group were learning fractions of quantities and I'd failed miserably, talking about dividing the quantity by the denominator and all that. I had to start looking at what I understood about maths and trying to figure out how I knew it, but I think I'd just learnt how to do it as opposed to ever thinking about why these little tricks worked. It's no wonder the kids had no idea what I was talking about.

I'd seen these laminated circles that looked like pies and cakes and pizzas on one side, which were split into fractions with the fractions written on the back. I made some of my own and then made some apple slices to go on the pies, cherries to stick on the cakes and salami slices for the pizzas. My idea was that, say if we were doing 1/7th of 21, we could use a pizza divided into seven equal pieces and talk about why they were sevenths, then divide 21 salami slices equally on the pizza to see how many were on each slice. Then we could look at how many were on 2/7ths of the pizza, 3/7ths and so on. Then we could use different quantities and different fractions and see if they got to understanding the concept so they could do it in their heads – you know, move from the concrete to the abstract like we'd been taught in uni.

It was brilliant – I think I learnt more than the kids did! I'd never really realised before that the whole dividing by the denominator then multiplying by the numerator thing actually meant something. I had a whole list of things that the kids got out of it by the end of the lessons I taught with this group for my uni assignment – fun, motivation, real life and all that, but the main thing was actually understanding what was going on. I could tell by the way the kids used the resource and talked to each other that they really got it and by the end some could do it mentally, some were drawing a little sketch to help them and some still needed the resource, but at least they still understood it.

I was really pleased in one of the class teacher's plenaries when one of my group got up to show what they'd learnt and she got four friends to sit in a circle with her and she got ten felt-tips. She announced that 3/5ths of 10 was 6 and proceeded to demonstrate by handing out the ten pens between the five of them and then she stood up and said 'I'm one-fifth of this circle and I have two pens' and got her friends all to do the same. It made me giggle as they were really concentrating. Then she nudged two of her friends to stand up with her and said 'We are 3/5ths of the group and we have six pens'. It was great, because the teacher then asked the rest of the class various questions and asked the children to demonstrate visually whether the answers were correct.

Post-Script: After play when we sat round some rectangular tables for literacy, my group were all talking about it and saying things like, 'Sir, there are five of us plus you sat here, so does being the man here make you 1/6th of our group?'. I wasn't sure if I should be doing a bit of maths there when we were supposed to be doing literacy but it seemed too good an opportunity to miss so I was asking them a few questions in that different context and they'd really got a handle on it.

Perspectives

It has been argued here that learners demonstrating difficulty with internalising mathematics and gaining knowledge without understanding in the lower two categories of the reflective framework experienced dualist pedagogy – one that views mathematics as a separate entity 'out there' waiting to be discovered. In contrast, from a non-dualist perceptive, mathematics does not exist separately as it is a human construct formed through individual learners' relationship with phenomena that brings about their own relational understanding. Martin's example exemplifies how his initial understanding of a mathematical concept was different from what he learnt through experience of teaching children, and that he was in turn able to guide children to develop their own understanding of the concept using different approaches.

It is worthwhile, therefore, summarising the contrasting perspectives that have arisen from the reflective framework so that you can draw together your thoughts based on your own experiences, as compared with those of the student teachers before you, in order to analyse in more depth your own perspective with regard to the kind of primary mathematics teacher you aspire to be.

Dualist perspectives

As shown in the reflective framework and as your own reflections may testify, one source of negative perceptions of mathematics is a teaching approach whereby learners take a passive, receptive role as teachers impart what is viewed as correct mathematics – a dualist perception where mathematics is seen as existing as a fixed set of facts to be remembered, rules to be followed and procedures to be undertaken. Such an approach can be termed an 'instrumentalist' view (Ernest, 1989) where teachers act as 'instructors' using a transmission approach frequently followed by expected bouts of practice by learners (Askew et al., 1997).

On the surface, such transmission is outmoded pedagogical practice – indeed over sixty years ago Polya advocated that if a teacher drills 'his students in routine operations he kills their interest, hampers their intellectual development and misses his opportunity. But if he challenges the curiosity of his students by setting them problems proportionate to their knowledge, and helps them to solve their problems with stimulating questions, he may give them a taste for and some means of independent thinking' (1945, p. 19). Some would hope that the transmission approach is no longer used – Anghileri, for instance, purporting that 'the mathematics classroom has changed from the days when the teacher told pupils what to do and how to do it' (1995, p. 74). However, as the reflective framework presented in this book indicates, there is evidence to suggest otherwise. Ernest, for instance, claims that 'too often the teaching and learning of mathematics involves little more than the practice and mastery of a series of facts, skills and concepts through examples and problems' (2000, p. 8) and recent literature evidences expectations of learning rules and procedures by rote without understanding (Haylock, 2010), teacher explanation followed up by learners' practice, with a lack of flexibility in strategies for either teaching or for problem-solving (Schuck, 2002) and Ofsted reporting that 'too often, pupils are expected to remember methods, rules and facts without grasping the underpinning concepts, making connections with earlier learning and other topics, and making sense of the mathematics so that they can use it independently' (2008, p. 5).

Government guidance (DfES, 2003a) suggested that remembering information is an important factor in learning mathematics, with the new National Curriculum aiming for children's 'ability to recall and apply knowledge rapidly and accurately' (DfE, 2013, p. 99). Memorisation of facts has been shown to extend to memorisation of rules that are presented as 'rigid' (Akinsola, 2008) and rule-based procedures (Boaler, 1997) applied in an equally rigid way, also to be remembered, as recalled facts are applied mechanically (Lampert, 1990), as 'knowing the tricks' (Boaler and Greeno, 2000), whereby use of different approaches is not encouraged. Such a rote-learning approach was evidently unsatisfactory for the student teachers who had experienced this and has been shown to be a factor of mathematics anxiety (Cornell, 1999).

The view of mathematics being a fixed entity to be transferred concentrates on the product or answer being the goal (Cross, 2009) and is reminiscent of Skinner's (1954) behavioural theory as the learners' apparent goals are to achieve required answers and be rewarded with a tick, leading to anxiety about getting answers wrong (Haylock and Thangata, 2007) and believing that correct procedure must be followed – even to the extent that if it is not, the answer cannot be right (Bibby, 2002b). Learner expectations become transmission of knowledge at a set pace, resulting in competition between individuals, often carried out at speed alongside a mysterious need for efficiency (Bibby, 2002b) and writing neatly (Boaler and Greeno, 2000), with Ofsted (2005, para 64), for instance, noting that 'in mathematics, teachers sometimes place too much emphasis on pupils' recording and presentation of their calculations, deflecting their attention from the necessary mathematical reasoning'. It is an approach without investigative open-ended mathematical thinking (Oxford and Anderson, 1995), and one where learners' motivation is limited by closed questions with set, correct answers (Boaler and Greeno, 2000) that the teacher already knows and since there is thought to be only one right answer (Lampert, 1990), mathematics is perceived to be logical at the expense of intuitive thinking (Frank, 1990).

Some student teachers clearly recalled such mathematical experiences which have been shown to lead to limited, fragmented understanding (Mji, 2003) as the facts remembered and rules followed are not necessarily understood (Grootenboer, 2008), resulting in '"rule-bound" adults possessing half-remembered rules without having any idea of how and why they work' (Davis, 2001, p. 137). As the 'teachers have children playing a passive, receptive role as learners' (Desforges and Cockburn, 1987, p. 7), they follow a structured curriculum that is taught in a linear fashion (Oxford, 1990) and in discrete components (Tobias, 1993) where connections are not made, concepts are not understood and learners consequently fall behind (Shodahl and Diers, 1984).

In research literature, classrooms have been described as non-participatory environments (Akinsola, 2008) where mathematics is perceived as solitary and performed in isolation of others (Lampert, 1990), with teachers espousing practical mathematics yet not using manipulative apparatus (Foss and Kleinsasser, 2001) and it is suggested that learners expect to be 'spoon-fed whatever information the teacher deems appropriate' (Howell, 2002, pp. 116–17) with resulting 'victim mentality' (Hwang, 1995), whereby students blame others for a lack of learning rather than seeing it as a process for which they take responsibility.

Existing literature thus paints a picture of some engaging with mathematics without really understanding why they are doing what they are doing – expected to be compliant and passive, their learning reliant on memorisation of facts (Wong, 2002), using rules without understanding (Nunes and Bryant, 1996) and learning being limited to following procedures (Kyriakides, 2009). Such a teaching approach is likely to result in a surface approach to learning (Cano, 2005) where learners perceive mathematics to be a predetermined set of knowledge to be absorbed without understanding and mathematical activity to be 'externally imposed' (Trigwell et al., 2005, p. 351). Research suggests that some teachers' own experiences involved individual and rote learning, leading to an assumption that mathematics is reliant on memorisation (Ambrose, 2004). It is crucial, therefore, that you establish your own philosophy on how mathematics should be taught and that in so doing, you analyse the effectiveness of your own experiences to ensure that poor mathematics pedagogy is not perpetuated.

Another dualist perspective is that which Ernest (1989) terms the platonist view. Although still based on the view of mathematics being a static body of knowledge, this focuses on both content (the body of knowledge) and understanding (by the learner) (Cross, 2009). Rather than instructing, the teacher attempts to give explanations to enable learners to 'discover' the existing body of knowledge, making logical connections to develop meaning and conceptual understanding (Ernest, 1991) through description of mathematical objects and relationships. Learning is, therefore, dependent on receiving knowledge and though there is more active construction than the instrumentalist model, through understanding explanations and the inclusion of problems and activities in textbooks, the focus is not on mathematical process. As exemplified by student teachers in the second tier of the reflective framework, this approach to mathematical learning did not inspire learners with enthusiasm or confidence.

While the concept of mathematics being discovered by learners has its merits, not least in the advocation of the use of practical apparatus (Brown, 2000), there have been claims of this more independent approach leading to underachievement (Boaler, 1997) and criticism of the notion of discovery as children are discovering a body of knowledge that has already been discovered by others (Papert, 1980). There also remains the element of received knowledge through teacher explanation and practising of skills and procedures using schemes or textbooks (Boaler, 2002) and what has been termed an 'over-reliance on worksheets' (Ofsted, 2005). It is an approach that has received criticism regarding the limitations of reproducing teachers' demonstrations (Desforges and Cockburn, 1987) that create learner dependency (Burton, 1994), with a lack of communication amongst learners (Anghileri, 1995) and also with a lack of connection to the real world (Romber and Kaput, 1999) and to other mathematics (Hopkins et al., 1999).

Similarly based on an existing body of proved knowledge is the absolutist view (Ernest, 2000) in which mathematical use and application is promoted. It is widely recognised that there is agreed mathematical knowledge (Koshy et al., 2000) that includes skills, such as drawing a measured straight line with a ruler; concepts, such as negative numbers; procedures that guide the use of these in solving problems; rules, such as BODMAS; and that these are linked to attitude and understanding. The previous National Curriculum (DfEE, 1999a) set out the required mathematical content for learning in schools and placed strong emphasis on the use and application of mathematics. The aim of such an approach is for children to be able to 'confidently apply their knowledge of mathematics to a range of situations in their subsequent working and domestic lives' (Hughes et al., 2000, p. 118) and it is suggested that integration of mathematical learning in other curriculum contexts both develops their ability to use and apply mathematics and to relate it to real life (Coles and Copeland, 2002). It is interesting to note that, despite previous advice (DCSF, 2008) flagging up the importance of children learning to use and apply mathematics, the current National Curriculum places less emphasis on this, stating only briefly that children should learn to 'apply knowledge rapidly and accurately' and to 'apply their mathematical knowledge to science and other subjects' (DfE, 2013, p. 99).

However, research suggests that using and applying mathematics in new contexts is problematic (Hughes et al., 2000), with indication that mathematical topics may be taught in isolation and that learners are unable to transfer skills to new situations due to a lack of understanding (Carpenter and Lehrer, 1999). While the government review of curriculum (DfE, 2010) suggests more teacher autonomy, guidance from the past two decades has been prescriptive and objective-led, and regarded as a contradiction to learner-focused pedagogy (Brown et al., 2007). This raises the issue of how government policy is interpreted by teachers, since the NNS and PNS were non-statutory and the statutory curriculum always contained encouragement to follow the more progressive mathematical philosophy of problem-solving. This was included in the 'Using and Applying Mathematics' (UAM) sections of the curriculum, but proved a difficulty in practice, with the 1999 revision of the curriculum (DfEE, 1999a) incorporating UAM into programmes of study instead of its original separation in an attempt at teacher engagement and recent guidance (DCSF, 2008) recommending more emphasis on UAM. The new National Curriculum

(DfE, 2013) now briefly sets out aims for children learning to apply knowledge and connects these to other subjects, with less actual content for teachers to follow in this respect.

Despite these changes, as so clearly represented in the literature, difficulties with mathematics education persist and in terms of the problem-solving aspect of UAM, there is evidence of a reduction of problem-solving to calculations wrapped up in word problems (Jones, 2003) and textbook problems that are closed tasks with little autonomy for the problem-solvers (Brown and Walter, 2005). Time is needed for a problem-solving approach to allow learners to think, reflect, make connections, recognise relationships, develop ideas and communicate (Carpenter and Lehrer, 1999), but in practice, the problem-solving aspect of UAM is sometimes seen as a 'bolt on' as opposed to an integrated teaching and learning approach (Fairclough, 2002), perhaps due to pressure of getting through the curriculum content and from parents (Orton and Frobisher, 1996). An added difficulty is that its active and practical nature can result in little written evidence which can put some teachers off in terms of accountability (Jones, 2003).

As a future primary teacher you have to contend with government guidance that, during frequent changes over the last two decades, has to date not resulted in satisfactory outcomes for learners of primary mathematics. Perhaps the inherent difficulty in all of this is the fundamental perception of the dualist view, that mathematics is a fixed body of knowledge, prescribed by government through curriculum content and not engaged with in practice in a relativist way.

Reflection points

- Look back over your reflections throughout the book to draw together your analysis of the extent to which your past experience of mathematics links with dualist perspectives as outlined above.
- To what extent have such approaches to teaching aided your mathematical learning?
- To what extent is it your intention to adopt such approaches in your future teaching of primary mathematics?

Non-dualist perspectives

Government guidance has been criticised on the basis of stilting creativity through structured lesson formats (Mooney et al., 2009) and from the perspective of autonomy, since research suggests that government initiatives are met with acceptance in schools, with a tendency to conform rather than critique and challenge (Andrews, 2007); and also from the perspective of teachers' confidence (Haylock, 2010). It is valuable to consider a non-dualist view that encapsulates more creative teaching and learning approaches through viewing mathematics, not as a fixed body of knowledge to be transmitted to the learner, but as a creation in itself from the human mind.

Espoused pedagogy of the student teachers in the upper level of the reflective framework intimated that learners are not instructed, nor are they expected to 'discover' things for themselves, but that teachers facilitate learning opportunities whereby children can engage in activities to build on and develop mathematical understanding, with teachers introducing ideas and strategies in context to support sense-making and meaning. In practical terms, while social collaboration enables children to bring ideas and suggested strategies to the learning group, teachers are also part of that social construction and therefore have the opportunity to introduce alternative ideas and methods. Rather than an expectation for learners to follow procedures without understanding, methods can be introduced when relevant to the learning circumstance and to the learner.

Because of school constraints, mathematical development needs to be shaped around the statutory curriculum. However, some student teachers believed that creative means should be taken to ensure that children learn as they need to. In conjunction with Nunes and Bryant's (1996) assertion that mathematics is an integral part of the culture from which it originates, this views mathematics not as a separate subject, but from a holistic viewpoint which promotes a non-dualist pedagogical approach that supports children's innate thinking aligned with the way they view their world; an approach advocated by Sakshang et al. (2002), whereby mathematics is integrated within the school curriculum.

In consideration of the relevance of mathematics across the presentation of student teachers' mathematical experiences in the reflective framework and in conjunction with existing theory (Hickman and Alexander, 1998; Hughes, et al., 2000; Mason, 2000), experience has encompassed mathematics as a sense of number, connections made between different aspects of mathematics, a means of communication and a purpose in everyday life, all these being a pragmatic and valuable part of learning mathematics (Ernest, 2000). However, alongside this non-dualist perception is mathematics experienced as a separate school subject (Tobias, 1993), with links made to other school curricular areas (Coles and Copeland, 2002) under question, supporting the findings of existing research whereby mathematics was shown to be taught in isolation (Hughes et al., 2000) and children experienced difficulties in applying the mathematics learnt to new situations (Carpenter and Lehrer, 1999). While such a mixed perception of non-dualist and dualist notions is observed in general practice, a question arises from this exemplification of a mixed approach in terms of how these mathematical perceptions and their associated practice of teaching resonate with children developing a holistic understanding of their world. The current statutory curriculum (DfE, 2013) is separated into subject areas and, while government proposals suggested schools would be at liberty to decide how to teach (DfE, 2010), there remains the suggestion that mathematics constitutes a separate core section of knowledge to be taught and learnt. There is therefore a need to consider how a holistic teaching approach can be taken and how a set mathematics curriculum can be incorporated into a wider curriculum.

Children's natural curiosity and enthusiasm for being inquisitive was a key element of mathematical development for student teachers' aspirations in the upper level of the reflective framework. Rather than being relevant to and applied to everyday life, accounts consistent with the final tier of the reflective framework describe mathematics as being a man-made framework created for the purpose of understanding and making use of our world, with Robert, for example suggesting that it is 'a framework of logical aspects of physical science. The world around us is governed by maths and maths as a subject is trying to understand that, trying to harness why things work.' It was also described as a means of communicating that understanding, or as Mimi defined it, as an 'all-encompassing communication device' whereby the world can be understood. Tanya summarised this idea in explaining her notion that

> mathematics is how numbers fit together to explain things in the world at large. It's like building blocks to patterns and creating. Our developed society, everything is built on maths, everything has to be worked out and measured and that's what maths is, little building blocks. You can actually physically build something, or create something like make a car or mix a recipe. You're working through a process of things to get to the other side, so I see maths like a little web I suppose – like a network to another level.

However, a critical perspective was taken in realising that putting ideologies into practice is not without difficulty, with recognition for instance that planning for differentiation is not easy and that teachers face constraints in the form of 'pressure on your time, fitting everything into the curriculum' together with government pressure, as Kora outlined 'pressure coming from above from statistics and government documentation. It's very difficult not to get into that mould, to forget why you're there, you're there to teach and encourage children' with specific reference made to 'testing in particular and the teachers feeling responsible themselves for results at the end of the year … when you've got a teacher who is too hung up on league tables, it's very difficult.'

Reflection upon this is worthwhile in both considering the origins of mathematics and hence the purpose for learning mathematics, and in ascertaining the value of an holistic approach to teaching mathematics, which has all-encompassing relevance to other school subjects and to life, since mathematics *is* the creation of understanding that is relevant to us.

One non-dualist approach is that of learning mathematics through problem-solving, a perspective described by Ernest (1989) as a product of creation whereby mathematics is viewed as an active element in society and culture. From the problem-solving perspective, mathematics is dynamic and continually open to expansion, involving a process of enquiry to reach understanding. However, it is not a finished product since the notion of mathematics being a human creation leaves it always open to revision, for as White and Gunstone (1992) suggest, understanding is a continuum. Indeed, the notion of mathematics being constituted of right or wrong can be contradicted in infinite ways for children learning mathematics – a simple example being a young child believing that a large integer cannot be subtracted from a small integer, but subsequently learning that this is possible, once the concept of negative numbers is understood. The problem-solving perspective is 'learner-focused' (Kuhs and Ball, 1986) as it is based on an individual's construction of knowledge. The teacher in this case does not directly transmit knowledge, but is instead a facilitator of knowledge acquisition, with an emphasis on process (Mikusa and Lewellen, 1999). However, as suggested previously, there is a perception presented in practice that 'the aim when doing mathematics is to get the right answer and thus please the teachers' (Cockburn, 1999, p. 108) as opposed to engaging in the process of mathematics. For teachers to focus on the latter, recognition is needed that mathematics is not just a body of knowledge, it is a 'disorganised and untidy, creative activity' (Orton, 1994a, p. 11).

Whereas transmitted instrumental learning is learnt through habit, the problem-solving approach is one of relational learning (Skemp, 1989). In contradiction of dualist perspectives is the constructivist approach, whereby mathematical knowledge is subjectively internalised, constructed and reconstructed by individuals. Schemes and texts may be used, but there is more teacher and school autonomy in the mathematics curriculum, with 'provision of meaningful problems designed to encourage and facilitate the constructive process' (Schifter and Twomey Fosnot, 1993, p. 9). Constructivist theory concerns itself with construction and modification of knowledge in the light of experience (Bruner, 1966), involving active participation as opposed to transfer of knowledge. Piagetian constructivist theory (Piaget, 1953) purports the development of schema as new experiences are assimilated into existing cognition, with accommodation when modification and reorganisation is necessary, although Piaget's accompanying claim to age-related development is open to criticism (Clemson and Clemson, 1994), despite the plethora of age-related objectives set out in the PNS (DfES, 2003a) and the new statutory curriculum for England (DfE, 2013).

With a problem-solving perspective, the construction of knowledge takes place in the learner's mind (Skemp, 1989) through experience and creation, and socially through communication that promotes the active construction of understanding by the individual in a community of talk, interaction and shared meaning (Vygotsky, 1978). A social constructivist perspective of teaching encourages 'social discourse involving explanation, negotiation, sharing and evaluation' (Kamii and Lewis, 1990, p. 35). In a socially constructive learning environment there is an ethos of shared understanding where learning is scaffolded by teachers and learners with support in developing understanding (Yackel and Cobb, 1996) and the classroom is 'characterised by a lively mix of discussion, questioning, debate and reasoning that can enhance interaction and as a consequence improve the quality of the children's mathematics understanding' (Bottle, 2005, p. 77). In contrast to the anxiety described earlier in this chapter, where mathematical performance can be affected by fear of the teacher (Cockburn, 1999), a constructive learning environment is one whereby children can 'feel free to try things out and make mistakes without any shame, fear or feeling the need to hide them, so that they can correct them and continue to learn without the interference of any bad feelings' (Ernest, 2000, p. 16).

Discussion plays a central role in the social construction of mathematical concepts (Askew, 1998), as children explain their mathematical thinking, to themselves and to others (Burton, 1994), both verbally and in written form (Floyd, 1981). This, however, relies on the careful development of mathematical language, which has been shown for some to be 'inaccessible' (Wilson, 2009, p. 95). Children, therefore, need the opportunity to develop their own means of communicating mathematically (Anghileri, 1995), gradually being introduced to associated formal language (Anghileri, 2000) which, as it is refined, enables them to more accurately explain their mathematical thinking and justifications (Nelson-Herber, 1986) and in turn develop understanding. Also important is collaborative working, whereby children describe their thinking to others as problems are tackled, making sense of both their own and others' reasoning (Anghileri, 1995), trying out ideas 'in a non-threatening environment' (Burton, 1994, p. 112) and, according to Billington et al. (1993, p. 40), those who 'take greater risks in posing questions … develop better strategies … support one another in their learning … are more likely to openly express doubts about their understanding.'

Hence the process is one of active learning, meaningful mathematical constructs being created through doing (Atkinson, 1992) and where children are engaged in 'playing around with and getting a sense of, noticing and describing, discussing and showing, articulating, asking questions, testing out, convincing, practising and consolidating, developing new situations and contexts' (Delaney, 2010, pp. 77–8) as 'active participation in problem solving through practical tasks, pattern seeking and sharing understanding' (Anghileri, 1995, p. 7) enables children to make sense of relationships that underlie mathematical knowledge. However, it is important to note that, as Kelly and Lesh (2000, pp. 28–9) purport, 'mathematical thinking does not reside in problems; it resides in the responses that students generate to problems' and is encouraged through the use of various methods as learners construct meaning and make connections, spot patterns and recognise relationships (Pound, 2008), linking the mathematics they engage with in school with their outside lives (Anghileri, 1995). Rather than the learning of isolated facts through an instrumentalist approach, learners are given the time and space (O'Sullivan et al., 2005) to make connections between mathematical facts and concepts (Suggate et al., 2006) as they build up a network of understanding related to their range of experience (Haylock, 2010). One of the benefits of the PNS (DfES, 2003a) was the encouragement of probing children's mathematical thinking and the promotion of different approaches (Pound and Lee, 2011) whereby children can be enabled to learn new strategies and relate these to their existing understanding. Through working collaboratively, they can be introduced to different ideas from peers as well as the teacher (Burton, 1994), although care needs to be taken that strategies are not taught in isolation and as abstract procedures (Anghileri, 1995) that result in instrumental instruction of mathematics without understanding and meaning.

The problem-solving approach is seen as 'one of the core elements in the development of mathematical thinking' (Pound, 1999), viewed by some researchers as fundamental to mathematics since it was created to solve mysteries, utilise that which is around us and communicate understanding (Ollerton, 2010). For the learner, it provides a 'purpose and reason to mathematics and allows children themselves to see why and how mathematics is relevant to their lives' (Jones, 2003, p. 88) and encourages them to become problem-finders (Pound, 2008, p. 59), especially since tackling problems leads to 'some reformulation of the original problem that is essentially a problem generating activity' (Brown and Walter, 2005, p. 126). It is also an opportunity for learners not to merely perceive mathematics as difficult, as previously described, but to accept that seeking solutions to problems and understanding our environment is challenging and that 'children need to come to terms with the frustrations and disappointments as well as the pleasures and satisfactions when they explore new territory' (Orton and Frobisher, 1996, p. 32). One of its criticisms, however, is that some teachers believe that 'time set aside for problem solving will eat into the time they have available for teaching facts and skills' (Jones, 2003, p. 90), an indication that the full nature of this integrated approach to teaching is not fully comprehended. Indeed, some of the advantages of planning mathematics learning through this medium are facilitation of an holistic approach of integration of mathematics into cross-curricular areas (Sakshang et al., 2002) and differentiation for varied learning needs through providing different levels of challenge, maintaining learners' interest and making connections to various aspects of mathematics and other curriculum areas.

It has been suggested, however, that teachers can feel out of control if mathematics is presented as open-ended and learners use different methods, find different solutions or do not reach a solution at all (Jones, 2003, p. 89).

Perhaps one of the difficulties in teachers taking this perspective on board, especially if their own learning experiences involved mechanistic methods, is that it may mean 'we are challenged to think differently' (Sakshang et al., 2002, p. vi), indeed, there is evidence of teachers who have 'had to make a shift in their own thinking and mathematical practice' (Fairclough, 2002, p. 85).

The perspective of recognising the importance of mathematical process as opposed to focusing on a product that may be correct but constitute little understanding, is also reflected in the purist view that Ernest (1991) describes as non-threatening and supportive, since it views all mathematical learners as equal in achievement of personal potential. Based on the purity of creativity, it encapsulates the non-dualist notion of the formation of mathematics where 'inventors doodled, made mistakes galore, agonised over problems for hours, days, weeks, even years, disposed of hoards of paper and chalk, and made haste slowly' (Dawson and Trivett, 1981, p. 125) and contradicts the instrumentalist views of formal mathematical procedures, rule following and right or wrong answers. However, while there is support for more progressive approaches to mathematics education where 'pupils need to see mathematics as a process that they can be actively and creatively involved in rather than a body of knowledge that "belongs" to someone else' (Anghileri, 1995, p. 9), there is indication that 'creativity and mathematics or creative mathematics appears for many to be a contradiction in terms' (Briggs, 2009, p. 94) and, according to Briggs and Davis (2008), teachers who regard mathematics as 'right or wrong' are unlikely to recognise the creativity inherent in mathematics.

The purist perspective focuses on the learner's development, based on construction of understanding. However, although teachers need to be aware of learners' existing understanding (O'Sullivan et al., 2005), there is a danger of deciding what they should learn next, for mathematics is not necessarily the linear progression of content that guidance such as the new National Curriculum (DfE, 2013) prescribes, nor should it be limited to Piagetian theory that suggests age-related learning. Development is based on the learners' construction and reconstruction as their understanding facilitates, and while ceilings should not be set on children's learning, teachers should recognise their innate ability, for as Desforges and Cockburn (1987, p. 4) suggest, 'before children come to school they are inventive mathematical thinkers', yet according to Skemp (2002, p. 75), 'children come to school having already acquired, without formal teaching, more mathematical knowledge than they are usually given credit for.'

Other non-dualist perspectives where mathematics is not externally imposed, but is socially constructed, include what Ernest (1991) terms the public educator view, which focuses on society. From this perspective, ability is not fixed, children's learning being affected by their environment and culture, for, as a human creation, mathematics is part and parcel of the culture in which it is produced (Nunes and Bryant, 1996). Rather than being passive recipients of knowledge, children take an active part in their learning through making their own decisions, the teacher's role being 'to provide opportunities in classrooms and throughout the day that require observation, wonder and time for children to make decisions on their own' (McVarish, 2008, p. 8). This approach involves children being encouraged to question, for as Pound and Lee (2011, p. 25) advocate, 'mathematics is actually about raising questions as much as it is about solving them. The ability to shape (or ask) and to solve mathematical problems is the essence of constructing mathematical reasoning.' Potential implications arising for practice here are the encouragement of mathematical enquiry amongst learners and the associated need for a classroom ethos where children are confident in asking questions of the teacher (O'Sullivan et al., 2005) and teachers who are sure of their own mathematical competence since 'it takes confidence to deal with questions from children to which you do not have a ready answer' (Boaler, 2009, p. 52).

Non-dualist perspectives are not new, Dewey's Pragmatist theory of the early twentieth century, based on the usefulness of mathematics and a focus on the practical and everyday life (Hickman and Alexander, 1998), being an example. Rather than transmission of a body of knowledge, the pragmatic approach focuses on 'creating worthwhile learning experiences' (Mason, 2000, p. 346) and values the relationship between the learner and the mathematics that leads to mathematical understanding. The non-dualist perception of mathematics is a view of the relational aspect between the learner and the object, since mathematics could not otherwise come into being, being, as it is, formed of that relational understanding. However, despite mathematics being all-encompassing, it has been described by some learners as pointless, a perception identified as contributing to the difficulties experienced in learning mathematics (Pound, 2008). It is important for learners to connect mathematics with the world around them (Nunes and Bryant, 1996), yet learners have been shown to find difficulty recognising mathematics that is relevant in their everyday lives (Bottle, 2005) and using school mathematics outside the classroom (Boaler, 1997). School mathematics should be set in 'meaningful situations' (Atkinson, 1992, p. 169), yet researchers warn of the dangers of imposing adult contexts that are outside the realms of children's interest (Ollerton, 2010), forcing them to 'suspend reality and accept the ridiculous' (Boaler, 2009, p. 45).

Focusing on the practical aspect of mathematics can help learners to 'rationalise their experience' (Edwards, 1998, p. 8), through the 'accessible, real and tangible' (Lee, 2006, p. 15), providing objects to touch and move to help them describe what happens (Anghileri, 2003, p. 90) and images and contexts to reach abstract mathematical concepts (Askew and Wiliam, 1995). While it is important to realise that 'there is no mathematics actually in a resource' (Delaney, 2001, p. 124), it is regarded that kinaesthetic experience can aid mathematical engagement although, as Ball (1992, p. 47) warns, 'understanding does not travel through the fingertips and up the arm' and as such learning will not automatically happen through the manipulation of resources. Resources are used as a focus for discussion, for modelling, explanation and demonstration (Bottle, 2005), although, rather than being limited to presentation by the teacher, they need also to be accessible for children to make their own choices about what might prove useful (Burton, 1994). Practical apparatus can be used by learners to create visual and mental images that can help reach understanding of abstract concepts (Moyer, 2001). However, there are indications that children do not necessarily make the link between the materials they use in the classroom to the outside world (Aubrey, 1997), and also that their understanding remains in the concrete (Andrews, 2007). As Askew (1998, p. 15) suggests, 'practical work is not at all useful if the children fail to abstract the mental mathematics from the experience' and it is therefore important to be aware that 'concrete embodiments do not convey mathematical concepts' (Gravemeijer, 1997, p. 316) and to ensure that teaching encourages children to use objects in a way that creates an understanding of representation (Harries and Spooner, 2000) through associated mental reflection and the development of mathematical thinking.

One of the major reasons for mathematics generally being perceived as difficult (Pound, 2008) is its abstract nature (Orton and Frobisher, 1996) and learners' associated difficulties in imagining (Pound, 1999) and communicating its concepts (Skemp, 1989). As such, there is strong argument for the non-dualist perspective that supports a social construction of understanding via the relationship between mathematics and learner through opportunities to question, pose problems, look for patterns (Pound, 2008), to learn to use abstract symbols, mathematical language and develop generalisations as they work with physical objects and practical situations (Bottle, 2005). Hence, although children may come to learn the mathematics of 'great abstractedness and generality, achieved by successive generations of particularly intelligent individuals each of whom has been abstracting from, or generalising, concepts of earlier generations' (Skemp, 1981, p. 83), they do so not by having a recognised body of mathematical knowledge presented to them for absorption, but by forming their own relationship with ideas about their world by reaching a mathematical understanding that is unique to their experience and relation with the subject as an individual learner. Rather than passive receipt, such learning derives from collaborative work and active construction (Von Glaserfeld, 1990, p. 22), and is dependent on learner autonomy developed through exploration, interest and engagement in mathematical activity as learners are encouraged to explain, reason and use a variety of methods to form relational understanding (Skemp, 1981), making connections between mathematical knowledge and methods to build on previous understanding (Nathan and Koedinger, 2000) and develop a 'strong conceptual knowledge base' (Garofalo and Lester, 1985, p. 88) where learners 'engage with what is being learnt in a way that leads to a personal and meaningful understanding' (Trigwell et al., 2005, p. 351).

While the perspectives presented here are not intended to be an exhaustive list of potential approaches to learning mathematics, they encompass a range within which mathematical purpose includes: its use in everyday life and the wider society, an attempt to understand that which is around us, a means of communicating that understanding and an essential element of culture. An added perception of mathematics is that of its intrinsic value. It is evident from both the reflective framework and associated literature that mathematics is perceived by some to be pointless and difficult, with evidence of disaffected learners. The notion described above of problem-solving being included in the school curriculum as a 'bolt-on' is supported by the observation of Briggs and Davis (2008, p. 16) that 'part of the problem with mathematics is that it can seem like you only get to the interesting parts of the subject after you have completed all the dull stuff' and it is purported that, 'if children ... feel ... that mathematics is boring, limited and about sums and that is all, it is small wonder that they begin to see mathematics as something not very pleasant or meaningful' (Clemson and Clemson, 1994, p. 10). There is a wealth of evidence that points to mathematics not being considered in the least bit fun. As Owen (1987, p. 17) purports, 'throughout history there has been conflict between mathematics seen as a subject growing out of economic and social necessity and the view that mathematics has a purity which transcends mere practicality' for mathematics can, for some, be a source of pleasure (Andrews and Hatch, 1999), wonder (Haylock and Thangata, 2007), power and enjoyment (Skemp, 1989) and 'intrinsic interest' (Pound, 2008, p. 8). To learn mathematics without experiencing this aspect is, according to Koshy et al. (2000, p. 8), 'superficial, mechanical and utilitarian' and is summed up proficiently by Ernest (2000, p. 8) in that 'to neglect the outer appreciation of mathematics is to offer the student an impoverished learning experience ... when an outer appreciation is neglected, not only does school mathematics become less interesting and the learner culturally impoverished, it also means that mathematics becomes less useful, as learners fail to see the full range of its connections with daily and working life, and cannot make the unexpected links that imaginative problem-solving requires.'

Reflection points

- How much autonomy do you think teachers have in the way they teach the statutory curriculum?
- What approaches will you take to this in your own practice?
- How do you envisage teaching mathematics creatively?

(Continued)

(Continued)

- How important is it for children to learn mathematics through practical means?
- What implications does this have for your planning?
- To what extent is social collaboration beneficial for learning mathematics?
- What challenges do you foresee in enabling this kind of learning environment?
- How can mathematics be learnt from an holistic perspective?
- How can teachers plan to ensure that children learn to make connections within mathematics?
- How can you help children develop their ability to communicate mathematically?
- How can you make real-life connections for children's mathematical learning?
- How can you plan to make mathematical connections across the curriculum in the primary school?
- How do you know if and when children are understanding their world through mathematics?
- Do your aspirations for teaching meet assessment requirements?
- In what ways is a problem-solving approach to learning mathematics useful?
- How would you plan this kind of approach?
- How do you aim to use the age-related National Curriculum content in practice?
- What is the value of discussion in mathematical learning?
- How can you plan to incorporate this into your lessons?
- How confident are you in being open to children's questions?
- What does 'active' learning mean to you in the context of mathematics lessons?
- How can you help children to develop their mathematical thinking?
- How will you know how this is developing?
- How important is it that children get to set the problems as well as try to solve them?
- How can you plan for children to be challenged without becoming overwhelmed?
- How can you ensure a positive and non-threatening learning environment in your classroom?
- What will you do if the next steps in children's learning do not match the next steps in the statutory curriculum?
- How can you harness children's natural curiosity and inquisitiveness?
- Do you believe children's mathematical ability is fixed?
- To what extent do you aspire to promote a love of learning mathematics not just for the purpose of its use in society, including passing examinations, and its real life connotations, but for intrinsic pleasure?

The issue here for you is a crucial one. Faced with a plethora of theory, initial teacher training courses concerning mathematics pedagogy relating to different philosophies of mathematics and connected to different psychologies of learning, it is little wonder that student teachers present with anxiety (Haylock, 2010). You enter teacher training at a time of political and educational change, with yet another version of a statutory curriculum (DfE, 2013) in the ongoing aftermath of teachers following what Hughes (1999, p. 4) described as 'undoubtedly the most prescriptive approach to primary mathematics ever developed in this country'. Alongside this, teachers have recently 'been positioned more as technically competent curriculum deliverers, rather than artistically engaged, research-informed curriculum developers' (Pound and Lee, 2011, p. ix) as they have followed the government-set curriculum and, according to Brown (2010), followed a procedure-based pedagogy as they teach with national testing in mind. There is a clear need for you to clarify underpinning principles for learning and teaching primary school mathematics and ascertain your own perceptions and values (Lang, 1995) in order to develop as an effective teacher and deal with future curriculum changes.

In reflecting upon the range of student teachers' experiences here, you are in a position to establish what you view effective teaching of mathematics to constitute and 'to be able to view it and appreciate it, from a range of perspectives' (Cockburn, 1999, p. 43). However, you first need to explore both your past experiences of mathematics and associated perceptions, and also reflect on your pedagogical aspirations. The range of theory available to you with which to engage within initial teacher training is challenging in itself, particularly in light of the changing face of teacher education where time spent on learning primary mathematics is reduced (Brown, 2010). Your perceptions are likely to have developed over time and may not have been explicitly articulated, and, as Orton and Frobisher (1996, p. 34) argue, 'they cannot be changed overnight, but they can be challenged'.

Chapter summary

The hierarchy of the reflective framework is based on the notion of mathematics being a non-dualist human conceptualisation dependent on relationality (Marton and Booth, 1997). Learning is dependent on the individual's relationship between themselves and what is learnt (Marton, 1986). As Martin found in the case study, enabling children to make sense and meaning to reach their own understanding of mathematical concepts involves their active participation in a learning process that is tailored to what they need.

This chapter presents the contrast between dualist and non-dualist perspectives, with the latter advocating a relativist conceptual framework whereby understanding is constructed by an individual's relationship with mathematics, as opposed to mathematics and learner being seen as separate entities. From this conception of mathematics, perceptions are formed through learners' experiences of mathematical engagement, although they may not be consciously held. These perceptions affect attitudes towards, understanding of and engagement with mathematics and result in potential implications for future teaching and learning. Reflection is needed in order for you to make your mathematical perceptions explicit, identify your aspirations for your future practice as teachers of primary mathematics, ascertain your personal philosophy for mathematics and determine your associated learning needs within your teacher training course.

11
Your relationship with mathematics

Learning objectives

Having read this chapter you will …

- Develop your understanding of your own relationship with mathematics
- Continue to build on the formation of your personal philosophy for learning and teaching mathematics
- Think about instigating changes in order to improve your relationship with mathematics

---

It is intended that your reflections throughout the preceding chapters, using the framework provided, have enabled you to raise your awareness of a range of perceptions, to clarify your own to raise your confidence in your own abilities, to set yourself goals to work on during your initial teacher training, to begin to create your personal philosophy for learning and teaching mathematics and to think about making any necessary changes.

In this chapter, you will be encouraged to draw together your reflections so far in order to bring some clarity to understanding your relationship with mathematics so that you can continue to develop your personal philosophy and to think about some of the changes you might want to bring about.

Case study

Fiona has worked for ten years in various schools and has taken up a new post in a small rural school. Here she talks about setting up her new classroom, based on her philosophy for teaching and learning mathematics. She says:

I had got quite disillusioned with teaching in general really. I'd just left a large urban school because I didn't feel comfortable with the way things were run there. Take maths, for instance, it was a case of children working in separate groups from text books all at different levels and on different books. It was a nightmare to try and provide support and the kids just seemed really cheesed off – there was no fun in it, especially for those who knew they were on the lower books.

The new school seemed much more amenable to different ideas and practice. I soon realised that people (including the advisers and inspectors!) seemed to think teaching in a small school was an easy ride, but in many ways it was a lot harder than my previous big schools and certainly a lot more work. The differentiation was enormous within the class across a range of ages which wasn't straightforward.

Over the holidays I'd gone in and sorted through all the cupboards and the caretaker helped me get rid of loads of bin bags of stuff that had been there for years and would never be used. Once school started I'd been able to choose a new scheme of work for maths but I'd also set up my own scheme so that the books would be used as part of that instead of the kids just working through them as they had in my previous schools. I'd set up all the activities at different levels so that it covered a whole range of ages and needs.

I'd gone through it all and made a huge list of all the resources I could possibly need throughout the scheme and sorted it alphabetically. The children loved helping out on wet playtimes and we got all the resources out of the cupboards and made piles of equipment in the classroom and down the hall so we had all that alphabetically sorted. Then I went down my list to see what we had and what we needed to get. The Head had let me know what budget there was and we set up a Parent Teachers Association who organised fundraising like jumbles sales. I spent the budget on the resources we needed and the PTA money on a cupboard with trays. I labelled the trays alphabetically and all the resources went back in – so it was really easy to find 'squared paper' or 'rulers'. It meant that the kids knew where everything was so they could choose the resources they thought they needed, or go and get what I suggested. It saved me loads of time as I couldn't set up the class prior to every lesson as I did playground duty every day, but the main thing was it made the children think about what they were doing and what would help them work things out.

When the children came in from playtime they'd automatically go to sit in friendship groups on the carpet area as until the lesson started they never knew where they would be sitting for groupwork as the groups would be different every day. The maths groups, for instance, would be different from the English groups depending on where various children were up to, but the maths groups would change as well as various children worked differently with number, say, than data handling. It was a bit of a quandary when I had, say a Year 6 child who really needed to work with Year 3 children, so I'd take them aside and give them the choice. Because we'd got such a family atmosphere in the class, they'd feel comfortable working with the younger kids at the level they needed at the time and I'd set them up as monitor. They'd do what the teaching assistant would do in another group – they'd be the one the other children had to ask permission from to go to the toilet or whether they could go and get scissors and things like that. It gave them that added respect from the group and I'd keep an eye on things unobtrusively from another group table. I'd always make sure those kids would get loads of praise and make a point of flagging up their strengths.

I think the most important thing for me was the ethos in the classroom. There was mutual respect between me and the kids but also between the kids. Anything untoward was always nipped in the bud – we'd use circle time to talk through things and use a buddy system, things like that. The children genuinely enjoyed learning as everything was set up for what they needed, but there was always the element of challenge and we played lots of games to put things into contexts.

There was a policy came through at the time saying we should be setting homework, but I knew the kids got plenty in school time and I thought they were better off spending their evenings at Brownies, football and all the things they were involved in. So, instead of formal homework, they'd leave with a sticky note with games to play on the way home. If I give you an example – Jess was learning about multiples of 4 and I knew her mum would be collecting her and have the twins in the car, so her 'homework' was for the four of them to count in turns in the car. It helped the twins with their counting but as Jess was the fourth each time, she had to shout the number – you know so it would be 1 from Mum, 2, 3 from the twins and Jess would shout 4, then it would be 5, 6, 7, 8 and so on. I knew Jess had got the idea of the multiples from the work we'd done that day with multilink but I wanted her to start thinking of the numbers in the abstract. She came in the next day and she'd coloured in blocks of four on some graph paper and brought it to me all excited, saying look Miss: 4, 8, 12, 16, 20, 24 ... I just loved seeing the children carry on with things outside school – they were just so interested in what they were learning.

I remember one parent coming in to see me quite early on and asking me what I'd done to their boy. I was a bit taken aback at first, until I realised he was saying, 'What have you done? He's coming home saying how much fun

(Continued)

(Continued)

maths is. I never had any fun learning maths – what's going on?' I invited him
in to an after-school event I'd set up for parents to try out some of the things
we were doing in school. It was a hoot and I got a handful of volunteers
coming in to help out after that which was fantastic as we didn't have much
funding for teaching support.

Don't get me wrong – it all involved a heck of a lot of work, especially at
the planning stage, but it all paid off. When we were inspected by Ofsted it
was obvious we weren't quite doing things conventionally perhaps like they
might have expected but they couldn't say the children didn't learn – our test
results spoke for themselves. Basically they said that in a small school you have
to be inventive and maybe do things a bit off the wall. I didn't argue with
them, but I tacitly disagreed as I think what we did there could work in any
school – you just have to build the strong foundations to work with.

Consideration of the reflective framework

The reflective framework that you have used throughout this book was formed
through research with actual student teachers who were themselves embarking
on teacher training. As has been seen, for example through Faye's case study
in Chapter 3, no one student is linked to any one level of the framework. The
framework itself was formed from pooling all the student teachers' accounts of
their previous learning of mathematics and aspirations for their future practice
as teachers, to 'capture the range of views present within a group, collectively,
not the range of views of individuals within a group' (Åkerlind, 2005a, p. 118).
There is no expectation that your perceptions will match a single category
(Barnacle, 2005) of the framework as these are 'compositions, formed out of an
aggregate of similar perceptions' (Barnacle, 2005, p. 50) incorporating 'key elements from the statements of a number of people' (Cherry, 2005, p. 57).

The reflective framework was formed from analysis of the pooled accounts
of the student teachers as a combined whole in terms of relationality (Leder
and Forgasz, 2006; Säljö, 1997), a method that allowed interpretation to move
beyond the individual description to the context of variation across the group
(Bradbeer et al., 2004; Green, 2005) to achieve a better understanding of the
range of mathematical perceptions (Dall'Alba, 2000; Marton, 1986).

Different perceptions of mathematics will exist for different student teachers
under different circumstances, but the reflective framework provides information
for engagement by all student teachers since it provides an holistic perspective

on collective experience, and can 'act as a powerful trigger for such meta-reflection' (Cherry, 2005, p. 59) by facilitating you to engage in thinking about your mathematical philosophy.

It is not expected that you move mechanically through the framework as some elements may not resonate with your own experiences, but they will serve to raise your awareness of the perceptions others may have, especially useful if you are in a position to support colleagues. The framework has been presented so that you can reflect on your own circumstances and where you aspire to be with your relationship with mathematics, for, as Åkerlind (2005b, p. 72) suggests, 'the aim is to describe variation in experience in a way that is useful and meaningful, providing insight into what would be required for individuals to move from less powerful to more powerful ways of understanding a phenomenon.'

You have been encouraged throughout to analyse your own experiences and to determine whether you have experienced dualist pedagogical practice whereby a transmission approach was used where learners were passive receivers (Desforges and Cockburn, 1987; Howell, 2002) of an external body of facts with little opportunity to construct meaning. Mainly confined to number facts, learnt through recitation and repetition, this kind of experience, as presented in the lower tier of the reflective framework, is similar to the Victorian methods outlined by Sharp et al. (2009) and leaves learners disassociated from a wider mathematics vocabulary. Perhaps your recollections of mathematical experience resonated with elements of the second layer of the reflective framework, where experienced pedagogy was dependent on a body of mathematical knowledge known to, and explained by, the teacher through whole class demonstration of set rules and procedures, as seen in primary schools by Askew et al. (1997), that are then used by learners, through limited internal relationship with mathematics, to reach a set of 'correct' answers, through reproduction (Desforges and Cockburn, 1987), to closed questions (Brown and Walter, 2005). You may also identify with aspects of the third tier of the reflective framework whereby mathematical experience was via a socially constructed learning environment with scaffolded support based on learners' identified needs from approachable teachers (Yackel and Cobb, 1996) available to provide help and of whom learners feel confident to ask questions, as advocated by O'Sullivan et al. (2005), and where an internal relationship with learning mathematics is enabled as teachers facilitate opportunities for mathematical thinking, doing and process. This non-dualist pedagogy comprises the highest level of the reflective framework as espoused practice for an active learning environment conducive to children internally relating to mathematical understanding through engagement. Included is concern for children's mathematical learning and a desire for inspirational pedagogical practice to effect approachable teachers who encourage enjoyment of learning mathematics and promote interest, fun and excitement amongst learners, encouraging children's confidence to do their best, through the kind of environment espoused by Billington et al. (1993) where children feel free to take risks with questions and strategies, support each other, query their understanding, work at their own pace and are not 'afraid to get things wrong' as advocated by Ernest (2000).

You have considered both your experienced and espoused pedagogical practice and begun to think about potential implications for your teaching development with regard to avoiding approaches that were associated in the lower categories of the reflective framework with limited engagement and relationship with mathematics leading to knowledge without understanding. When reflecting on the upper end of the reflective framework, you have considered pedagogy perceived as encouraging development of mathematical understanding through emphasis on process via active engagement and scaffolded support (Yackel and Cobb, 1996) from teachers who are aware of learning needs (O'Sullivan et al., 2005). In aspiring to be the best possible teachers of primary mathematics, you have considered the desire for children to perceive mathematics as enjoyable and the intention to implement a socially constructive, supportive and interactive learning environment (Billington et al., 1993; Bottle, 2005; Pound and Lee, 2011) with a focus on mathematical process and where connections are made (Anghileri, 1995), independent thinking is encouraged (Burton, 1994), children's needs are acknowledged (Nathan and Koedinger, 2000) and where mathematical understanding is constructed through doing (Atkinson, 1992). It is recommended that you consider planning development of this aspect of mathematical learning through teacher training to increase awareness of the creative nature of mathematics in noticing patterns, exploring, describing, questioning and probing (Anghileri, 1995; Delaney, 2010); socially constructed understanding via discussion, explanation, sharing, evaluation and negotiation (Askew, 1998; Kamii and Lewis, 1990); the process of mathematics and associated development of mathematical thinking within knowledge construction (Desforges and Cockburn, 1987; Skemp, 1981, 1989, 2002); gradual development of mathematical communication from children's own representations to formal symbols and vocabulary (Anghileri, 2000; Nelson-Herber, 1986); and autonomy based on teacher confidence, understanding and pedagogical awareness for relational mathematical understanding to be facilitated.

Starting point: awareness

If you have any anxieties about mathematics, the prospect of teaching it and being back in a mathematics classroom, you might feel that you are the only one experiencing such concerns, yet engaging with the reflective framework will hopefully have assured you that such worries are not unique. It has been suggested that learners tend 'to assume that their fellow students think in the same way that they do' (Petocz and Reid, 2005, p. 798), in which case the wide variation of mathematical perceptions in the reflective framework will have proved that this is not the case. Raising your awareness of others' mathematical perceptions is useful if you find yourself in a position to support others in their relationship with mathematics and so that you can compare and contrast the range of perceptions to clarify your own and consider how they could affect your future learning and teaching.

It is evident from the reflective framework that there are student teachers who have a negative relationship with mathematics. It is hoped, however, that working through the chapters you are aware that rather than an irrational phobia (Hodges, 1983), mathematics has been shown to cause rational anxiety and negative perceptions amongst some learners which can affect their ability to engage. Since there is apparently 'an urgent need to teach mathematics differently' (Hogden and Askew, 2007, p. 470) and it has been established that teachers themselves have an enormous influence on what is taught and on learning (Cross, 2009), to consider your own relationship with mathematics and the potential influence of this on your teaching is valuable. In addition to the reflective framework, it is recognised that there is generally a range of perceptions associated with mathematics (Ambrose, 2004) that are likely to influence the practice of teachers. The intention has been that you work to facilitate improvement in your own relationship with mathematics as appropriate to ensure that you have or develop positive perceptions (Noddings, 1992) since these have shown to have a strong influence on understanding how to teach effectively (Hofer and Pintrich, 2002).

Teachers have different experiences, attitudes, knowledge and pedagogical understanding of mathematics and flexible opportunities for development are needed to meet individual needs (Smith, 2004). Your teacher training institution has a responsibility to prepare you for teaching mathematics effectively and as such there is a need for teacher education providers to be aware of the variation in mathematical perceptions in order to plan for student teachers' learning. However, perceptions are a personal and intrinsic entity and so direct involvement on behalf of the learner is also needed in terms of taking responsibility for learning (Tolhurst, 2007). It is therefore essential that you examine your own perceptions of mathematics at the outset of teacher training to take control of a subject that may have caused you anxiety in the past. The means to reflect on your own mathematical experience and practice (Cooney and Krainer, 1996) here will help you to develop an increasingly positive relationship with mathematics as the starting point for addressing and potentially changing perceptions as may be warranted.

You have been encouraged to reflect on your mathematical experience and to analyse the pedagogy you have experienced to determine benefits and drawbacks, to be aware of alternative approaches, to compare and contrast other student teachers' experiences with your own and to form your personal philosophy of what mathematics is, how it can be learnt and how it should be taught. As you analyse your personal relationship with mathematics and decide whether that needs to change, you may have reflected on beliefs that until now may have been unconsciously held (Ambrose, 2004; Bishop, 1991). For example, you may have always seen mathematics as a challenge, perceiving that to be a negative aspect, resulting in the subject appearing difficult. However, you have read about some student teachers seeing that challenge as enjoyable, as they like the stimulation of having to think about things that are not easy and finding solutions to difficult problems. Just as mathematics can be seen to be challenging, perhaps you now find yourself challenging your own thinking, as you develop your philosophy for learning and teaching mathematics and your pedagogical aspirations for practice. The process is certainly not straightforward, not least because mathematical perceptions are not necessarily part of conscious thought (Cross, 2009), and are probably not notions that you have previously consciously considered (MacNab and Payne, 2003). Indeed, working through this book may have proved quite a painful process if you have recalled bad experiences and tried to come to terms with negative perceptions as it is recognised that establishing viewpoints can at times be complex and emotive (Cherry, 2005). However, given that perceptions can influence practice (Nespor, 1987), it is a worthwhile process to undergo if you are to fulfil your potential as a teacher.

Previous research supports that an individual's relationship with mathematics can change. You may be encouraged to know that negative perceptions can be challenged (Uusimaki and Nason, 2004) and that 'adults can get over a negative disposition towards maths' (Pound and Lee, 2011, p. 16). Mathematics anxiety is learnt and as such can be unlearnt (Ashcraft and Kirk, 2001), and student teachers' concerns regarding mathematics can be improved during initial teacher training (Hopkins et al., 2004). Nevertheless, changing people's ingrained beliefs is always difficult, but being aware of others' perceptions is an effective starting point for considering and heightening your own awareness (Houssart, 2009).

Mathematical perceptions can be challenged (Edwards, 1998) but first need to be identified, which is a process entirely personal and unique to an individual. By working through the reflective framework here you have been able to both identify and challenge your perceptions by comparing them with those of others. Although you may have held your mathematical perceptions for many years and they may be difficult to change, it is a worthwhile process in order to determine your personal teaching philosophy, for as Pound and Lee (2011, p. 16) suggest, 'we owe it to them (children) to do all that we can ... to develop our own enthusiasm and, in the process, our expertise.'

This process of development is far from straightforward since mathematical perceptions are 'the indirect outcome of a student's experience of learning mathematics over a number of years' (Ernest, 2000, p. 7), developed over considerable time, with individuals perhaps unaware of them (Ambrose, 2004). By identifying with the range of student teachers' mathematical perceptions throughout this book, you have enabled reflection and taken the opportunity to examine your beliefs. Such a reflective process may confirm your perceptions of mathematics as being valid and worthwhile, expand your awareness and extend your understanding (Valderrama, 2008) as your critical reflection leads to change as necessary. While it is recognised that it can be difficult to change perceptions, according to Ernest (1989, p. 249), 'teaching reforms cannot take place unless teachers' deeply held beliefs about mathematics and its teaching and learning change'.

Challenging and potentially changing established perceptions is problematic, for beliefs are hard to change, and can be particularly painful and elicit strong emotions. According to literature, there appears to have been little engagement with philosophising about primary school mathematics in terms of teachers questioning their views and associated perceptions and what they are teaching (Bibby, 2002b). Perhaps the lack of research is due to the difficulty that lies in capturing something so elusive (Hofer and Pintrich, 2002) and so your personal engagement to determine your individual mathematical perceptions is of value for you to move your relationship with mathematics forward.

Relationality

It is likely that your experiences are not confined to any one aspect of the reflective framework, but that in comparing your own mathematical experience with others you have been able to ascertain what you consider to be effective approaches to learning and teaching mathematics and are thus developing your own teaching philosophy. You may have also been asking how you instigate changes to your perceptions, beliefs, engagement and subject knowledge. As stressed at the outset, this book does not constitute a magic wand and only you can bring about change, but your raised awareness and in-depth reflections are an excellent starting point from which to make this happen.

So, with your honed awareness of your personal mathematical perceptions and aspirations, let us consider the non-dualist theme that has permeated the higher levels of the reflective framework. We will now focus on you as the learner in your forthcoming initial teacher training and how you can develop into an effective mathematician and teacher of mathematics. The relational aspect between you, as the experiencer of mathematics, and the experienced mathematics is vital (Bowden, 2005; Pang, 2003). It is your relationship with mathematics that is the cornerstone of developing your own mathematical understanding, the way in which you will learn in initial teacher training, shaping your own future teaching practice. This concept of relationality (Marton, 1986) is illustrated in Figure 11.1 as you, the individual with the mathematical perceptions you hold as a result of your previous experience, engage in mathematical activity as you behold phenomena around you and naturally seek meaning and make sense of those phenomena using your existing mathematical understanding. In doing so you develop further understanding, so that as your mathematical experience develops, you continue to form mathematical perceptions through the relationship you have with the phenomena you experience.

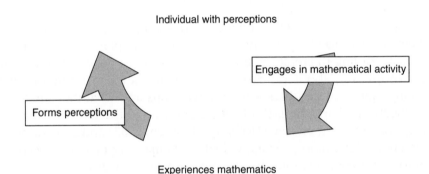

Figure 11.1 Relationality – perceptions and experience

You are not considered separate to this process (Marton, 2000) of continuous engagement with developing mathematical thinking and understanding, since the focus is the relational aspect between mathematics and learner through a 'non-dualist view of human cognition that depicts experience as the internal relationship between human and the world' (Pang, 2003, p. 147). You have your own unique 'relational view of the world' (Bowden, 2005, p. 11) because only you have had those particular mathematical experiences. By comparing yourself with the experiences of others, through the reflective framework throughout this book, you can examine others' perceptions to set yourself goals for your own aspirations as the development of mathematical learning, thinking and understanding is a unique process of which you yourself have control. You are no longer dependent on past experiences and can instead decide for yourself how you are going to approach your teacher training. You fundamentally influence your practice as a learner and future teacher, and you have the power to determine what shape that practice will take (Christou et al., 2001).

As you embark on initial teacher training, a circle of development is hence formed as your continual experience leads to ongoing reflection that will continue into your career in the classroom, which is illustrated in Figure 11.2. As you experience being taught mathematics and teaching yourself, either conscious or unconscious perceptions form that will add to your raised awareness of your relationship with mathematics. Hence you can make explicit your mathematical perceptions and use these to develop your philosophy for future teaching and determine if change is needed in order to facilitate this and put into practice what you ascertain is necessary in your teaching.

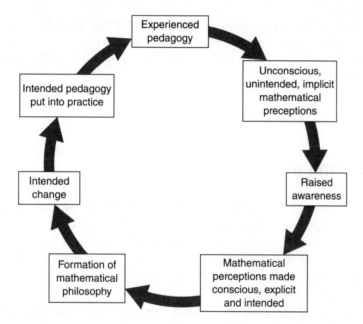

Figure 11.2 Reflective cycle for ITT and beyond, based on mathematical experience

It is crucial that you engage in such a reflective cycle for, as Ernest (2000) purports, perceptions cannot be taught. You may feel secure with your mathematical perceptions and aspirations and see no need to change, but it is nevertheless worthwhile expanding awareness and gaining understanding of the perspectives of colleagues you will work alongside (Valderrama, 2008). If you do identify a need for change, use the reflective framework to establish your relationship with mathematics and consider potential implications and actions for your practice as a means to engage with a process of change, starting with personally challenging assumptions and beliefs (Edwards, 1998; Orton and Frobisher, 1996).

Reflection points

- You have engaged in critical reflection of your mathematical experiences, beliefs and goals throughout the chapters in this book.
- Take some time now to make a list of all the factors you think are important to learning mathematics.
- How do you think children learn mathematics?
- How do you think mathematics should be taught?
- List the attributes which you think a teacher of primary mathematics should have.
- Consider your lists and decide the extent to which you can match up to those ideals.
- Make a list of the things you want to learn more about during your ITT course.
- Make a list of the things you would like to improve.
- Be practical and make a list of what you think you can do about it and what you will need to set up.

Chapter summary

You will have spent considerable time throughout this book analysing your own position and comparing your experiences with others and determining, through academic reading and critical reflection what your aspirations are for teaching primary mathematics. In this chapter you have built on your evolving philosophy for learning and teaching mathematics and have begun to consider not only what your goals are for teacher training and beyond, but more specifically what you need to develop if you are to become the teacher you envisage. The central element to developing mathematically is understanding your relationship with mathematics, as it is this relationality which forms your unique position as a mathematician, the way you think mathematically and the way you understand phenomena mathematically. If your relationship with mathematics has been negative, it need not stay that way and you hold the power to start developing mathematically by acknowledging and then leaving behind your baggage and gradually engaging with the subject through a different pair of eyes. You can use your previous experiences to help you understand how some of your children or colleagues perceive mathematics. You can also build on them to see yourself as a mathematician and develop greater awareness of how you want to learn and teach the subject.

Change of any sort is not without difficulties and there is no claim that the journey is going to be an easy one, but with raised awareness, a clear philosophy, an openness to see things differently and determination to learn, you have already begun and can travel as far as you like!

12
Making changes

Learning objectives

Having read this chapter you will ...

- Acknowledge your prior mathematical experiences and assumptions and prepare to be open-minded about making changes
- Consider how you can change the way you think and engage mathematically
- Apply creative thinking to your own learning needs in initial teacher training
- Be mindful of what you can do to develop your teacher identity with an increasingly positive relationship with mathematics

Throughout this book, you have reflected upon your mathematics perceptions based on your previous mathematics experience and compared these with the accounts of experiences of other student teachers. You have thought about your aspirations for teaching primary mathematics and set goals for your learning in initial teacher training so that you can develop as you wish to. In considering different approaches to teaching and learning and the nature of mathematics itself you may have begun to make changes in your thinking and your practice. This chapter is intended to give you more food for thought as you continue to develop your mathematics philosophy and change the way you think and engage mathematically.

Potential for change

As intimated in previous chapters, change is not straightforward. Raising aware-ness is a starting point for developing knowledge of a range of mathematical perceptions in order to identify your strengths and the areas you wish to develop. In particular, you have been encouraged to reflect on any 'baggage' you may be bringing to your teacher training so that you are in a position to effectively deal with it, first by making yourself aware of it and secondly by considering how you can make your relationship with mathematics better. Although you may have been previously unaware of your mathematical beliefs, research (Dweck, 2006) suggests that people's beliefs are very powerful in shaping success in achieving what we want. Dweck (2006) suggests, based on a range of research she has carried out with various learners, that our belief system underpins the way we live our lives and it is no surprise, therefore, that the student teachers within the reflective framework have found their mathe-matical perceptions to have a profound effect not only on their learning, but also intrinsically linked to their self-belief and self-esteem. They have demon-strated that mathematics can evoke strong negative emotions and if you identify with this, then it is likely that your mathematical learning has been and will continue to be affected unless you change how you perceive mathematics.

Emotions can strongly affect achievement, and, as Claxton (1999, p. 15) sug-gests, 'learning itself is an intrinsically emotional business'. What is perhaps involved here is 'emotional intelligence', defined by Goleman (1998, p. 317) as 'the capacity for recognising our own feelings and those of others, for moti-vating ourselves, and for managing emotions well in ourselves and in our relationships'. However, although you have reflected at length, being able to motivate yourself and manage your emotions is no simple act, especially given the years of mathematical experiences that have led you to your current emotions, beliefs and perceptions.

According to Mortiboys (2012), there is a need for learners to create an emo-tional state that is conducive to learning, which may not be straightforward for those who have historically held negative perceptions of mathematics. It begins with the development of self-awareness and by working through the various reflections in this book, you are on the road to developing the emotional state that will allow you to move forward. By acknowledging the way you feel you have moved away from what De Bono (2004, p. 17) terms 'selective perception', whereby an individual is tied to perceptions supporting pre-formed ideas, and are now in a position to be more open-minded about the possibilities of your relationship with mathematics and open to the notion of change.

This should not continue to be detrimental to your self-esteem if you are perhaps reaching the stage of regretting the way that you have engaged with mathematics previously. Your relationship with mathematics has been a direct outcome of your experiences, and as an adult you now have the chance to make new experiences. De Bono (2004, p. 5) describes people acting within a 'logic bubble' whereby they act logically within the bubble that is 'made up of the perceptions, values, needs and experience of that person'. You have the wherewithal to create your own logic bubble based on changing perceptions, values and needs as you experience mathematics from now on in the way you choose.

Reflection points

- Look back over your various reflections on the range of aspects of mathematics that have been covered in this book.
- If you were to draw a logic bubble of the way you viewed mathematics prior to reading the book, what words best describe your perceptions, values, needs and experience?
- Now draw a new logic bubble to include the ways in which you have either changed your mathematical perceptions, values, needs and experience or have set goals to do so.

Thinking creatively to begin the process of change

Through your reflections, you have made conscious your mathematical beliefs and are now in a position to work with them and change them. However, while it is widely accepted that reflection is important, exactly how teachers use theory such as that contained in this book to create teacher identity is not clear-cut (Cooper and He, 2012). What is suggested here is that you begin to see yourself with more confidence and autonomy as a mathematician, based on the premise that we are all mathematicians with our varying relationship with mathematics and as your identity as a teacher emerges, you will find it will continually evolve as you gain further experience (Sutherland et al., 2010).

Bringing about change is probably the most difficult stage of this process. The student teachers within the reflective framework advocated that creativity was necessary to teaching mathematics, as they set out their aspirations for teaching primary mathematics in a variety of ways that encouraged children to work practically and socially to make sense and meaning from phenomena, and to teach a statutory curriculum through creative means that facilitated children to reach their potential whatever their stage of learning mathematically. As an ideal to strive for in your own teaching, perhaps creative thinking needs to be applied to your own learning, just as you would most likely want to utilise it to guide children's learning.

Let us therefore consider how you can think creatively in order to use your increased awareness of mathematical perceptions to put into practice the philosophy you have already created for learning and teaching mathematics. According to Lucas (2001, p. 38), 'creativity is a state of mind in which all of our intelligences are working together. It involves seeing, thinking and innovating.' In contemplating how mathematics can be viewed and how an individual can think mathematically, it is time for you to take an innovative approach to your own relationality with mathematics. Lucas (2001, p. 38) purports that 'creative people question the assumptions they are given' and you have already questioned assumptions you had about mathematics and yourself as a mathematician. Now that you have a clearer idea of how you want to learn and teach mathematics you have begun to change your perceptions and how you choose to engage with the subject. You have the choice to develop a teacher identity whereby you see yourself as a budding mathematician who is open to new challenges and forming a new relationality with mathematics. Lucas (2001, p. 38) suggests that creative people 'see the world differently, are happy to experiment, to take risks and make mistakes' so it is time to look at mathematics differently, and experiment with it. Take risks and do not be afraid to make mistakes along the way.

Reflection points

Would you encourage the children you teach:

- to be creative?
- to look at what they see around them?
- to think mathematically about what they see in order to make sense of it?
- to be innovative in their thoughts and actions?
- to question?
- to experiment?
- to take risks?
- to not be afraid to make mistakes?

If you have answered yes to any of those questions, then is there any reason you should not encourage yourself to do the same?

Developing a mind open to change

You may feel that you are not a creative person and that this is going to be a difficult process. According to De Bono (2004, p. 47), 'there is a silly myth that creativity is a sort of mystical talent which some people have and which others can only envy'. In contrast, he suggests that we are all naturally creative, but that creativity is a skill that may not be a habit for you, in which case he advocates learning and practising skills as everyone can have ideas that can then lead to others. So, just as you would encourage creativity in the children you will teach, cut yourself some slack and try thinking about mathematics creatively and experiment!

In doing so you need to have an open mind and adopt a strategy of mindfulness, defined by Langer (1997, p. 4) as 'the continuous creation of new categories, openness to new information and an implicit awareness of more than one perspective'. Instead of hanging on to old beliefs, informed by past experience, you have begun to create a philosophy for learning and teaching mathematics, taking on board different perspectives in order to develop your personal aspirations. Being open to new and different perspectives and questioning those of your own and of others is a part of mindfulness, according to Safran (2001, p. 81), who suggests that 'whether learning takes place depends on the learner'. The development of yourself in your mathematics learning and teaching is therefore down to you, for 'in mindful learning it is the learner who controls the relationship between him or herself and the subject matter' (Safran, 2001, p. 82). At this stage you may still not be feeling very confident as a mathematician, but you have begun the journey of change through raising your awareness, identifying your goals and aspirations and being prepared to do something about it through questioning your assumptions and being open-minded to new perspectives. As this develops, so too will your mathematical understanding and your confidence as a mathematician, for, as Safran (2001, p. 90) purports, 'mindful learning allows the learner to develop self-knowledge and self-confidence' based on your desire to learn.

If you have the desire to learn and to improve your relationship with mathematics, then you need to be prepared to make the effort, since the responsibility and wherewithal for learning lies within you. According to Dweck (2006, p. 4), making the effort is the key to development as she saw in her research that 'human qualities, such as intellectual skills, could be cultivated through effort'. This effort needs to run alongside the willingness to make mistakes as learning naturally involves a less than perfect journey. If we already knew, could already do and already understood, then we would not be learning. There are always going to be aspects of mathematics that we do not understand – such is the nature of life, its phenomena and our experiences. However, there are aspects of mathematics you know you need to understand better so that you are able to teach and so, rather than considering yourself any sort of failure, you will need to open your mind to new experience and set your mind to what you want to achieve and how you want to achieve it.

Reflection points

Are you prepared to:

- have an open mind with regard to mathematics?
- be creative in your approach to mathematics?
- try new strategies?
- learn new skills?
- challenge old beliefs?
- be mindful of your mathematical perceptions?
- take control of your learning?
- put in the effort?

Changing your mindset

It was clear from the student teachers' accounts that some were in danger of almost writing themselves off where mathematics was concerned, finding the subject too difficult, engagement with mathematics too fraught with anxiety and seeing themselves as lacking the confidence and ability to 'do' mathematics. However, their ambitions to become primary teachers and indeed their willing-ness to take part in the research that led to the formation of the reflective framework, together with their descriptions of their aspirations, showed that their minds were not fixed on negativity. With no exception, all the student teachers wanted to overcome any concerns they had about mathematics and to develop into the best teachers of primary mathematics that they could be, which was absolutely to their credit in that they were choosing to return to learning mathematics and to confront and overcome their anxieties. Similarly, if you have chosen to work through this book you are probably in the same position: not over-confident in your mathematical ability but determined to learn what you need in order to be able to teach it effectively to primary school children.

Dweck's (2006) mindset theory distinguishes between a 'fixed mindset', where an ability is set in stone never to be developed, and a 'growth mind-set', clearly demonstrated by the student teachers in the reflective framework since every one of them, aside from their past experiences and 'baggage' they carried, believed they could, with effort and the desire to learn, develop mathematically in order to be able to teach. According to Dweck (2006, p. 7), such a growth mindset 'is based on the belief that your basic qualities are things you can cultivate through your efforts. Although people may differ in every which way – in their initial talents and aptitudes, interests, or temperaments – everyone can change and grow through application and experience.' This applies to you too – if you are prepared to learn and to make the effort to develop, then you can.

It does not matter if you think you are not as 'good' at mathematics as others. Indeed, I have seen really gifted mathematicians struggle to teach mathematics to children as they find it difficult to break down mathematical concepts, or more importantly, see how a child's mind can come to understand these. In contrast, I have seen student teachers who do not consider themselves to be the best mathematicians teach the subject well, as they have gone through similar processes as the children to reach an understanding. This is not to say that either student teacher lacks mathematical intelligence, but that they are different, just as we are all different in our understandings of a multitude of concepts. The fundamental basis is that our mathematical intelligence is not fixed, but rather is open to development, and so increasing your mathematical experience, engaging in your initial teacher training course, making the effort to learn and being open to that development means you are able to foster the relationship with mathematics that you desire. In other words, you have a choice – you can choose to have a growth, as opposed to a fixed, mindset.

Consider, then, whether your mind is fixed on not being able to do mathematics or not being good at mathematics. If you have a fixed mindset, you will believe that your goal of becoming an effective teacher cannot be achieved because you think that a person either can do mathematics or they can't, and you are set on thinking that you can't. If, like some of the student teachers in the reflective framework, your past experiences include being told by your teachers that mathematics was not your strong point, it would be no surprise for you to feel that way as people, especially children, have a tendency to believe what those in authority tell them, and such negativity can stay with them into adulthood. Feeling that mathematics is beyond you is a fixed mindset and potentially damaging, as shown amongst student teachers in the reflective framework and in Dweck's research (2006, p. 34), for she remarks that 'the loss of one's self to failure can be a permanent, haunting trauma'. She describes the process whereby 'failure has been transformed from an action (I failed) to an identity (I am a failure)' (Dweck, 2006, p. 33), shown in student teachers' descriptions in the reflective framework as they recall years of failing to succeed in mathematics leading to a lack of confidence, self-esteem and self-belief in their ability to engage. However, the fact that you have taken the trouble to read this book means that, just like the student teachers in the framework, you have the desire to improve and therefore believe that you can. You are an adult and have the freedom to challenge what people may have led you to believe in the past, or what you allowed yourself to believe.

According to Dweck (2006, p. 202), 'the fixed mindset makes people complicated. It makes them worried about their fixed traits ... and it makes them judgemental'. However, try not to be hard on yourself. If, like some of the student teachers, you were subject to judgemental behaviour yourself as a learner then it is no wonder if you ended up feeling judgemental about your relationship with mathematics. As seen in the reflective framework, it can lead to learners feeling embarrassed and ashamed of their apparent lack of mathematical ability, which links to a fixed mindset whereby 'imperfections are shameful' (Dweck, 2006, p. 73). By adopting a growth mindset you can change that and decide to stop being hard on yourself and instead do something about changing things. Those with a fixed mindset would believe that if you have to work at mathematics, then you must not be any good at it, whereas those with a growth mindset would believe that you can improve with effort. Which mindset do you choose to follow? It is possible to change your mindset if you are prepared to let go of the past and replace it with new experience.

There is no suggestion that this change is easy to make, but if you need to change your relationship with mathematics, then you may decide it is worth endeavouring to do so. As Dweck (2006, p. 225) suggests, 'it's not easy to just let go of something that has felt like your "self" for many years' but if it is a change you wish to make it will be worth the effort. Adopting a growth mindset, Dweck (2006, p. 12) purports, can lead to 'the love of challenge, belief in effort, resilience in the face of setbacks and greater (more creative) success'. Consider, for a moment, the ways in which you want to teach and advocate that children learn mathematics. According to Dweck (2006, p. 16), 'as soon as children become able to evaluate themselves, some of them become afraid of challenges. They become afraid of not being smart.' Would you want children in your care to adopt such a fixed mindset over their relationship with mathematics whereby they try to take the easy route, avoid situations where they might get things wrong and choose options where they think they will be assured of success? If the answer is no, then would you want to hold a fixed mindset yourself? Or are you prepared to be challenged, to work hard, to put in the effort and to develop your relationality with mathematics via a growth mindset based on a belief that 'abilities can be cultivated' (Dweck, 2006, p. 50)?

Working on developing your relationship with mathematics may not be straightforward and there are likely to be mistakes made and hurdles met along the way, but a growth mindset would mean an acceptance that this is the nature of learning. We cannot all excel at everything and difficulties in learning are inevitable and can at times be painful. The difference in learning with a growth mindset is that you recognise and acknowledge that there will be problems and you are prepared to meet and deal with them. Another aspect of a growth mindset is that any perceived failure 'does not define you' (Dweck, 2006, p. 33), for just as you would expect children to find learning hard at times yet you would encourage them to find ways to solve problems and overcome what is difficult by trying out different strategies, you can adopt that perspective for your own learning. Dweck's (2006) research with children showed that those with a growth mindset were prepared for and expected to stretch themselves, they enjoyed the challenge and indeed appeared to thrive on it. You may be far from feeling that way yourself about mathematics, but if you are not prepared to try, then you may never know! It is perhaps a societal belief that people who appear to be mathematical seem simply to understand it and be able to do it, yet there has most probably been a lot of effort undertaken to get to that stage and it is no reflection on a learner if hard work has to go into learning. Indeed, Dweck (2006, p. 42) describes the importance of hard work as 'the transformative power of effort – the power of effort to change your ability and to change you as a person'.

In addressing your relationship with mathematics, then, it is worthwhile to consider the lens through which you have, up until now, perceived your mathematical learning and to 'think about where you'd like to go and which mindset will take you there … mindsets are just beliefs. They're powerful beliefs, but they're just something in your mind and you can change your mind' (Dweck, 2006, p. 16). Using the reflective framework, you have been able to consider a range of perceptions held by student teachers in order to make conscious your own experiences, think about your aspirations for learning and teaching mathematics and to consider how you will achieve your goals. You may have found that your developing philosophy differs from what you thought at the outset, and can now think about the mindset you need to take your development further to be able to put your mathematics philosophy into practice. With a growth mindset, it is not a question of whether you can learn mathematics, but *how* you learn and it is hoped that reflecting on various aspects of mathematics has enabled you to consider how mathematics is best learnt. It is heartening to know that Dweck (2006, p. 53) suggests that, with a growth mindset, 'even when you think you're not good at something, you can still plunge into it wholeheartedly and stick to it. Actually, sometimes you plunge into something *because* you're not good at it … you don't have to think you're already great at something to want to do it and to enjoy doing it.' It could still be the case that re-entering a mathematics classroom is the last thing you want to do, but because you have set your sights on becoming a primary teacher, you have decided to forge ahead and learn more about how to teach mathematics. The focus, with a growth mindset, is the learning and to think about different ways in which mathematical understanding can be created so that you are able both to progress personally and professionally as a learner and teacher of mathematics. You may need to put behind you any anxiety and negativity that you may harbour from past experience and instead use those experiences to inform your philosophy. Your past mathematical experiences can be both a foundation of how not to proceed but also a valuable source of knowing what does not work well and what you need to change. You may recognise that you were once a learner of mathematics with a fixed mindset who thought you could get no further, thinking that your lack of confidence in the subject was due to a limited intelligence in that area. Perhaps that was when circumstances were out of your control and now they are not. You can now choose a growth mindset and become one of the successful individuals who 'love learning, … seek challenges, … value effort and … persist in the face of obstacles' (Dweck, 2000, p. 1).

As seen in the student teachers' perceptions, some people think that you are clever if you are good at mathematics. A fixed mindset would mean that if you perceive yourself to be no good at maths, then you are not clever. Student teachers' descriptions in the lower tier of the reflective framework recounted such perceptions, yet if you identify with this, then, just like the student teachers, this does not mean that you are in any way stupid or a failure mathematically speaking. Remember that Faye in the case study of Chapter 3 was far from a mathematics failure and yet she identified very closely with the lower tiers of the framework. The difference is that she had, or made, or developed new experiences. She was not prepared to settle for such experience fixing a mindset that did not facilitate her to progress. Developing a growth mindset means that you can set about learning mathematics in your teacher training with determination. It is not about being clever or proving you can do it – it is about being prepared to learn, being open to new experience and seeing what you *can* develop.

Reflection points

- If you recognise in yourself a fixed mindset and you are still clinging to the idea that you are not much good at mathematics and, although you might be convinced by the general premise of this book, you are still convinced that mathematics is beyond you, then consider a different perspective.
- Would you have a fixed mindset towards the children you teach? Do you expect children to be able to do mathematics and if they do not have natural ability then do you think there is no point trying to teach them?
- Will you expect them to succeed without making mistakes?
- Will you expect them to be clever without needing to make any effort?
- Will you expect them to find learning easy and have no difficulties?

- Will you expect them to not want to challenge themselves?
- Will you expect them to find no stimulation or fun in challenge?
- If the answers are no, and you do not have a fixed mindset towards the development of children's learning, can you justify having a fixed mindset towards your own learning?

Mindset for teaching mathematics

In considering the mindset with which you have, or will, approach mathematics, it is worth also thinking about the relevance of mindset in teaching, whether this aids your reflections on past experiences or helps in forming your philosophy for your own teaching. The recollected mathematics teaching in lower tiers of the student teachers' reflective framework corresponds to a fixed mindset whereby the teacher's role seemed to be transmission of knowledge as opposed to a growth mindset of developing knowledge, as seen in the upper tiers of the framework. Adopting a growth mindset for your own teaching means you will be open to creative thinking and looking at different strategies to use in developing mathematical understanding for the children you teach and also prepared to learn alongside them.

There is value in thinking about the message, overt or implicit, that you give to children in terms of focus on product rather than process. As seen in the reflective framework, teachers focusing on 'right' answers using 'correct' methods proved limited with regard to their learning mathematics and confidence in themselves as mathematicians. A focus on product rather than process leads to performance-related goals, where learners are led to think that the number of right answers is far more important than the learning journey and the extent to which they understand. Performance-related goals and associated assessment gives the impression that learning is dependent on ability and if learners do not reach the expected answers, then they consider themselves 'unable' to 'do' mathematics. Student teachers felt both judged by their teachers and by themselves as their self-esteem was affected and a vicious circle was formed whereby they thought they were no good at mathematics and therefore did not set themselves very high expectations.

To focus on the process of understanding mathematics through a variety of means, to engage in different strategies, to try even when things seem impossible, to face problems with enthusiasm and to enjoy the stimulation of having to think creatively to try to find solutions and not be phased by what seems very challenging echoes a growth mindset. How you teach children to learn is dependent on your mindset and the way in which you go about this will send a message to children, who are exceptionally astute at picking up on such things. Is it therefore your intention for children to feel comfortable in your class, to take an active part in learning and to not worry about making mistakes because they will not be judged and so that they know you are interested in their development? Children need to know they are praised for doing their best and putting in the effort, working hard and trying even when things are difficult, as opposed to getting hung up on assessment, for as Dweck suggests:

> A performance goal is about measuring ability. It focuses students on measuring themselves from their performance and so when they do poorly they may condemn their intelligence and fall into a helpless response. A learning goal is about mastering new things. The attention here is on finding strategies for learning. When things don't go well, this has nothing to do with the student's intelligence. It simply means that the right strategies have not yet been found. Keep looking. (2000, p. 16)

It is hoped you will be the kind of teacher who teaches children 'to love challenges, be intrigued by mistakes, enjoy effort and keep on learning' (Dweck, 2006, p. 177). You therefore need to reflect upon whether you see yourself as that kind of learner, and what kind of teacher you will be.

Watching children develop is the greatest job satisfaction for a teacher and well worth the effort in figuring out how you can help to make it happen, but as Dweck (2006) suggests, you have to care about the learners you will teach. By the same token, you have to care about yourself as a learner and make sure you do yourself justice in your initial teacher training to do the best you can to become the best teacher you can. We are very privileged to be employed as teachers – 'we are entrusted with people's lives. They are our responsibility and our legacy. We now know that the growth mindset has a key role to play in helping us fulfil our mission and in helping *them* fulfil their potential' (Dweck, 2006, p. 211).

That magic wand has still not been waved to suddenly make you feel confident with mathematics, but just as raising your awareness of a range of different mathematical perceptions has led you to consider your beliefs and your philosophy for your future learning and teaching of mathematics, 'just learning about the growth mindset can cause a big shift in the way people think about themselves and their lives' (Dweck, 2006, p. 216). It could be the case that it is not that you cannot 'do' mathematics, you just have not yet found the strategies that suit the way you learn. In other words, just as you will work with children, learning *how* is the key. With a growth mindset you can think differently, be creative, motivate yourself, develop skills, work hard, put in the effort, be determined to develop, embrace challenge and not be put off by problems.

Reflection points

- Do you tend towards performance goals based on ability?
- What are you good at?
- Were you always that good from the outset?
- Or have you developed with experience?
- How did you get to your level of expertise in your field?
- Was it from limiting your perception of getting better through putting the effort in?

Mathematics philosophy

The reflective framework has two distinct and fundamental elements within its hierarchy: teacher-centred approaches, where learning is, in simple terms, a process of imparting information (Trigwell et al., 1999), and student-centred approaches that focus on the learners' ways of thinking about the phenomena studied (Kember, 1997). You may recall having been taught via teacher-centred approaches, and, either through your own learning or more recent experiences observing practice in primary schools, student-centred approaches.

Perhaps you have decided that it is your mindset that needs to change; but, as Dweck (2006) would argue, changing mindset is a challenge. Change of any kind can be problematic yet frequently necessary, and even experienced teachers can find it difficult to change their practice, especially conceptual change (Kember 1997). It is not straightforward to unpick what you have always believed about mathematics and yourself as a mathematician and to perhaps begin to view the subject and yourself from a different perspective.

You have the autonomy to choose your mindset and adopt the strategies and tools you will need for your individual circumstance. As you have seen from the student teachers' descriptions, you are not the first and certainly will not be the last student teacher to undergo this process. Indeed, Flores and Day (2006, p. 219) state that 'learning to become an effective teacher is a long and complex process ... which entails an interplay between different, and sometimes conflicting, perspectives, beliefs and practices, which are accompanied by the development of the teacher's self'. Your learning and teaching and relationship with mathematics is unique to you and reflection upon your experiences and beliefs will be a continual process throughout your future career in the classroom.

It has been recognised throughout that this reflective process can be tiring and at times painful. Flores and Day (2006, p. 221) suggest that 'because of their emotional investments, teachers also inevitably experience a range of negative emotions when control of long held principles and practices is challenged'. Their research into teachers' professional identities indicated that these are constructed, deconstructed and reconstructed as teachers examine their past experience, teacher education and their teaching contexts. You have reflected upon very real events that have led to the way you feel about and engage with mathematics, but that is not the end of the story. What you have been able to do here is theorise on different ways of looking at mathematics and you can now choose how you want to approach mathematics in the future.

You are in control of how you wish to shape your identity as a mathematician, a learner of mathematics and a teacher of mathematics. As indicated earlier in this book, children deserve better – but so do you! Cooper and He (2012) describe a model of teacher development as identified by Fuller (1969), whereby student teachers are naturally concerned about themselves, and this book has guided you to explore your own personal mathematical experiences to compare and contrast with others so that you can understand your own relationship with mathematics. The next stage in Fuller's model is that student teachers then question their adequacy as teachers, and in this respect you have been encouraged here to unpick how you think children should learn mathematics and what approaches to teaching mathematics may be the most effective so that you can set future teaching goals. The third stage of the model is where student teachers concern themselves with the impact you have on those you teach. This final stage should have been at the heart of your reflections throughout this process, for as you have examined your mathematical beliefs, you have been creating not only your personal philosophy for mathematics but your professional philosophy, based on the interests of the children you will be teaching.

A way forward

As Scott Peck suggests:

> Life is difficult. This is a great truth, one of the greatest truths. It is a great truth because once we truly see this truth, we transcend it. Once we truly know that life is difficult – once we truly understand and accept it – then life is no longer difficult. Because once it is accepted, the fact that life is difficult no longer matters. (Scott Peck, 1990, p. 13)

Throughout this book you have acknowledged your relationship with mathematics, difficult as that process may have been, and your conclusion might be that mathematics is hard. But that's OK – maths *is* hard! Once you accept this and decide to stop blaming yourself for thinking it is, you can begin to decide with a clear head what you are prepared to do about it. Instead of fixing your mind to the notion that you cannot do it or you cannot get much better at it, you can set your mind to a growth mindset; you can accept that the journey ahead may be difficult, but embark on it anyway, facing it as a challenge, prepared to put in the effort to improve your relationship with mathematics and thereby improve the potential for your learning and teaching mathematics.

According to Scott Peck:

> We are daily bombarded with new information as to the nature of reality. If we are to incorporate this information, we must continually revise our maps, and sometimes when enough new information has accumulated, we must make very major revisions. The process of making revisions, particularly major revisions, is painful, sometimes excruciatingly painful. (1990, p. 46)

Over your lifetime you have mapped out your mathematical beliefs and your relationship with mathematics has developed accordingly. Through the process of reflection in this book, you now have new information and the nature of reality where mathematics is concerned may be changing for you. However, Scott Peck (1990, p. 46) puts forward the question, 'What happens when one has striven long and hard to develop a working view of the world, a seemingly useful, workable map and then is confronted with the new information suggesting that that view is wrong and the map needs to be redrawn?' Having worked through this book you may find that your view of mathematics is beginning to change to such an extent that coming to terms with that change and the effort that is needed in bringing about change is overwhelming. However, it is down to you – only you can decide you want to change and decide what you need to do in order to bring about change. You can adopt a fixed mindset and convince yourself that mathematics is beyond you, or you can choose a growth mindset and use your reflections here to decide if and how you want to improve your relationship with mathematics.

The depth of feeling that has been shown throughout this book to exist amongst some student teachers with regard to mathematics leads me to apply both psychological and psychiatric perspectives to what is evidently a huge deal for such learners of mathematics setting out to seek to be able to teach it confidently in the primary classroom. Bruch (1974, p. ix cited in Scott Peck, 1990, p. 44) indicates that mankind has a common problem – 'the sense of helplessness, the fear and the inner conviction of being unable to "cope" and to change things'. At its worst case, fear of mathematics paralyses learners, and student teachers described their severe anxieties about their relationships with mathematics as based on their prior experiences, experiences that in some cases were so demoralizing that the student teachers had almost fallen victim to them – almost, but not quite, since without exception they showed a growth mindset in wanting to change and wanting to improve their relationship with mathematics. Given that you have chosen to read this book, perhaps you also feel that depth of despair about mathematics or you know people who do that you would like to be able to help. According to Scott Peck (1990), the main factor underlying a fear of being able to cope or change lies in accepting responsibility. While Dweck's (2006) notion of the fixed mindset would contribute to student teachers' fixing blame on, for example, past mathematical experience for feeling the way that they do about maths, the growth mindset does not focus on blame, but looks ahead to development. From a psychotherapy perspective, those who feel helpless have given away their power but

> sooner or later, if they are to be healed, they must learn that the entirety of one's adult life is a series of personal choices, decisions. If they can accept this totally, then they become free people. To the extent that if they do not accept this they will forever feel themselves victims. (Scott Peck, 1990, p. 44)

It is sincerely hoped that, like the student teachers who contributed to the reflective framework presented in this book, you are not prepared to be a victim to fear of mathematics and instead are prepared to make the choice to change your mindset and seek ways in which you can make improvements. To be a free and confident mathematician, you have the choice as an adult, no matter what your prior experience, to make your own decisions about how you choose to approach learning and teaching and developing your relationship with mathematics.

Sense of mystery

This book hinges on the valuable insight provided by the student teachers whose recollections of past mathematical experience were used to create the reflective framework and must culminate with a statement from a student teacher, Diane, that sums up the essence of our joint enquiry here, for mathematics has: 'that sense of mystery to me – that I don't really understand it all'.

The phenomena of life *are* a mystery and nobody can claim to understand it all. If only mathematics could be universally accepted as the means by which we attempt to understand according to our *own* conceptualisation and relationality, without pressure or expectation, instead of the imposition of others' ways of understanding, the mysterious nature of mathematics might be more widely recognised as synonymous with the mysterious nature of the phenomena that surround us and embraced as a source of enjoyment, stimulation and challenge. Its undoubted frustrations, complexities and sometimes sheer impossibility could then be welcomed with confident wonder.

References

ACME – Advisory Committee on Mathematics Education (2006) *Ensuring Effective Continuing Professional Development for Teachers of Mathematics in Primary Schools.* ACME Policy Report PR/09. September, 2006. London: The Royal Society.

Adler, S. (1991) 'The reflective practitioner and the curriculum of teacher education', *Journal of Education for Teaching: International Research and Pedagogy*, 17 (2): 139–50.

Åkerlind, G. (2005a) 'Phenomenographic methods: a case illustration', in J.A. Bowden and P. Green (eds), *Doing Developmental Phenomenography*. Melbourne: RMIT University Press. pp. 103–27.

Åkerlind, G. (2005b) 'Learning About Phenomenography: Interviewing, data analysis and the qualitative research paradigm', in J.A. Bowden and P. Green (eds), *Doing Developmental Phenomenography*. Melbourne: RMIT University Press. pp. 63–73.

Akinsola, M.K. (2008) 'Relationship of some psychological variables in predicting problem solving ability of in-service mathematics teachers', *The Montana Mathematics Enthusiast*, 5 (1): 79–100.

Alexander, R. (ed.) (2010) *Children, Their World, Their Education: Final Report and Recommendations of the Cambridge Primary Review.* London: Routledge.

Alexander, R., Rose, J. and Woodhead, C. (1992) *Curriculum Organisation and Classroom Practice in Primary Schools – A Discussion Paper.* London: Department of Education and Science.

Alexander, R.J. and Flutter, J. (2009) *Towards a New Primary Curriculum: A Report from the Cambridge Primary Review. Part 1: Past and Present.* Cambridge: University of Cambridge Faculty of Education.

Ambrose, R.A. (2004) 'Initiating change in prospective elementary school teachers' orientations to mathematics teaching by building on belief', *Journal of Mathematics Teacher Education*, 7: 91–119.

Andrews, P. (2007) 'The curricular importance of mathematics: a comparison of English and Hungarian teachers' espoused beliefs', *Journal of Curriculum Studies*, 39 (3): 317–38.

Andrews, P. and Hatch, G. (1999) 'A new look at secondary teachers' conceptions of mathematics and its teaching', *British Educational Research Journal*, 29 (2): 203–23.

Anghileri, J. (1995) *Children's Mathematical Thinking in the Primary School*. London: Cassell.

Anghileri, J. (2000) *Teaching Number Sense*. London: Continuum.

Anghileri, J. (2003) *Children's Mathematical Thinking in the Primary School*. London: Cassell.

Ashcraft, M. and Kirk, E. (2001) 'The relationships among working memory, math anxiety and performance', *Journal of Experimental Psychology*, 130 (2): 224–371.

Askew, M. (1998) *Teaching Primary Mathematics: A Guide for Newly Qualified and Student Teachers*. London: Hodder and Stoughton.

Askew, M. and Wiliam, D. (1995) *Recent Research in Mathematics Education 5–16*. London: Ofsted.

Askew, M., Brown, M., Rhodes, V., Johnson, D. and Wiliam, D. (1997) *Effective Teachers of Numeracy*. London: King's College.

Atkinson, S. (ed.) (1992) *Mathematics with Reason – The Emergent Approach to Primary Mathematics*. London: Hodder and Stoughton.

Aubrey, C. (1997) 'Children's early learning of number in school and out', in I. Thompson (ed.), *Teaching and Learning Early Number*. Buckingham: Open University Press.

Ball, D. (1992) 'Magical hopes: manipulatives and the reform of math education', *American Educator*, 16 (2): 14–18, 46–7.

Barnacle, R. (2005) 'Interpreting interpretation: a phenomenological perspective on phenomenography', in J.A. Bowden and P. Green (eds), *Doing Developmental Phenomenography*. Melbourne: RMIT University Press. ch. 4.

Battista, M.T. (1999) 'The mathematical mis-education of America's youth: ignoring research and scientific study in education', *Phi Delta Kappa*, 80 (6): 425–33.

Beswick, K. (2007) 'Teachers' beliefs that matter in secondary mathematics classrooms', *Educational Studies in Mathematics*, 65: 95–120.

Bibby, T. (2002a) 'Shame, an emotional response to doing mathematics as an adult and a teacher', *British Educational Research Journal*, 28 (5): 705–22.

Bibby, T. (2002b) 'Primary school mathematics: an inside view', in P. Valero and O. Skovsmose (eds), *Proceedings of the Third International MES Conference*. Copenhagen: Centre for Research in Learning Mathematics. pp. 165–74.

Bibby, T., Moore, A., Clark, S. and Haddon, A. (2007) *Children's Learner-Identities in Mathematics at Key Stage 2: Full Research Report*. ESRC End of Award Report, RES-000-22-1272. Swindon: ESRC.

Biggs, J.B. (1987) *The Learning Process Questionnaire (LPQ): Manual*. Hawthorn, Victoria: Australian Council for Educational Research.

Billington, J., Fowler, N., MacKernan, J., Smith, J., Stratton, J. and Watson, A. (1993) *Using and Applying Mathematics*. Nottingham: ATM.

Bishop, A.J. (1991) 'Mathematical values in the teaching process', in A.J. Bishop, S. Mellin-Olsen and J. Van Dormorlen (eds), *Mathematical Knowledge: Its Growth through Teaching*. Dordrecht: Kluwer. pp. 195–214.

Boaler, J. (1997) *Experiencing School Mathematics*. Buckingham: Open University Press.

Boaler, J. (2002) *Experiencing School Mathematics: Traditional and Reform Approaches to Teaching and their Impact on Student Learning*. Mahwah, NJ: Lawrence Erlbaum Associates.

Boaler, J. (2009) *The Elephant in the Classroom*. London: Souvenir Press.

Boaler, J. and Greeno, I.G. (2000) 'Identity, agency and knowing in mathematics worlds', in J. Boaler (ed.), *Multiple Perspectives on Mathematics Teaching and Learning*. Westport, CT: Ablex.

Bottle, G. (2005) *Teaching Mathematics in the Primary School*. London: Continuum.

Bowden, J. (2005) 'Reflections on the phenomenographic team research process', in J.A. Bowden and P. Green (eds), *Doing Developmental Phenomenography*. Melbourne: RMIT University Press. ch. 2.

Bradbeer, J., Healey, M. and Kneale, P. (2004) 'Undergraduate geographers' understandings of geography, learning and teaching: a phenomenographic study', *Journal of Geography in Higher Education*, 28 (1): 17–34.

Brady, P. and Bowd, A. (2005) 'Mathematics anxiety, prior experience and confidence to teach mathematics among pre-service education students', *Teachers and Teaching: Theory and Practice*, 11 (1): 37–46.

Briggs, M. (2009) 'Creative mathematics', in A. Wilson A. (ed.), *Creativity in Primary Education*, 2nd edn. Exeter: Learning Matters. pp. 94–104.

Briggs, M. and Crook, J. (1991) 'Bags and baggage', in E. Love and D. Pimm (eds), *Teaching and Learning Mathematics*. London: Hodder and Stoughton.

Briggs, M. and Davis, S. (2008) *Creative Teaching: Mathematics in the Early Years and Primary Classroom*. London: Routledge.

Brown, M. (2000) 'Effective teaching of numeracy', in V. Koshy, P. Ernest and R. Casey (eds), *Mathematics for Primary Teachers*. London: Routledge. pp. 149–57.

Brown, M. (2010) 'Swings and roundabouts', in I. Thompson (ed.), *Issues in Teaching Numeracy in Primary Schools*, 2nd edn. Maidenhead: Open University Press. ch. 1.

Brown, S. and Walter, M. (2005) *The Art of Problem Posing*. Mahwah, NJ: Lawrence Erlbaum Associates.

Brown, T. (2005) 'The truth of initial training experience in mathematics for primary teachers', in D. Hewitt (ed.), *Proceeding of the British Society for Research into Learning Mathematics*, 25 (2): 19–24.

Brown, T., McNamara, O., Hanley, U. and Jones, L. (1999) 'Primary student teachers' understanding of mathematics and its teaching', *British Educational Research Journal*, 25 (3): 299–322.

Brown, T., Hanley, U., Darby, S. and Calder, N. (2007) 'Teachers' conceptions of learning philosophies: discussing context and contextualising discussion', *Journal of Mathematics Teacher Education*, 10: 183–200.

Bruch, H. (1974) *Learning Psychotherapy*. Cambridge, MA: Harvard University Press.

Bruner, J. (ed.) (1966) *Studies in Cognitive Growth*. New York: Wiley.

Buckley, P.A. and Ribordy, S.C. (1982) 'Mathematics anxiety and the effects of the evaluative instructions on math performance', *Proceedings of the Mid-Western Psychological Association*, Minneapolis, MN, May 6–8.

Burton, L. (1994) *Children Learning Mathematics: Patterns and Relationship*. Hemel Hempstead: Simon and Schuster Education.

Buxton, L. (1981) *Do You Panic About Maths? Coping with Maths Anxiety*. London: Heinemann Educational Books.

Cano, F. (2005) 'Epistemological beliefs and approaches to learning: their change through secondary school and their influence on academic performance', *British Journal of Educational Psychology*, 75: 203–21.

Carpenter, T.P. and Lehrer, R. (1999) 'Teaching and learning mathematics with understanding', in E. Fennema and T.A. Romberg (eds), *Classrooms That Promote Understanding*. Mahwah, NJ: Lawrence Erlbaum. ch. 2.

Carré, C. and Ernest, P. (1993) 'Performance in subject matter knowledge in mathematics', in S.N. Bennett and C. Carré (eds), *Learning to Teach*. London: Routledge.

Carson, T.R. (1995) 'Reflective practice and a reconceptualization of teacher education', in M. Wideen and P.P. Grimmett (eds), *Changing Times in Teacher Education: Restructuring or Reconceptualization*. London: Falmer. ch. 11.

Chambers (2003) *The Chambers Dictionary*, 9th edn. Edinburgh: Chambers.

Chapman, O. (2007) 'Facilitating preservice teachers' development of mathematics knowledge for teaching arithmetic operations', *Journal of Mathematics Teacher Education*, 10: 341–9.

Cherkas, B.M. (1992) 'A personal essay in math', *College Teaching*, 40 (3): 83.

Cherry, N. (2005) 'Phenomenography as seen by an action researcher', in J.A. Bowden and P. Green, P. (eds), *Doing Developmental Phenomenography*. Melbourne: RMIT University Press. ch. 5.

Christou, C., Phillipou, G. and Menon, M.B. (2001) 'Pre-service teachers' self esteem and mathematics achievement', *Contemporary Educational Psychology*, 26: 44–69.

Clarke, D.M. (1994) 'Ten key principles from research for the professional development of mathematics teachers', in D.B. Aichele and A.F. Coxford (eds), *Professional Development for Teachers of Mathematics: The 1994 Yearbook of the National Council of Teachers of Mathematics*. Reston, VA: National Council Of Teachers of Mathematics.

Claxton, G. (1999) *Wise Up: The Challenge of Lifelong Learning*. London: Bloomsbury.

Clemson, D. and Clemson, W. (1994) *Mathematics in the Early Years*. London: Routledge.

Cockburn, A.D. (1999) *Teaching Mathematics with Insight – The Identification, Diagnosis and Remediation of Young Children's Mathematical Errors*. London: Routledge Falmer.

Cockcroft, W.H. (1982) *Mathematics Counts*. London: HMSO.

Coles, D. and Copeland, T. (2002) *Numeracy and Mathematics Across the Primary Curriculum*. London: David Fulton.

Cooney, J. and Krainer, K. (1996) 'In-service mathematics teacher education: the importance of listening', in A.J. Bishop, K. Clements, J. Kilpatrick and C. Larbode (eds), *International Handbook of Mathematics Education*. Dordrecht: Kluwer Academic Publishers. pp. 1155–86.

Cooper, J.E. and He, Y. (2012) 'Journey of "becoming": secondary teacher candidates' concerns and struggles', *Issues in Teacher Education Journal*, Spring: 89–108.

Cooper, S.E. and Robinson, D.A. (1989) 'The influence of gender and anxiety on mathematics performance', *Journal of College Student Development*, 30: 459–61.

Cornell, C. (1999) '"I hate math! I couldn't learn it, and I can't teach it!" – childhood education', cited in P. Brady and A. Bowd (2005) 'Mathematics anxiety, prior experience and confidence to teach mathematics among pre-service education students', *Teachers and Teaching: Theory and Practice*, 11 (1): 37–46.

Cross, D.I. (2009) 'Alignment, cohesion, and change: examining mathematics teachers' belief structures and their influence on instructional practices', *Journal of Mathematics Teacher Education*, 12: 325–46.

Dall'Alba, G. (2000) 'Reflections on some faces of phenomenography', in J.A. Bowden and E. Walsh (eds), *Phenomenography*. Melbourne: RMIT University Press. ch 6.

Davis, A. (2001) 'Teaching for understanding in primary mathematics', *Evaluation and Research in Education*, 15 (3): 136–42.

Dawson, A.J. and Trivett, J.V. (1981) 'And now for something different: teaching by not teaching', in A. Floyd (ed.), *Developing Mathematical Thinking*. London: Addison–Wesley.

DCSF – Department for Children, Schools and Families (2008) *Independent Review of Mathematics Teaching in Early Years Settings and Primary Schools – Final Report – Sir Peter Williams*. Nottingham: DCSF Publications.

DCSF – Department for Children, Schools and Families (2009) *Independent Review of the Primary Curriculum: Final Report (Rose Review)* Nottingham: DCSF Publications.

De Bono, E. (2004) *How to Have a Beautiful Mind*. London: Vermilion.

De Corte, E., Op't Eynde, P. and Verschaffel, L. (2002) 'Knowing what to believe: the relevance of students' mathematical beliefs for mathematics education', in B.K. Hofer and P.R. Pintrich (eds), *The Psychology of Beliefs about Knowledge and Knowing*. London: Lawrence Erlbaum Associates. ch. 15.

Delaney, K. (2001) 'Teaching mathematics resourcefully', in P. Gates (ed.), *Issues in Mathematics Teaching*. London: Routledge Falmer. pp. 123–45.

Delaney, K. (2010) 'Making connections: teachers and children using resources effectively', in I. Thompson (ed.), *Issues in Teaching Numeracy in Primary Schools*, 2nd edn. Maidenhead: Open University Press. ch. 5.

DES – Department of Education and Science (1967) *The Plowden Report – Children and their Primary Schools*. London: Her Majesty's Stationery Office.

DES – Department of Education and Science and Welsh Office (1985) *Better Schools – A Summary*. London: HMSO.

DES – Department of Education and Science (1988) *Education Reform Act 1988*. London: HMSO.

DES – Department of Education and Science (1989) *The Education National Curriculum – Attainment Targets and Programmes of Study*. London: HMSO.

Desforges, C.W. and Cockburn, A.D. (1987) *Understanding the Mathematics Teacher: A Study of Practice in the First School*. Lewes: Falmer Press.

DfE – Department for Education (2010) *The Importance of Teaching: The Schools White Paper 2010*. London: TSO.

DfE – Department for Education (2013) *The National Curriculum in England*. December 2013. Reference: DfE-00178-2013.

DfEE – Department for Education and Employment (1999a) *The National Curriculum – Handbook for Primary Teachers in England*. London: DfEE and QCA.

DfEE – Department for Education and Employment (1999b) *The National Numeracy Strategy – Framework for Teaching Mathematics from Reception to Year 6*. Suffolk: DfEE Publications.

DfES – Department for Education and Skills (2002a) Education Act 2002. London: Her Majesty's Stationery Office.

DfES – Department for Education and Skills (2002b) *Qualifying to Teach – Professional Standards for Qualified Teacher Status and Requirements for Initial Teacher Training*. London: Teacher Training Agency.

DfES – Department for Education and Skills (2003a) *Primary National Strategy*. [National Strategies website: closed on Tuesday 28 June 2011.] www.education.gov.uk.

DfES – Department for Education and Skills (2003b) *Excellence and Enjoyment: A Strategy for Primary Schools*. Nottingham: DfES Publications Ref DfES/0377/2003.

Dodd, M. (2008) 'The mathematical competence of adults returning to learning on a university foundation programme: a selective comparison of performance with the CSMS study', in E. Nardi and T. Rowland (eds), *Research in Mathematics Education*. Volume 10, Number 2. Abingdon: Routledge Taylor and Francis. pp. 203–4.

Dunne, M. (2011) 'Who do you think you are … and who do you think you will be as a teacher?', in L. Cartwright and D. McGregor (eds), *Developing Reflective Practice: A Guide for Beginning Teachers*. Maidenhead: Open University Press/McGraw Hill. pp. 39–54.

Dweck, C.S. (2000) *Self-Theories – Their Role in Motivation, Personality and Development*. London: Taylor and Francis.

Dweck, C.S. (2006) *Mindset: How You Can Fulfil Your Potential*. London: Random House.

Edwards, S. (1998) *Managing Effective Teaching of Mathematics 3–8*. London: Paul Chapman.

Ernest, P. (1989) 'The impact of beliefs on the teaching of mathematics', in P. Ernest (ed.), *Mathematics Teaching: The State of the Art*. London: Falmer Press. pp. 249–54.

Ernest, P. (1991) *Philosophy of Mathematics Education*. New York: Falmer.

Ernest, P. (2000) 'Teaching and learning mathematics', in V. Koshy, P. Ernest and R. Casey (eds), *Mathematics for Primary Teachers*. London: Routledge.

Fairclough, R. (2002) 'Developing problem-solving skills in mathematics', in V. Koshy and J. Murray (eds), *Unlocking Mathematics Teaching*, 2nd edn. London: Routledge. pp. 84–109. ch. 5.

Fennema, E. and Franke, M.L. (1992) 'Teachers' knowledge and its impact', in D.A. Grouws (ed.), *Handbook of Research On Mathematics Teaching and Learning*. New York: Macmillan Publishing Company. pp. 147–64.

Ferraro, Joan M. (2000) *Reflective Practice and Professional Development*. Washington, DC: Teaching and Teacher Education.

Flores, M.A. and Day, C. (2006) 'Contexts which shape and reshape new teachers' identities: a multi-perspective study', *Teaching and Teacher Education*, 22: 219–32.

Floyd, A. (ed.) (1981) *Developing Mathematical Thinking*. Wokingham: Addison–Wesley.

Foss, D.H. and Kleinsasser, R.C. (2001) 'Contrasting research perspectives: what the evidence yields', *Teachers and Teaching: Theory and Practice*, 7 (3): 271–95.

Frank, M. (1990) 'What myths about mathematics are held and conveyed by teachers?', *Arithmetic Teachers*, 37 (5): 10–12.

Fuller, F.F. (1969) 'Concerns of teachers: a developmental conceptualisation', *American Educational Research Journal*, 6: 207–26.

Furner, J.M. and Duffy, M.L. (2002) 'Equity for all students in the new millennium: disabling math anxiety', *Intervention in School and Clinic*, 38 (2): 67.

Garofalo, J. and Lester, F.K. (1985) 'Metacognition, cognitive monitoring and mathematical performance', *Journal for Research in Mathematics Education*, 16: 163–76.

Gattegno, C. (1971) *What We Owe Children*. London: Routledge and Kegan Paul.

Goleman, D. (1998) *Working with Emotional Intelligence*. London: Bloomsbury.

Goulding, M., Rowland, T. and Barber, P. (2002) 'Does it matter? Primary teacher trainees' subject knowledge in mathematics', *British Educational Research Journal*, 28 (5): 689–704.

Gravemeijer, K. (1997) 'Mediating between the concrete and the abstract', in T. Nunes and D. Bryant (eds), *Learning and Teaching Mathematics – An International Perspective*. Hove: Psychology Press.

Green, P. (2005) 'A rigorous journey into phenomenography: from a naturalistic inquirer viewpoint', in J.A. Bowden and P. Green (eds), *Doing Developmental Phenomenography*. Melbourne: RMIT University Press. ch. 3.

Grootenboer, P. (2008) 'Mathematical belief change in prospective primary teachers', *Journal of Mathematics Teacher Education*, 11: 479–97.

Gullberga, A., Kellnera, E., Attorpsa, I., Thorena, I. and Tarnebergb, R. (2008) 'Prospective teachers' initial conceptions about pupils' understanding of science and mathematics', *European Journal of Teacher Education*, 31 (3): 257–78.

Harries, T. and Spooner, M. (2000) *Mental Mathematics for the Numeracy Hour*. London: David Fulton.

Harvard, G.R. and Hodkinson, P. (eds) (1995) *Action and Reflection in Teacher Education*. Norwood, NJ: Ablex Publishing.

Haylock, D. (2010) *Mathematics Explained for Primary Teachers*, 4th edn. London: Sage.

Haylock, D. and Thangata, F. (2007) *Key Concepts in Teaching Primary Mathematics*. London: Sage.

Hersh, R. (1986) 'Some proposals for revisiting the philosophy of mathematics', in T. Tymoczko (ed.), *New Directions in the Philosophy of Mathematics*. Boston, MA: Birkhauser. pp. 9–28.

Hickman, L. and Alexander, T. (1998) *The Essential Dewey: Volume 1, Pragmatism, Education, Democracy*. Bloomington, IN: Indiana University Press.

Hodges, H. (1983) 'Learning styles for mathophobia', *Arithmetic Teacher*, 30 (7): 17–20.

Hofer, B.K. and Pintrich, P.R. (eds) (2002) *The Psychology of Beliefs About Knowledge and Knowing*. London: Lawrence Erlbaum Associates.

Hogden, J. and Askew, M. (2007) 'Emotion, identity and teacher learning: becoming a primary mathematics teacher', *Oxford Review of Education*, 33 (4): 469–87.

Hopkins, C., Gifford, S. and Pepperell, S. (1999) *Mathematics in the Primary School – A Sense of Progression*, 2nd edn. London: David Fulton.

Hopkins, C., Pope, P. and Pepperell, S. (2004) *Understanding Primary Mathematics*. London: David Fulton.

Houssart, J. (2009) 'Latter day reflections on primary mathematics', in J. Houssart and J. Mason (eds), *Listening Counts – Listening to Young Learners of Mathematics*. Stoke-on-Trent: Trentham Books. pp. 143–56.

Howell, C.L. (2002) 'Reforming higher education curriculum to emphasize student responsibility – waves of rhetoric but glacial change', *College Teaching*, 50 (3): 116–18.

Hughes, M. (1999) 'The National Numeracy Strategy – are we getting it right?', *The Psychology of Education Review*, 23 (2): 3–7.

Hughes, M., Desforges, C. and Mitchell, C. (2000) *Numeracy and Beyond*. Buckingham: Open University Press.

Hwang, Y.G. (1995) 'Student apathy, lack of self-responsibility and false self-esteem are failing American schools', *Education*, 115 (4): 484–9.

Jackson, C.D. and Leffingwell, R.J. (1999) 'The role of instructors in creating math anxiety in students from kindergarten through college', *Mathematics Teacher*, 92 (7): 583.

Jackson, E. (2007) 'Seventies, eighties, nineties, noughties … a sequence of concerns', *University of Cumbria: Practitioner Research in Higher Education*, 1 (1): 28–32.

Jackson, E. (2008) 'Mathematics anxiety in student teachers', *University of Cumbria: Practitioner Research in Higher Education*, 2 (1): 36–42.

Jones, L. (2003) 'The problem with problem-solving', in I. Thompson (ed.), *Enhancing Primary Mathematics Teaching*. Maidenhead: Open University Press. ch. 8.

Kamii, C. and Lewis, B.A. (1990) 'What is constructivism?', *Arithmetic Teacher*, 38 (1): 34–5.

Kelly, A. and Lesh, R. (eds) (2000) *Handbook of Research Design in Mathematics and Science Education*. Mahwah, NJ: Lawrence Erlbaum Associates.

Kember, D. (1997) 'A reconceptualisation of the research into university academics' conceptions of teaching', *Learning and Instruction*, 7: 255–75.

Kogelman, S. and Warren, J. (1978) *Mind Over Math*. New York: McGraw-Hill.

Koshy, V., Ernest, P. and Casey, R. (2000) *Mathematics for Primary Teachers*. London: Routledge.

Krantz, S.G. (1999) *How to Teach Mathematics*. Providence, RI: American Mathematical Society.

Kuhs, T. and Ball, D. (1986) *Approaches to Teaching Mathematics: Mapping the Domains of Knowledge, Skills and Disposition*. Lansing, MI: Center of Teacher Education, Michigan State University.

Kyriakides, A.O. (2009) 'Learning to add fractions: a progression of experiences or an experience of the progression?', in J. Houssart and J. Mason (eds), *Listening Counts – Listening to Young Learners of Mathematics*. Stoke-on-Trent: Trentham Books. pp. 85–100.

Lampert, M. (1990) 'When the problem is not the question and the solution is not the answer – mathematical knowing and teaching', *American Educational Research Journal*, 27: 29–63.

Lang, P. (1995) 'Preparing teachers for pastoral care and personal and social education: to train or educate?', *Pastoral Care*, 13 (4): 18–23.

Langer, E.J. (1997) *The Power of Mindful Learning*. Reading, MA: Addison–Wesley.

Larrivee, B. (2000) 'Transforming teaching practice: becoming the critically reflective teacher', *Reflective Practice: International and Multidisciplinary Perspectives*, 1 (3): 293–307.

Leder, G.C. and Forgasz, H.J. (2006) 'Affect and mathematics education: PME perspectives', in A. Gutierrez and P. Boero (eds), *Handbook of Research on the Psychology of Mathematics Education: Past, Present and Future*. Rotterdam: Sense. pp. 403–27.

Lee, C. (2006) *Language for Learning Mathematics*. Maidenhead: Open University Press.

Liljedahl, P.G. (2005) 'Mathematical discovery and affect: the effect of AHA! Experiences on undergraduate mathematics students', *International Journal of Mathematical Education*, 36 (2–3): 219–35.

Lockhead, J. (1990) *Knocking Down the Building Blocks of Learning*. Educational Studies in Mathematics, No. 23. Dordrecht: Kluwer.

Lucas, B. (2001) 'Creative teaching, teaching creativity and creative learning', in A. Craft, B. Jeffrey and M. Leibling (eds), *Creativity in Education*. London: Continuum. ch. 2.

MacNab, D.S. and Payne, F. (2003) 'Beliefs, attitudes and practices in mathematics teaching: perceptions of Scottish primary school student teachers', *Journal of Education for Teaching*, 29 (1): 55–68.

Marton, F. (1986) 'Phenomenography – a research approach to investigating different understandings of reality', *Journal of Thought*, 21: 28–49.

Marton, F. (2000) 'The structure of awareness', in J.A. Bowden and E. Walsh (eds), *Phenomenography*. Melbourne: RMIT University Press. ch. 7.

Marton, F. and Booth, S. (1997) *Learning and Awareness*. Mahwah, NJ: Lawrence Erlbaum Associates.

Mason, M. (2000) 'Teachers as critical mediators of knowledge', *Journal of Philosophy of Education*, 34 (2): 343–52.

Mathematical Association (MA) (1955) *The Teaching of Mathematics in Primary Schools. A Report Prepared for the Mathematical Association for Consideration by All Concerned with the Development of Young Children*. London: G Bells and Sons Ltd.

Maxwell, J. (1989) 'Mathephobia', in P. Ernest (ed.), *Mathematics Teaching: The State of the Art*. London: Falmer Press. pp. 221–6.

McGregor, D. (2011) 'What can reflective practice mean for you … and why should you engage in it?', in L. Cartwright and D. McGregor (eds), *Developing Reflective Practice: A Guide for Beginning Teachers*. Maidenhead: Open University/McGraw-Hill. pp. 1–20.

McNamara, D. (1994) *Classroom Pedagogy and Primary Practice*. London: Routledge.

McVarish, J. (2008) *Where's the Wonder in Elementary Mathematics?* Abingdon: Routledge.

Metje, N., Frank, H.L. and Croft, P. (2007) 'Can't do maths – understanding students' maths anxiety', *Teaching Mathematics and Its Applications*, 26 (2): 79–88.

Mewborn, D. (2001) 'Teachers' content knowledge, teacher education, and their effects on the preparation of elementary teachers in the United States', *Mathematics Teacher Education and Development*, 3: 28–36.

Mikusa, M.J. and Lewellen, H. (1999) 'Now here is that authority on mathematics reform, Doctor Constructivist', *Mathematics Teacher*, 92: 158–63.

Miller, L.D. and Mitchell, C.E. (1994) 'Mathematics anxiety and alternative methods of evaluation', *Journal of Instructional Psychology*, 21 (4): 353.

Mji, A. (2003) 'A three-year perspective on conceptions of and orientations to learning mathematics of prospective teachers and first year university students', *International Journal of Mathematical Education in Science and Technology*, 34 (5): 687–98.

Mooney, C. and Fletcher, M. (2003) *Achieving QTS Primary Mathematics: Audit and Test Assessing Your Knowledge and Understanding*, 2nd edn. Exeter: Learning Matters.

Mooney, C., Briggs, M., Fletcher, M., Hansen, A. and McCullouch, J. (2009) *Primary Mathematics Teaching: Theory and Practice*, 4th edn. Exeter: Learning Matters.

Morris, J. (1981) 'Math anxiety: teaching to avoid it', *Mathematics Teacher*, 74 (6): 413–17.

Mortiboys, A. (2012) *Teaching with Emotional Intelligence: A Step By Step Guide for Higher and Further Education Professionals*, 2nd edn. London: Routledge.

Moyer, P. (2001) 'Are we having fun yet? How teachers use manipulatives to teach mathematics', *Education Studies in Mathematics*, 47 (2): 175–97.

NACCCE – National Advisory Committee On Creative and Cultural Education (1999) *All Our Futures: Creativity, Culture and Education*. London: DfEE.

Napper, R. and Newton, T. (2000) *Tactics*. Ipswich: TA Resources.

Nathan, M.J. and Koedinger, K.R. (2000) 'An investigation of teachers' beliefs of students' algebra development', *Cognition and Instruction*, 18 (2): 209–37.

Nelson-Herber, J. (1986) 'Expanding and refining vocabulary in content areas', *Journal of Reading*, 29: 626–33.

Nespor, J. (1987) 'The role of beliefs in the practice of teaching', *Journal of Curriculum Studies*, 19: 317–28.

Noddings, N. (1992) *The Challenge to Care in Schools: An Alternative Approach to Education*. New York: Teachers College Press.

Nunes, T. and Bryant, P. (1996) *Children Doing Mathematics*. Oxford: Blackwell.

Ofsted – Office for Standards in Education (2005) *The National Literacy and Numeracy Strategies and the Primary Curriculum*. London: Ofsted.

Ofsted – Office for Standards in Education (2008) *Mathematics: Understanding the Score*. London: Ofsted.

Ollerton, M. (2010) 'Using problem-solving approaches to learn mathematics', in I. Thompson (ed.), *Issues in Teaching Numeracy in Primary Schools*, 2nd edn. Maidenhead: Open University Press. pp. 84–96.

Orton, A. (1994a) 'The aims of teaching mathematics', in A. Orton and G. Wain (eds), *Issues in Teaching Mathematics*. London: Cassell. pp. 1–20.

Orton, A. (1994b) 'Learning mathematics: implications for teaching', in A. Orton and G. Wain (eds), *Issues in Teaching Mathematics*. London: Cassell. pp. 35–57.

Orton, A. and Frobisher, L. (1996) *Insights Into Teaching Mathematics*. London: Continuum.

O'Sullivan, L., Harris, A. and Sangster, M. (2005) *Reflective Reader – Primary Mathematics*. Exeter: Learning Matters.

Owen, D. (1987) 'Teaching and learning mathematics in the primary school', in M. Preston (ed.), *Mathematics in Primary Education*. Lewes: Falmer Press. pp. 17–41.

Oxford, R.L. (1990) *Language Learning Strategies: What Every Teacher Should Know*. New York: Newbury House/HarperCollins.

Oxford, R.L. and Anderson, N.J. (1995) 'A crosscultural view of learning styles', *Language Teaching*, 28: 201–15.

Paechter, C. (2001) 'Gender reason and demotion in secondary mathematics classrooms', in P. Gates (ed.), *Issues in Mathematics Teaching*. London: Routledge Falmer.

Pang, M.F. (2003) 'Two faces of variation: on continuity in the phenomenographic movement [1]', *Scandinavian Journal of Educational Research*, 47 (2): 145–56.

Papert, S. (1980) *Mindstorms*. Brighton: Harvester Press.

Perry, A.B. (2004) 'Decreasing math anxiety in college students', *College Student Journal*, 38 (2): 321.

Petocz, P. and Reid, A. (2005) 'Something strange and useless: service students' conceptions of statistics, learning statistics and using statistics in their future profession', *International Journal of Mathematical Education in Science and Technology*, 36 (7): 789–800.

Piaget, J. (1953) 'How children form mathematical concepts', *Scientific American*, 189 (5): 74–81.

Polya, G. (1945) *How to Solve It*. Princeton, NJ: Princeton University Press.

Pound, L. (1999) *Supporting Mathematical Development in the Early Years*. Buckingham: Open University Press.

Pound, L. (2008) *Thinking and Learning About Mathematics in the Early Years*. Abingdon: Routledge.

Pound, L. and Lee, T. (2011) *Teaching Mathematics Creatively – Learning to Teach in the Primary School Series*. London: Routledge.

Prosser, M. and Trigwell, K. (1999) *Understanding Learning and Teaching*. Birmingham: Society for Research into Higher Education and Open University Press.

Prosser, M., Crawford, K., Gordon, S. and Nicholas, J. (1998) 'University mathematics students' conceptions of mathematics', *Studies in Higher Education*, 23 (1): 87–94.

Prosser, M., Martin, E., Trigwell, K., Ramsden, P. and Lueckenhausen, G. (2005) 'Academics' experiences of understanding of their subject matter and the relationship of this to their experiences of teaching and learning', *Instructional Science*, 33: 137–57.

Romberg, T.A. and Kaput, J.J. (1999) 'Mathematics worth teaching, mathematics worth understanding', in E. Fennema and T.A. Romberg (eds), *Classrooms That Promote Understanding*. Mahwah, NJ: Lawrence Erlbaum. ch. 1.

Ryan, J. and Williams, J. (2007) *Children's Mathematics 5–13: Learning from Errors and Misconceptions*. Maidenhead: Open University Press.

Safran, L. (2001) 'Creativity as "mindful" learning: a case from learner-led home-based education', in A. Craft, B. Jeffrey and M. Leibling (eds), *Creativity in Education*. London: Continuum. ch. 5.

Sakshang, L., Ollson, M. and Olson, J. (2002) *Children Are Mathematical Problem Solvers*. Reston, VA: National Council of Teachers of Mathematics.

Säljö, R. (1997) 'Talk as data and practice – a critical look at phenomenographic inquiry and the appeal to experience', *Higher Education Research And Development*, 16(2): 173–90.

Schifter, D. and Twomey Fosnot, C. (1993) *Reconstructing Mathematics Education: Stories of Teachers Meeting the Challenge of Reform*. New York and London: Teachers College Press, 1993.

Schön, D.A. (1996) *Educating the Reflective Practitioner: Toward a New Design for Teaching and Learning in the Professions*. San Francisco, CA: Jossey-Bass.

Schuck, S. (2002) 'Using self-study to challenge my teaching practice in mathematics education', *Reflective Practice*, 3 (3): 327–37.

Scott Peck, M. (1990) *The Road Less Travelled*. London: Arrow.

Sharp, J., Ward, S. and Hankin, L. (eds) (2009) *Education Studies: An Issues-Based Approach*, 2nd edn. Exeter: Learning Matters.

Shodahl, S.A. and Diers, C. (1984) 'Math anxiety in college students: sources and solutions', *Community College Review*, 12 (2): 32–6.

Silverman, J. and Thompson, P.W. (2008) 'Toward a framework for the development of mathematical knowledge for teaching', *Journal of Mathematics Teacher Education*, 11 (6): 499–511.

Skemp, R.R. (1978) 'Relational understanding and instrumental understanding', *Arithmetic Teacher*, 26 (3): 9–15.

Skemp, R.R. (1981) *Psychology of Learning Mathematics*. Harmondsworth: Penguin Books.

Skemp, R.R. (1989) *Mathematics and Primary School*. London: Routledge.

Skemp, R.R. (2002) *Mathematics in the Primary School*. London: Routledge Falmer.

Skinner, B.F. (1954) 'The science of learning and the art of teaching', *Harvard Educational Review*, 24 (2): 86–97.

Smith, A. (2004) *Making Mathematics Count – The Report of Professor Adrian Smith's Enquiry into Post 14 Mathematics Education*. London: TSO.

Smith, S.S. (1997) *Early Childhood Mathematics*. Boston. MA: Allyn and Bacon.

Sowder, J. (2001) 'Connecting mathematics education research to practice', in J. Bobis, B. Perry and M. Mitchelmore (eds), *Numeracy and Beyond* (Proceedings of the 24th Annual Conference of the Mathematics Education Research Group of Australasia). Sydney: MERGA. pp. 1–8.

Speer, N.M. (2005) 'Issues of methods and theory in the study of mathematics teachers' professed and attributed beliefs', *Educational Studies in Mathematics*, 58: 361–91.

Suggate, J., Davis, A. and Goulding, M. (2006) *Mathematical Knowledge for Primary Teachers*. London: David Fulton.

Sutherland, L., Howard, S. and Markauskaite, L. (2010) 'Professional identity creation: examining the development of beginning pre-service teachers' understanding of their work as teachers', *Teaching and Teacher Education*, 26 (3): 455–65.

Swars, S.L., Smith, S.Z., Smith, M.E. and Hart, L.C. (2009) 'A longitudinal study of effects of a developmental teacher preparation program on elementary prospective teachers' mathematics beliefs', *Journal of Mathematics Teacher Education*, 12: 47–66.

Szydlik, J.E., Szydlik, S.D. and Benson, S.R. (2003) 'Exploring changes in pre-service elementary teachers' mathematical beliefs', *Journal of Mathematics Teacher Education*, 6: 253–79.

Taylor, B. (2006) *Reflective Practice*. New York: McGraw-Hill.

TDA – Training and Development Agency for Schools (2007) *Professional Standards for Teachers Qualified Teacher Status*. London: Training and Development Agency for Schools.

Thompson, A.G. (1992) 'Teachers beliefs and conceptions: a synthesis of the research', in D.A. Grouws (ed.), *Handbook of Research on Mathematics Teaching and Learning*. New York: Macmillan. pp. 127–46.

Tobias, S. (1978) *Overcoming Math Anxiety*. Boston, MA: Houghton Mifflin.

Tobias, S. (1993) *Overcoming Math Anxiety Revised and Expanded*. New York: Norton.

Tolhurst, D. (2007) 'The influence of learning environments on students' epistemological beliefs and learning outcomes', *Teaching in Higher Education*, 12 (2): 219–33.

Townsend, M.W. and Wilton, K. (2003) 'Evaluating change in attitude towards mathematics using the then–now procedure in a cooperative learning programme', *British Journal of Educational Psychology*, 73(4): 473–87.

Trigwell, K., Prosser, M. and Waterhouse, F. (1999) 'Relations between teachers' approaches to teaching and students' approaches to learning', *Higher Education*, 37: 57–70.

Trigwell, K., Prosser, M. and Ginns, P. (2005) 'Phenomenographic pedagogy and a revised approaches to teaching inventory', *Higher Education Research and Development*, 24 (4): 349–60.

Uusimaki, L. and Nason, R. (2004) 'Causes of underlying pre-service teachers' negative beliefs and anxieties about mathematics'. *Proceedings of the 28th Conference of the International Group for the Psychology of Mathematics Education*, 4: 369–76.

Valderrama, C.A. (2008) 'The power of Colombian mathematics teachers' conceptions of social/institutional factors of teaching', *Educational Studies in Mathematics*, 68: 37–54.

Van Nieuwerburgh, C. (2014) *An Introduction to Coaching Skills – A Practical Guide*. London: Sage.

Von Glaserfeld, E. (1990) 'An exposition of constructivism: why some like it radical', in R.B. Davies, C.A. Maher and M. Noddings (eds), *Constructivists' Views on the Teaching and Learning of Mathematics*. Reston, VA: National Council for Teachers of Mathematics. pp. 19–30.

Vygotsky, L.S. (1978) *Mind in Society: The Development of the Higher Psychological Processes*. Cambridge, MA: Harvard University Press.

White, R. and Gunstone, R. (1992) *Probing Understanding*. London: Falmer Press.

Whitmore, J. (2009) *Coaching for Performance: Growing Human Potential and Purpose: The Principles and Practice of Coaching and Leadership*, 4th edn. London: Nicholas Brealey.

Wilkins, J.L.M. (2008) 'The relationship among elementary teachers' content knowledge, attitudes, beliefs and practices', *Journal of Mathematics Teacher Education*, 11 (2): 139–64.

Wilson, A. (ed.) (2009) *Creativity in Primary Education*, 2nd edn. Exeter: Learning Matters.

Wong, N.Y. (2002) 'Conceptions of doing and learning mathematics', *Journal of Intercultural Studies*, 23 (2): 211–29.

Yackel, E. and Cobb, P. (1996) 'Socio mathematical norms, argumentation, and autonomy in mathematics', *Journal for Research in Mathematics Education*, 27 (4): 459–77.

Index